GOD THE PARENT

NATE DAVIS

CONTENTS

Follow God's example, therefore, as dearly loved children
and walk in the way of love, just as Christ loved us and gave
himself up for us as a fragrant offering and sacrifice to God.
Ephesians 5:1-2, NIV

INTRODUCTION

For many years, I didn't think that the Bible said much about how to raise children. I began to realize that the Scriptures offered more when I was introduced to several child-training programs that claimed to be Bible-based. By then, I was a dry sponge in need of help, so I relished any insight I could get. These teachers gave me hope that the Bible provided answers, but over time I realized that their instructions were lacking deep biblical content and, at times, contradicted the Bible. I began to believe that there was need for a more thorough search of the Scriptures. This book is the result of my endeavor to do that.

The Bible verses that address parenting directly are helpful for moms and dads, but there are several other ways to learn about parenting from God's Word. There are parents and children in the Bible, and lessons can be learned from their experiences, too. The fact that God acted as a father to the nation of Israel during the Exodus and the wanderings in the desert leaves us with an example that will be pursued in depth in this book. Of course, God is a father to all who are born again, providing us with more examples. On a few occasions, those who wrote the letters to the early believers (which now make up most of the New Testament) said that their care, concerns and actions were similar to a parent with his child, leaving us with more upon which to meditate. I wish that I could have considered all facets of every phrase, passage or historical record on parenting in the Bible. The fact is that God's wisdom for parents runs so deep that it offers a lifetime supply of encouragement and direction to any parent who earnestly searches God's Word.

Your Resident Expert

By some people's standards, I don't have the technical qualifications to be an expert on children. I am not a psychiatrist or psychologist. I am not a child development specialist. This might be a problem if I were writing in order to defend a particular behavioral hypothesis, but I am not. Instead, I am writing as a student of the Bible, believing that God gave us an instruction manual that tells us how to live our lives. I am starting with the premise that whatever God said works.

For our family, following God's teaching and example as best we can has helped. We have a great time, we love one another, and our children are great friends. Very often, when we pack our crew and go out for an event, people offer compliments such as, "What sweet children you have," and "They are so well behaved." Or, from acquaintances, we often hear, "You have the best kids," or "I'd rather watch six of your children than two of somebody else's." As much as we appreciate the kind words, we know that we don't always feel like the perfect family at home. Why not? We are acutely aware of the struggles that each child brings to us. We can count our shortcomings as parents as well. This does not feel like utopia. What we do have is all by God's grace and instruction. Therefore, I can say with great confidence that your resident expert is not me. God is your resident expert.

On a similar note, I do not use anecdotes from my own family to validate the advice in this book. I don't tell stories about our family and then suggest the reader trust us or follow us. The only thing that makes the advice in this book reliable is that it comes from God's Word. He invented the family and showed us how to love its members, and for that I am grateful.

Audience

Primarily, I am writing for those Christian parents who would benefit by reading in hours what would take months to study. If this is you, please know that you are on my heart, and my desire is to help you. I have also realized that some who are not parents might benefit from this book. It has a lot to say to any believer about the way God cares for those who call him Father. The book can also help newlyweds or those working toward marriage to be both sober-minded and hopeful about family. Finally, I hope *God the Parent* will serve as a valuable resource for my own children and yours as they seek to raise their children in the future. My hope is to bless generations yet to come.

When writing, I decided to read each chapter to my family. To my surprise, they liked them and thanked me. Consider whether you might want to read *God the Parent* to your children, too.

Items of Clarification

I need to mention that I prefer not to use certain religious words that have come into English by transliteration from Greek or Latin. For example, in place of the word "church," I prefer a term like "meeting," "fellowship," "group of believers" or "worship." Instead of "baptism," I would say "immerse." In a Bible verse, I simply put brackets around the words I have replaced. By doing this, I hope to communicate the original intention of the passage more clearly.

In this book, I typically quote the New King James Version (NKJV) or the New International Version (NIV). Although I seldom cite the King James Version (KJV), a person can use it with tools like Strong's numbering system to study the meaning of Greek and Hebrew words. For example, with Strong's, one can see how a word found in a particular verse was used elsewhere in the Bible. The website www.blueletterbible.org offers free access to the KJV, Strong's and other linguistic tools.

I may quote only part of the verse referenced (sometimes just a few words). The short reference is meant to guide the reader to a concept embodied in the passage. Consider what lies before and after the part I cite in order to better understand the events taking place or instructions given.

Chapter 1

Good Parenting is Important

How one parents matters. If you willingly pick up a book like this to read, you probably already believe parenting is important. Still, I want to devote this first chapter to laying out the case from a biblical standpoint, not only because I think people should approach this topic seriously, but because God makes that case and it is right to think about what he said. The fact is that life is full of concerns, and parenting must take priority. We should know how and why good parenting matters so much to God to help us stay focused from day to day. The Bible gives us good reason to be particular in the way we parent.

In the beginning, in Genesis 1 and 2, God's relationship with his two greatest earthly creations was quite wonderful and simple. He was with them (Genesis 3:8). Had Adam and Eve's children been born in the garden, they, too, would have walked with God; but that is not the way it worked out. Sin entered the world, and things got complicated. In due time, God would solve the sin problem. He would do something drastic, something passionate, and the concept of family would be central to those events.

In Genesis 22, God asked Abraham to sacrifice his only son, Isaac. At first glance, this situation seems far from the ideals of family, that members are to care for one another and protect each other. One can imagine the tension between obedience, sorrow and faith as this loving father struggled with such an unthinkable command. In the end, God provided a ram to take Isaac's place, showing that he would ultimately provide the penalty for sin. This is why the events matter so much: in Genesis 22, God used the relationships made through family to show, from his viewpoint, the cost of our salvation. God would suffer as a family suffers loss, yet he would be willing to endure it for the benefit of adding to his family a multitude of redeemed children.

The Genesis of Parenting

Since family is such an important institution for understanding the passion of Christ, one might expect to find great examples of families in the first book of the Bible. Quite to the contrary, we find families bitten by the sting of the evil human heart. In fact, in Genesis, families were problematic.

The first relationship between brothers ended with one violently murdering the other. Cain burned with jealousy over Abel's righteous sacrifice, so he killed him (Genesis 4). We don't know much about what happened in the next 1,600 years or so, but we know it got very bad: mankind became exceedingly wicked. This was not a small group of troublemakers. The earth's population could easily have been hundreds of millions (1.11% annual growth) or billions (1.26% annual growth).[1] Eventually, the circumstances became so dire that God decided to start over with Noah and his family by destroying the earth in a giant and prolonged deluge (Genesis 6 and 7). If we think parent and child behavior is often bad now, we should consider that it was very likely worse back then (Genesis 6:5, 11-13).

Through Noah, humanity was saved by the preservation of one family through the faith of the father, yet not all was well in Noah's family (Hebrews 11:7). After the Flood, Noah got drunk and ended up cursing his own grandson. In Genesis 9, Ham "saw his father naked and told his two brothers outside" (Genesis 9:22, NIV). When Noah awoke from his wine and found out what Ham had done to him, he said, "Cursed be Canaan! The lowest of slaves will he be to his brothers [or relatives]" (Genesis 9:25, NIV).

Based only on what is provided in the text, I must conclude that the real tragedy of Genesis 9 lay in Noah's treatment of his own family. First, his curse was not directed at Ham, who found Noah naked. It was directed at Ham's son, Canaan, but that was not logical or just. What did Canaan do wrong? He wasn't even mentioned as part of the events. Using him

---

1. Annual Growth Rate =(Population Final, 100 million or 1 billion/Population Initial, 2)^(1/ Years, 1,600) - 1

was just Noah's way to get at Ham. Yet we know that this way is not the way of God. Ezekiel 18:20 states that "The son shall not bear the guilt of the father." (NKJV, see also Deuteronomy 24:16). Second, we should wonder why in the world Noah would curse his own family. Had Ham done anything wrong, Noah could have talked with him and urged him to repent, but Noah chose to curse, which instituted strife between his children's families for generations to come. This event should be noted as one of several in Genesis that show that sin corrupts the family.

What can we learn here? Noah and his family had the unique opportunity to start over after the Flood. In a similar way, certain occasions renew the souls of family members and give hope for a new direction. These are times for blessing, not cursing. Parents shouldn't waste these opportunities. They must be careful not to blurt out a curse in anger or call their children or grandchildren anything curse-like. Children may do something foolish, but a parent or grandparent shouldn't speak into existence their stupidity. Instead, they should bless them and correct their foolish behavior.

Not too many generations after the Flood, God found a man who would trust him: Abraham. However, while Abraham and Sarah showed unique faith, both did some things that might make one scratch one's head in wonder (Genesis 15:6, Hebrews 11:8-11). Their lives included some self-induced family heartaches. How would these go over in your family life? Abraham let another man court his wife on two occasions because he was afraid he would get hurt if it were known that she was his wife. With this, he nearly lost her (Genesis 12:11-20, 20:2-18). Abraham also had a child with his servant, which was not what God had in mind at all (Genesis 16:4). Taking a servant as a concubine was Sarah's idea, but Sarah quickly became jealous of and cruel toward Hagar (Genesis 16:4-5, 21:9-10). Is this the kind of family one would want to emulate?

Genesis also records several significant events in Lot's family's life. Lot, who was Abraham's nephew, offered his daughters to a rowdy mob of men, saying, "...do to them as you wish" (Genesis 19:8, NKJV). Lot's wife disobeyed God and died because she looked back at Sodom, presumably still longing for what it had offered (Genesis 13:10-13, 19:26). After they escaped the city, Lot's daughters got Lot drunk and then slept with him (Genesis 19:30-36). The daughters then became pregnant and bore sons whose descendants became two nations, the Ammonites and Moabites, which contended with Moses and the Israelites centuries later (Genesis

19:37-38). Lot's family provides more evidence that the Genesis records are not always a good source of examples of good family decisions.

Later, Abraham and Sarah's son, Isaac, and daughter-in-law, Rebekah, also did some things that were not worthy to be esteemed. Like his father, Isaac was willing to give his wife away out of fear (Genesis 26:7-11). Much of the family troubles concerning Isaac's immediate and extended family, however, had to do with jealousy, selfishness, greed and revenge. In their family, Isaac and Rebekah had favorites. Rebekah loved their son Jacob, and Isaac loved their son Esau. This was a what-can-you-do-for-me kind of love, each picking the child who satisfied some daily want. Esau provided wild game, and Jacob provided companionship (Genesis 25:27-28).

Then came a time when Rebekah and Jacob teamed up to lie to Isaac in order to get Esau's blessing.

> So Esau hated Jacob because of the blessing with which his father
> blessed him, and Esau said in his heart, "The days of mourning for
> my father are at hand; then I will kill my brother Jacob."
>
> Genesis 27:41, NKJV

Once again in Genesis, one brother was willing to murder another. However, Jacob fled to live with Laban, Esau and Jacob's uncle, and did not come back until after his mother had died. (The days of mourning Isaac's death were not at hand as Esau had suspected; Isaac in fact lived many more years. (Genesis 35:27-29).)

Jacob had problems with Laban. Laban cheated Jacob out of the seven years he had worked in order to marry Rachel, giving him Leah as a wife instead. Jacob later also married Rachel, but Leah was constantly seeking her husband's approval, and Rachel was jealous (Genesis 30:1, 8, 20). She was barren, but Leah had children (Genesis 29:30-35, 31:7). In desperation, Rachel asked her husband to sleep with her servant (Genesis 30:5-8). The name of one of the sons from those relations, Naphtali, expressed Rachel's feelings; "With great wrestlings I have wrestled with my sister, and indeed I have prevailed." (Genesis 30:8, NKJV). The child's name spoke of the discord between the sisters; they were determined opponents.

Esau's marital woes were not as well documented. He had married two Hittite wives who caused Isaac and Rebekah much distress. Eventually, Esau added a third wife, a descendant of Ishmael, in order to make his mother and father happy (Genesis 26:34-35, 27:46, 28:8-9).

When it was time for Jacob to return to the Promised Land, Rachel and Leah spoke pointed words about their father, Laban: "Are we not considered strangers by him? For he has sold us, and also completely consumed our money." (Genesis 31:15, NKJV). So, Rachel stole her father's idols and lied about it (Genesis 31:19, 34-35). Why would Rachel want an idol? Because the family was worshipping idols (Genesis 35:2). These are the parents and grandparents featured in the book of Genesis.

How did Jacob's children fare? Consider what some of them did. Reuben defiled his father's bed (Genesis 35:22, 49:4). Simeon and Levi lied and murdered (Genesis 34:13, 26-31, 49:5-6). The brothers, minus Benjamin and Reuben, agreed to kill Joseph and, when they had second thoughts, sold him as a slave (Genesis 37). Judah hired a prostitute who turned out to be his widowed daughter-in-law (Genesis 38:1-26).

In Genesis 49, we find out from Jacob what would happen to each of his sons: "Gather around so I can tell you what will happen to you in days to come" (v. 1, NIV). Much of what was said would not be considered complimentary or optimistic.

Repeatedly in Genesis, we see a family in conflict, ensnared by sinful decisions. How could these problems have been avoided? How are parents to care for their children in such a way as to steer clear of these types of failures?

I am afraid that sometimes people read about what family life was like in Genesis and concede that Christian family life is destined to be similarly messy, but that is not a good concession at all. We have the rest of the Bible to show us how to steer clear of the family problems found here.

A bad family situation created by bad parenting will have short-term and long-term ramifications. Children do not get to pick their families, and if there are bad circumstances, one can't simply leave. If there is cruelty, jealousy or annoyance, it likely goes on year after year. It is hard to be in a family when all is not going well. But on the other hand, it does not have to go badly. One family can foster adversity, and another can foster honor and respect.

> Children's children *are* the crown of old men, And the glory of children *is* their father.
>
> Proverbs 17:6, NKJV

Here, we have a picture of how a child might look up to his father and how a grandfather might treasure his grandchildren. God wants family members to enjoy and love one another, and parenting plays a significant role in the process.

The book of Genesis does not offer examples of great families. Viewing it in isolation, a person might wonder if parenting matters much. The rest of the Bible, however, debunks that conclusion. Of course, showing what happens naturally to families is a convincing argument for the importance of doing it differently, and Genesis does serve to communicate clearly the need for something better. It shows that people don't have what it takes to parent well on their own, so they need new insights from God. Without committing to receiving his wisdom on the matter, a family could turn into quite a mess.

The Importance of Parenting Throughout Proverbs

Proverbs' emphasis on parenting suggests its importance. Much of the wisdom in Proverbs specifically coaches parents.[2] Also, the book regularly addresses the writer's child.[3] For example, it says, "Listen, my son, to your father's instruction and do not forsake your mother's teaching. They are a garland to grace your head and a chain to adorn your neck." (Proverbs 1:8-9, NKJV). Most of the rest of the book is meant to teach wisdom to the children of the king. It is a father's bequest of wisdom to his children. It is a father taking his role as parent seriously.

If you are wondering how imperative good parenting is, consider what Proverbs has to say about it.

> Chasten your son while there is hope, And do not set your heart on his destruction.
>
> Proverbs 19:18, NKJV

Parents who choose to leave a child to his own devices could be accessories in his early death. For those who exert discipline, there is hope. Parenting can provide a child with a bright future, or it can result in his destruction. It is that significant.

Even the person who was the example of living a rebellious life in Proverbs 5:11-14 knew that good parenting offered him hope (NKJV).

---

2. Proverbs 10:1, 5; 13:1, 24; 15:20; 17:6, 21, 25; 19:13, 18, 26-27; 20:11, 20; 22:6, 15; 23:13, 22, 24-25; 28:7, 24; 29:3, 15, 17; 30:11, 17

3. Proverbs 1:10, 15; 2:1; 3:1, 11, 21; 4:1, 10, 20; 5:1, 7, 20; 6:1, 3, 20; 7:1, 24; 8:32; 23:15, 19, 26; 24:13, 21; 27:11; 31:1-2

And you mourn at last, When your flesh and your body are consumed, And say: "How I have hated instruction, And my heart despised correction! I have not obeyed the voice of my teachers, Nor inclined my ear to those who instructed me! I was on the verge of total ruin, In the midst of the assembly and congregation."

In the passage, the person whose flesh and body were spent received correction when he was a child. Good guidance allowed the rebellious adult to realize the mistakes he had made, even after years of rebellion.

In Proverbs, the consequences of either listening to or rejecting a parent's discipline and teaching are clarified.

A fool despises his father's instruction, But he who receives correction is prudent.

Proverbs 15:5, NKJV

He who disdains instruction despises his own soul, But he who heeds rebuke gets understanding.

Proverbs 15:32, NKJV

Proverbs is packed with these kinds of comparisons. One's decisions make one either a fool who despises himself or a prudent person with understanding. By providing discipline, parents give children a chance to respond well to it and to gain life and honor (Proverbs 10:17, 13:18). When parents provide a moral code and show children when they are wrong, it can save them from more ruinous behavior in the future (Proverbs 6:20-24). These rules provide a better life. Similarly, Ephesians 6:1-3 promises a fruitful and long life for obeying the instructions of parents (NKJV, see also Exodus 20:12 and Deuteronomy 5:16).

Children, obey your parents in the Lord, for this is right. *"Honor your father and mother,"* which is the first commandment with promise: *"that it may be well with you and you may live long on the earth."*

Good parents provide children with the guidance necessary for a good life and the blessing of God.

Another reason why parenting must secure a high priority is because "He who begets a scoffer *does so* to his sorrow, And the father of a fool has no joy." (Proverbs 17:21, NKJV). And, "A foolish son *is* a grief to his father, And bitterness to her who bore him." (Proverbs 17:25, NKJV, see also Proverbs 10:1, 30:17).

Children who do not learn restraint end up in a mess. The world may love them, but by God's standards their actions will finish in disgrace. They will be torn apart by the temptations of the devil, who "prowls around like a roaring lion looking for someone to devour" (1 Peter 5:8, NIV). Parents who do not provide discipline are greatly increasing the likelihood that a child will fail, act stupidly, be poor, be shameful, die prematurely and deny what is right (Proverbs 10:17, 12:1, 13:18, 15:10). Wisdom says that parents should earnestly provide biblical instruction and discipline. God's plan for raising children is not to leave them alone and hope they grow out of it. Parents need to get serious about their jobs. Proverbs' warnings make the risks clear, and the spread between potential outcomes described by the writer serves to intensify the message of the importance of parenting well.

The book of Proverbs promotes the fostering of a self-disciplined life by combining teaching (e.g., 4:1), warning (e.g., 4:14-15), correction involving loss or discomfort (e.g., 3:11, 5:12, 23:14), and wisdom (e.g., 4:5-6). To refer to the concept of discipline from a biblical perspective, one must think of all of these ideas at the same time. Discipline can't be just one or two of them.

We tend to use the English word *discipline* to speak only of a parent-designed consequence involving loss or discomfort, but we do use forms of the word that communicate the interconnected concepts presented in Proverbs. The aim of leading, teaching and instructing (discipleship) and correction involving loss or discomfort (discipline) is a life of self-control (self-discipline) and dedicated focus (a discipline). Proverbs says that the route to a self-disciplined life in which one practices the ways of God as a discipline is through discipleship and appropriate discipline. This holistic concept of discipline is what Proverbs considers important.

Punishment of a Rebellious Son

Good parenting matters! The Old Testament Law bears it out. Could you have handled the pressure of being a parent in Israel?

> If a man has a stubborn and rebellious son who will not obey the voice of his father or the voice of his mother, and *who*, when they have chastened him, will not heed them, then his father and his

mother shall take hold of him and bring him out to the elders of his city, to the gate of his city. And they shall say to the elders of his city, "This son of ours is stubborn and rebellious; he will not obey our voice; he is a glutton and a drunkard." Then all the men of his city shall stone him to death with stones; so you shall put away the evil from among you, and all Israel shall hear and fear.

Deuteronomy 21:18-21, NKJV (see also Exodus 21:15, 17;
Leviticus 20:9; Deuteronomy 27:16 and Proverbs 30:17)

What if a parent's laissez-faire style reared a sinful young adult? A parent would have had to hand him over to be killed by stoning.

If you were living in Old Testament times and if you had any affection for your children, you would have been desperate to raise them properly. Can you feel the weight of responsibility that parents under this law would have felt? There was significant pressure not to fail. Things haven't changed, really. There is still significant pressure not to fail because children will face eternal judgment for what is done during this life (Romans 2:6-8). Parents, this matters.

Eli and Sons

One can learn something by watching another family. Consider God's displeasure with the priest Eli and his sons, who were also priests.

> Now Eli was very old; and he heard everything his sons did to all Israel, and how they lay with the women who assembled at the door of the tabernacle of meeting.

1 Samuel 2:22, NKJV

Eli's sons were sleeping with women who were not their wives and participating in other deplorable but unspecified behavior. After hearing the news, Eli presented an ineffectual rebuke (1 Samuel 2:23-25), and God responded to his family with judgment.

> So the messenger answered and said [to Eli], "Israel has fled before the Philistines, and there has been a great slaughter among the people. Also your two sons, Hophni and Phinehas, are dead; and the ark of God has been captured." Then it happened, when he made mention of the ark of God, that Eli fell off the seat backward by the side of the gate; and his neck was broken and

he died, for the man was old and heavy. And he had judged Israel forty years.

1 Samuel 4:17-18, NKJV

Eli's sons' behavior provoked a just response. The judgment was not only for Eli's sons, but also for Eli (1 Samuel 3:14 and 4:18). This was the reason for the verdict against Eli: "his sons made themselves vile, and he did not restrain them." (1 Samuel 3:13, NKJV). Unfortunately, these men missed the message of self-control, and perhaps Eli had an air of carelessness about parenting over the course of his life.

The deaths of Eli and his sons were meant to be an example to anyone who heard what happened, and they should be an example to us (1 Samuel 3:11). Eli did hear from God. In the end, however, he was judged by how he handled his children.

This account of Eli's life doesn't mean that every father is responsible for his grown children's sinful actions; however, Eli's predicament gives those who do not plan to teach self-restraint reason for concern. We should consider 1 Samuel 2-4 when we are trying to understand how God feels about the role of parents. Stated simply, God expects parents to teach their children to control their behavior.

Manage His Own Family

First Timothy 3:4-5 speaks of requirements for servant-overseers in the fellowship of believers. This person "must manage his own family well and see that his children obey him, and he must do so in a manner worthy of full respect. (If anyone does not know how to manage his own family, how can he take care of God's [fellowship of followers]?)" (NIV). Christians who can act as older, guiding brothers to others need to prove that they are effective in their own home because effective parenting is a sampling of a Christian man's capability.

If a person is trying to decide what great things he might do for our Lord, he should look to his own family first. In the order of responsibilities, parenting takes priority. Staying away from serving roles to focus on family shows that a person loves his family, other believers and God.

What should one do if he is serving in the fellowship and has a rebellious teenage son or daughter? Should he carry on in his role? Should he wish things were different but decide this is the way it is with teenagers? No. He should leave his role for as long as it takes (weeks, months, or years) and get things in order at home because good parenting is that important.

Set Apart for God's Purpose

People often use the term *holy* to mean perfect, but its meaning is broader than that. To be holy is to be set apart. Perfection is one way God is set apart from humans, so he, indeed, is holy in that unique respect. On the other hand, most things that were considered set apart in the Old Testament were not too different than the common versions—bowls, lamp stands, animals for sacrifice, etc. The difference was that God said they were holy, and at that point, they were. For Jesus-followers, this understanding is significant because the Bible says our children are not common, but are holy (1 Corinthians 7:14).

Holy items were to be treated with great concern. Those who thought anyone could burn incense before God all died the day they tried it because they did not treat the activity with proper, holy respect (Numbers 16). Also, Nadab and Abihu, the sons of Aaron, might have thought God would appreciate their plan when they offered unauthorized sacrifices on the altar; however, fire consumed them (Leviticus 10:1-3). The record makes it clear that God really did want holy activities to be done in a certain way.

If the Spirit of God were present in the Tent of Meeting, how would you have handled priestly duties? Would you have been flippant or careless? Or, would you have been thoughtful, patient and deliberate? Would you have gone through all the necessary preparations? Since children are holy, a parent's attitude should be one of carefulness, similar to what was required of priests. This is no ordinary calling, making the children of believers no ordinary children. Therefore, parents should care for them with dignity, teach them carefully and treat life with them as a serious matter.

Defining how to handle children who are set apart for God is the goal of this book. How do we prepare? What should our attitude be? What do we do? What do we teach? Raising children well is not a matter of good intentions but a matter of doing what God wants, the way he wants it. We must be very deliberate to find out exactly what pleases the Lord, committing ourselves to the Holy Spirit and his Word. It is about following him as closely as possible, and it precludes many activities as well. For example, degrading children contradicts the notion that they are holy. We should not conclude that God is concerned about some details, but not all. We should not conclude that God is more interested in our creativity and happiness than in his holy representation. We should not add God to only one compartment of our lives but should honor him with every moment, every decision and every action.

Vitally Important

The record of the families of Genesis reveals the great need for help. From Proverbs, we learn that parents put their children in danger when they neglect to provide discipline. Also, through discipline, children receive some of God's most wonderful blessings. The Old Testament Law showed the urgency of good parenting because it required that rebellious young adults be put to death for their rebellion. We see how God dealt with Eli when he neglected to restrain his sons. From the New Testament, we learn that a person who wants to be a servant-overseer must first prove himself a good leader of his family and that our children are to be handled as holy treasures. God is clear: good parenting is important! Now, we must decide whether we are going to take him seriously or not.

This survey of passages that express the importance of good parenting is brief, especially when we consider that God chose to relate to his redeemed creation as a father. Every event recorded speaks to the importance of this relationship. One should not underestimate the extent to which God has encouraged parents to deem their job important.

Parents, devote yourselves to God, his life in you and the Scriptures. Find some counselors who make children a priority. You can read books that teach about parenting, but you should always compare the advice that authors give to the teachings of the Bible. Take any good ideas and leave behind bad philosophies. God calls parents to a great ambition with their families, and they should commit to the task wholeheartedly.

For Discussion

1. To you, how important is good parenting? Has this changed over time?
2. What distracts you from parenting well?
3. If you were to convince a friend to put more focus on parenting, what would you say?
4. Which section of this chapter motivates you most? Why?
5. Think of an individual or couple who has parented well. Why did you choose that person or couple? How would you describe their style of parenting?

Chapter 2

Goals

"For I [God] have known him [Abraham], in order that he may command his children and his household after him, that they keep the way of the LORD, to do righteousness and justice, that the LORD may bring to Abraham what He has spoken to him."

Genesis 18:19, NKJV

What are your top ten goals for your children? This is a valuable question, one worth thinking and talking about. The following chapter is a collection of some of the Bible's lessons on what a child, or any person for that matter, should be when he becomes mature.

The Bible does not lay out the kind of strategy that would lead only to raising well-adjusted and independent children, nor does it suggest that socially acceptable behavior or self-determination should be a parent's aim. God expects much more. Parents are to concern themselves with the pull of sin and the pull of God in a child's heart and to encourage their children to practice extra-ordinary obedience to their Maker.

Godly Character

God is good. Parents should want their children to be like him, displaying all his good attributes. We learn about his character by studying his ways. For example, we can think about the fruit of the Spirit (Galatians 5:22-23) or consider the ways of genuine love (1 Corinthians 13). Several books, guides and articles have been written to expound godly characteristics and to help children understand how these can be put into everyday practice. Parents should want their children to embrace these concepts, which need to be explained carefully with examples. What is kindness? What is courage? What is gentleness?

> Finally, brethren, whatever things are true, whatever things *are* noble, whatever things *are* just, whatever things *are* pure, whatever things *are* lovely, whatever things *are* of good report, if *there is* any virtue and if *there is* anything praiseworthy—meditate on these things.
>
> Philippians 4:8, NKJV

These "things" are worth thinking through with children.

Dependent

In order to have the fruit of the Spirit, children must believe they died with Christ and that they now live by God's Spirit. The aim is not to have children who follow a set of rules, have learned about Christianity and appear to comply. The goal of parents should be to raise children who know, trust, love and submit to the Spirit of the Living God. Studying character is valuable and important, but parents must also teach that a person can't produce in himself Christian character. The only way to see good fruit is to cling to Jesus.

> Remain in me, as I also remain in you. No branch can bear fruit by itself; it must remain in the vine. Neither can you bear fruit unless you remain in me. I am the vine; you are the branches. If you remain in me and I in you, you will bear much fruit; apart from me you can do nothing.
>
> John 15:4-5, NIV

Children can do nothing truly good without Jesus. So, parents should wish for their children to produce the fruit of the Spirit, and they should wish for their children to hear from Jesus and abide in his power during each day. These two are inseparable. The fruit represents the goal and dependence on Jesus is the means to attain it.

God's aim is that we would fellowship with the Holy Spirit in such a way that we do what he wants. Children are no different. Teaching them to think of themselves as fully dependent on God is a truth that enables that life.

Bound

Is God opposed to defining his own as slaves? Not at all.

> For to me the people of Isra'el are slaves; they are my slaves whom I brought out of the land of Egypt; I am ADONAI your God.
> Leviticus 25:55, Complete Jewish Bible

> For it is God's will that by doing good you should silence the ignorant talk of foolish people. Live as free people, but do not use your freedom as a cover-up for evil; live as God's slaves.
> 1 Peter 2:15-16, NIV (see also 1 Corinthians 7:22)

A positive or negative notion of the concept of slavery is completely dependent on the master. The experience could be horrible because people can be horrible. On the other hand, what if the master was perfect, full of love, brilliant, powerful and unchanging? Slavery could be fantastic. One who committed himself to another could receive protection, provision and meaningful work. He could instantly experience a higher standard of living and enjoy many of the perks of his master's social status.

Everyone is bound to something. The Bible says that one is either a slave to sin (the horrible master) or a slave to God. God's free gift of eternal life is the opportunity to become a slave to a good and loving master, to be bound to him.

> But now having been set free from sin, and having become slaves of God, you have your fruit to holiness, and the end, everlasting life. For the wages of sin *is* death, but the gift of God *is* eternal life in Christ Jesus our Lord.
> Romans 6:22-23, NKJV, see also verses 16-21 and
> 1 Corinthians 6:20

Parents should want their children to be totally submissive to God as loving, willing slaves. Parents should ask their children, "If you were to consider Jesus as your master in this situation, what decision would you make?"

The Bible says that Jesus-followers are to consider themselves to be both slaves and God's adopted children (Ephesians 1:5). This is not a contradiction. With a perfect God, living as a slave and living as a son are equally desirable roles. Again, it is all about the quality of the master.

Love, Honor and Friendship

Jesus said, "If you love me, keep my commands." (John 14:15, NIV). True love will prove itself: "But if anyone obeys his word, love for God is truly made complete in them. This is how we know we are in him" (1 John 2:5, NIV). "Dear children, let us not love with words or speech but with actions and in truth." (1 John 3:18, NIV). Love is a word of action.

Similarly, children demonstrate love toward parents by jumping to obey. Parents can say to their children, "The best way for you to show mom and dad that you love them is to do what we ask you right away, okay?" This truth about loving each other with action needs to loom large in parents' hearts because the meaty part of life is more about love and relationships than it is about rules and performance. Rules, it turns out, are a vehicle for love. Parents should be consistently proposing that children love God and others with action.

Love differs from honor, but obedience will communicate them both.

> Children, obey your parents in the Lord, for this is right. "Honor your father and mother..."
>
> Ephesians 6:1-2, NIV

Honor entails thoughtful reflection on the person to whom the honor is given, whereas love is born in the heart. Children should want to obey family rules and goals (which should be aligned with God's goals) out of love and respect, engaging their minds and hearts in this endeavor.

Jesus spoke about loving by keeping his father's commandments, which led to speaking about friendship, too:

> If you keep My commandments, you will abide in My love, just as I have kept My Father's commandments and abide in His love. These things I have spoken to you, that My joy may remain in you, and *that* your joy may be full. This is My commandment, that you love one another as I have loved you. Greater love has no one than this, than to lay down one's life for his friends. You are My friends if you do whatever I command you. No longer do I call you servants, for a servant does not know what his master is doing; but I have called you friends, for all things that I heard from My Father I have made known to you.
>
> John 15:10-15, NKJV

Think about this statement in light of all the events recorded in the Bible. One simple, life-changing truth is revealed, refreshing those who would fear and follow God: Jesus loves by laying down his life and proclaims, "I have called you friends."

If Jesus calls us friends, we must be friends with the Father as well. Father, son and adopted children are friends. If he had in his mind to call us friends, wouldn't he want us to love our children as friends, too? Parents should enjoy their children's camaraderie every day. Anything less seems cold. For me, under five-year-olds make great buddies for investigating a construction project in the neighborhood. Six- to ten-year-olds provide companionship for outdoor games. Pre-teens and teens make grocery shopping and work projects more enjoyable. I love to be with my children. Furthermore, I look forward to seeing how these friendships will develop as life unfolds from one season to the next. The goal is friendship now and continued friendship as our children grow older.

Friendship with a child, as John 15 says, ideally includes obedience to Jesus and producing fruit for the Father. It includes knowing God's will and making sacrifices for brothers and sisters. The best friendships will be founded on these ambitions.

As parents and children abide in God's love, special relationships can be formed. We have a glimpse into this type of friendship thanks to the words Paul wrote about Timothy.

> For this reason I am sending to you Timothy, my son whom I love, who is faithful in the Lord. He will remind you of my way of life in Christ Jesus, which agrees with what I teach everywhere in every [group of believers].
>
> 1 Corinthians 4:17, NIV

Although they were not blood relatives, Paul had a father-son relationship with Timothy, loving him as a co-worker, friend and son. Paul expressed how he felt about the one he referred to as a "son" in this letter:

> I thank God, whom I serve with a pure conscience, as my forefathers did, as without ceasing I remember you [Timothy] in my prayers night and day, greatly desiring to see you, being mindful of your tears, that I may be filled with joy, when I call to remembrance the genuine faith that is in you, which dwelt first

in your grandmother Lois and your mother Eunice, and I am persuaded is in you also.

2 Timothy 1:3-5, NIV

Parents can think of this kind of relationship between Paul and Timothy as a long-term goal with their own children, hoping for a sincere, genuine, glorious relationship focused on the friendship that Jesus introduces in John 15:10-15—friendship with their Maker.

Some parents believe that they can't be friends with their children until their children become adults. I bought into this philosophy at one time, committing to being the "bad guy" until my children were old enough to be friends. Please consider this very important truth regarding my mistake here: Jesus said that he called his followers friends and he said, by the Holy Spirit, that those he loved he disciplined as children (John 15:15, Hebrews 12:5-6). God disciplines his children-friends. Similarly, parents can and should discipline well and, at the same time, love their children as friends.

If parents don't have a feeling of friendship and thoughts of respect and adoration for their children now, then they have not met the friendship goal and need to ask God for a solution to this problem. The commitment to friendship is a good foundation for teaching that love and honor, whether for friends, parents, children or God, are best shown with action.

Self-Control

Many moms and dads, whether followers of Jesus or not, would hope for their children to be loving, joyful, patient, kind and good; but the concept of self-control competes with the you-only-live-once worldview. The idea of self-control can scare those who aren't believers because it gets to the heart of the cost of commitment to Jesus. On the other hand, when someone accepts salvation, he can begin to plan for eternity rather than getting temporary pleasure.

In Paul's day, the issue of self-control, eternity and righteousness was a turn-off to Felix, the unrepentant governor. When Paul brought up the subjects, Felix pulled back and said, "That's enough for now!" (Acts 24:25, NIV).

Self-control matters greatly to God. Consider the growth of a believer.

But also for this very reason, giving all diligence, add to your faith virtue, to virtue knowledge, to knowledge self-control, to self-control

perseverance, to perseverance godliness, to godliness brotherly
kindness, and to brotherly kindness love. For if these things are
yours and abound, *you* will be neither barren nor unfruitful in the
knowledge of our Lord Jesus Christ.

2 Peter 1:5-8, NKJV

Believers must add self-control to their faith, among other things. This is
how one is fruitful for Jesus.

The person without self-control is at risk.

Whoever *has* no rule over his own spirit *Is like* a city broken down,
without walls.

Proverbs 25:28, NKJV

Walls were a city's most reliable defense. Without them, enemies had an
easier time attacking. Self-control is a child's wall. Parents should not send
children into a hostile, tempting, devil-led world without it, but should
raise them in such a way that they will accept discipline and instruction,
leading to a life of restraint.

Take note that without self-control, every other good character trait
produced by the Spirit is impossible. For example, children cannot be
loving or gentle unless they can control their own selfish desires. Similarly,
if one possesses self-control, it is helpful any day of the week, at any age
and under any tempting situation. This means that lessons learned in
childhood can translate to good choices when a person is an adult. Parents
might think of it like this: teaching a child to come when he is called
requires the same self-control as learning not to steal. Teaching a child not
to yell at her brother requires the type of self-control that may save her
marriage. On the other hand, when a child does not learn restraint, it may
haunt him for years to come, and he may blame God for the condition
of his life: "A man's own folly ruins his life, yet his heart rages against the
LORD." (Proverbs 19:3, NIV).

Although the Bible does not mention strength of will on every page, it
implies its necessity from beginning to end. If parents teach their children
to be self-controlled, they may not get a lot of support from unbelievers,
who might prefer to raise children to be self-determined, that is, able to
decide on and get what they want. However, to believers it should be
obvious that, if God wants us to raise children who live a moral lifestyle,
they will need the will and ability to do so.

Self-Evaluation

Self-control goes one step further when children grow up to become their own disciplinarians, evaluating their actions on their own and correcting what needs to be corrected. They will look to God and others to catch what they miss. This, too, is part of God's goal for children.

The great lament urges self-searching.

> Let us examine our ways and test them, and let us return to the LORD.
>
> Lamentations 3:40, NIV

The necessity of self-evaluation was passed on to believers in the first century, too.

> Examine yourselves to see whether you are in the faith; test yourselves.
>
> 2 Corinthians 13:5, NIV

> Each one should test his own actions. Then he can take pride in himself, without comparing himself to somebody else.
>
> Galatians 6:4, NIV

> But let a man examine himself, and so let him eat of the bread and drink of the cup. ...For if we would judge ourselves, we would not be judged. But when we are judged, we are chastened by the Lord, that we may not be condemned with the world.
>
> 1 Corinthians 11:28, 31-32, NIV

Self-evaluation pleases our Lord, as does asking for God's help in the evaluation. In the Old Testament, one of the great God pleasers, David, poured out his heart.

> Test me, LORD, and try me, examine my heart and my mind; for I have always been mindful of your unfailing love and have lived in reliance on your faithfulness.
>
> Psalms 26:2-3, NIV

> Search me, O God, and know my heart; test me and know my anxious thoughts.
>
> Psalm 139:23, NIV

How wonderful it would be to have children who would one day cry out like David.

Self-evaluation can't function fully apart from a committed human will and the presence of the Holy Spirit. For example, in the context of the statement, "Each one should test his own actions," it says, "For he who sows to his flesh will of the flesh reap corruption, but he who sows to the Spirit will of the Spirit reap everlasting life." (Galatians 6:8, NKJV). The Spirit of Jesus will lead his followers to the self-evaluative life. Parents need to raise children who see the value of correction and seek after it later in life.

Welcoming Correction

Parents and children should welcome advice and correction.

> A fool despises his father's instruction, But he who receives correction is prudent.
>
> Proverbs 15:5, NKJV

> *It is* better to hear the rebuke of the wise than for a man to hear the song of fools.
>
> Ecclesiastes 7:5, NKJV

Families should foster an environment in which those willing to rebuke are thanked and honored. Consider how David thought of rebukes received.

> Let not my heart be drawn to what is evil, to take part in wicked deeds with men who are evildoers; let me not eat of their delicacies. Let a righteous man strike me—it is a kindness; let him rebuke me—it is oil on my head. My head will not refuse it.
>
> Psalm 141:4-5, NIV

"Let a righteous man strike me" makes it sound as if David did not care in the least how the correction was delivered: he just wanted it. If parents can teach their children to be this passionate about wanting to do the right thing, they have blessed them for life.

God rebuked David through his companion, Nathan (2 Samuel 12), and it was well received, but this is not always the case. The person who offers unwanted advice often ends up in this situation: "Have I now become your enemy by telling you the truth?" (Galatians 4:16, NIV). When someone corrects another, it is common for the corrected person to respond by defending himself or by claiming that the one who confronted him is mean and unfair. Similarly, he might mock or give the other person the silent treatment. All of these effectively block the benefit of any advice given.

Because many respond to correction negatively, few people are willing to give it. For this reason, parents need to teach their children to ask for critical advice and to be grateful when it comes. Parents should also want their children to be willing and able to communicate what they did wrong and why it was immoral. Finally, children need an example. Parents need to be thankful when they are corrected, too. Parents should believe this: "Better is open rebuke than hidden love." (Proverbs 27:5, NIV).

From a Child to a Parent

In the Garden, God's first instruction for Adam and Eve was to be fruitful parents (Genesis 1:28). If family was high on God's plan for creation, it should be important and valuable to us, too. A good goal for children is that they learn, over time, how to be good parents themselves.

Too often today, parents' ambitions for their children to be successful in a career crowd out time spent encouraging them to be good moms and dads. True, some won't have the opportunity to have children when they grow older. The solution to this problem is for parents to qualify their teaching. For example, a parent could say, "If you get married, your wife will appreciate the way you are learning to take care of that, and it will help your family." Or, a parent could ask, "How would a mom handle this situation?" A parent can also explain that even if a child does not marry when he is older, the process of preparing for the possibility will be healthy.

If moms and dads don't encourage their children to think about how to be godly spouses and parents, their silence on the issue may make their children think the roles aren't really that important compared to other activities in life. This would be the opposite of what God wants. It is important that parents promote the idea that children should be getting ready to be parents.

The bottom line is that a person should start thinking about the responsibility of family well in advance of his or her wedding day. Parents should teach good behavior, social skills, logic, compassion, etc., not primarily so that children can meet career goals, but so that they can become great husbands or wives, moms or dads.

A Family Blessed to Bless Others

After the flood, God split the people up by giving them different languages at Babel (Genesis 11:5-9). They spread out in different directions, but God had a plan to reach the people of these family groups. In Genesis 12, God outlined this plan.

> I will make you [Abraham] a great nation; I will bless you and make your name great; and you shall be a blessing. I will bless those who bless you, and I will curse him who curses you; and in you all the families of the earth shall be blessed.
>
> Genesis 12:2-3, NKJV

God decided to bless one family so that they, in turn, would bless the world. His plan was family-centric and global in nature. Deuteronomy 4:6 furnishes a good example of a part of the plan at work (NKJV).

> Therefore be careful to observe *them* [the commands]; for this *is* your wisdom and your understanding in the sight of the peoples who will hear all these statutes, and say, "Surely this great nation *is* a wise and understanding people."

Abraham's descendants were to be like a light shining in the world to show the people of every culture of the earth ("peoples") how to get back to the true God. Through Moses, Joseph, David, Solomon, Daniel, the prophets, etc., people of other nations learned about the God of the Israelites. For example, when Israel left Egypt, "Many other people went up with them" (Exodus 12:38, NIV). These were non-Israelites who had come to believe in the Israelite God. Also, consider that after Daniel came out of the lion's den, "King Darius wrote to all the nations and peoples of every language in all the earth: 'May you prosper greatly! I issue a decree that in every part of my kingdom people must fear and reverence the God of Daniel. For he is the living God and he endures forever; his kingdom will not be destroyed, his dominion will never end. He rescues and he saves; he performs signs and wonders in the heavens and on the earth. He has rescued Daniel from the power of the lions.'" (Daniel 6:25-27, NIV)

The Savior came from Abraham's family, which was the ultimate fulfillment of the promise that all people groups would be blessed through him, but God didn't stop blessing one group of people so that they could bless others. Who is the blessed-to-bless promise for now? "…those who rely on faith are blessed along with Abraham, the man of faith." (Galatians 3:9, NIV) For what purpose are they blessed? They are blessed to bless all the people groups of the earth (Matthew 28:19, Galatians 3:8). Will God accomplish his goal? He will. In the end, Jesus will have redeemed people from "every tribe and tongue and people and nation" (Revelation 5:9, NKJV, also 14:6-7).

God wishes to bless us in many ways and that blessing is to be for the sake of others, both near and far. Our finances, our speech, our prayers and our time should show our family's commitment to give to the people of the world for God's glory. "And blessed *be* His glorious name forever! And let the whole earth be filled *with* His glory. Amen and Amen." (Psalm 72:19, NKJV).

God has a family-blessing strategy today. He wants to bless you, your children and your grandchildren, so that "all peoples on earth will be blessed through you." I am not saying that you are Abraham but that God, the inventor of family, likes to bless families so that they can bring glory to him. Blessing comes in the form of wisdom, wealth, understanding, experience, the miraculous, love, faith, peace, etc. So, bless strangers. Bless those who stand against you. Bless those who don't know Jesus. Bless the poor believers around the world. Stick together as a family in order to bless whenever possible because one of God's goals is for children to be part of a family that is blessed to bless others. Therefore, fellowships should be sending out families, testifying as families, learning as families, and serving as families. Others will be watching and discovering this "wise and understanding people."

Peace for Today

Grand concepts like being blessed to bless the people of the world dwell together in the Bible with simple instructions that would affect a family every day. The grand and the routine are not independent of each other, but the great ambitions of God have their start in the everyday dealings of life. Day to day, parents should use discipline to help develop delightful children.

> Correct your son, and he will give you rest; Yes, he will give delight to your soul.
>
> Proverbs 29:17, NKJV

According to the Bible, without a determined disciplinarian, joy may be lost in the home.

When life's troubles weigh on parents' hearts and disappointment threatens their joy, what happens when children come near? Do parents say, "That brings me peace and delights my soul"? Or, do they say, "Oh no, not more trouble!"

A popular children's book called <u>Love You Forever</u>[4] attempts to capture the concept of a mother's unconditional love toward her growing boy. Consider the description of this boy's childhood. Would this bring peace to your house and delight to your soul? The two-year-old boy "ran all around the house. He pulled all the books off the shelves. He pulled all the food out of the refrigerator and he took his mother's watch and flushed it down the toilet." The mother's response was, "This child is driving me crazy." When the boy was nine years old, "...he never wanted to come in for dinner, he never wanted to take a bath and when grandma visited he always said bad words." As a teenager he "...had strange friends and wore strange clothes and he listened to strange music." The mother expressed that a zoo cage would be a more fitting home for the boy.

The fictitious mother in this book did not have a disciplined child who brought peace and made her soul delight. Her philosophy of parenting did not make these goals attainable, and it makes quite a sad story. The author of <u>Love You Forever</u> seems to hold to the notion that if a mother shows affection toward a child, he will eventually become a well-adjusted adult. To raise a child, in that case, a parent must put up with him for twenty (or thirty) years. Is this what a parent should want?

God says that parents can enjoy their children now. He intends for children to be a source of peace and soulish delight: "Yes, he will give delight to your soul." If parents are not blessed by the presence of their children, they should adjust the way they parent them. They should be careful not to confuse peace with quiet. God made children to be, at times, playful and full of energy. Parents should delight in these times, too. However, if a child rebels against his parents' rules, correction is necessary to maintain a peaceful home.

Parents whose discipline brings about peace on a daily basis will be more likely to raise children capable of blessing others. This short-term goal for children will help keep them on the path toward those long-term goals that impact the world.

---

4. Robert Munsch, *Love You Forever*, (Ontario, Canada: Firefly Books, 2000)

The Way He Should Go

God wants parents to have long-term goals for their children.

> Train up a child in the way he should go: and when he is old, he will not depart from it.
>
> Proverbs 22:6, KJV

This verse suggests that parents should think and plan long term.

The simplistic reading of the verse says that children would certainly follow God if the parents do exactly what they are supposed to do. However, Proverbs is a book of wisdom and should not be understood simplistically. The book presents actions and results that are generally true, but it will not tell us how to get what we want from every scenario. Consider Proverbs 10:3: "The Lord will not allow the righteous soul to famish" (NKJV). Have the righteous never gone hungry? What, then, should we say about Paul in Philippians 4:12? The wisdom of Proverbs 10:3 says that, in general, the righteous should not go hungry, but at times it does happen. Likewise the admonition to "Train up a child in the way he should go" will normally work out well, but not always. King Solomon himself turned from the wisdom that he had earlier in his life and worshipped other gods and goddesses in spite of his father, David's, commitment to teach him reverence for God (1 Kings 11:33, Proverbs 4:3-9). The point is that the wise understand that the sayings of Proverbs are concise truths, not absolute guarantees.

Another mistake one might make with Proverbs 22:6 is to claim that "the way he should go" is a vocation or personal interest. The parent's job, in that case, would be to figure out exactly how a particular child is wired to find his special educational strategy, pastime or career, but that way of thought is exclusive to modern society. In an agrarian society, people did not have as many ways to express talents or interests. Instead, they helped out with the family and eventually inherited their parent's work. Therefore, the thought that Proverbs 22:6 is concerned with personality, interests or vocation is misguided. Additionally, the point of the Bible is almost never, "find what you love," but instead to be content in all circumstances.

Along the same lines, some have suggested that the word "train" in this verse indicates that a unique type of education, a certain rule system, a particular method of discipline or a specific catechism should be applied.

The promise, one might say, is only good if a parent figures out the secret meaning behind the word "train." This is unnecessary speculation.

Perhaps it would help to get down to the basics of Proverbs 22:6 to understand its meaning and purpose. The Hebrew word *chanak*, translated here as "train," refers to the holy dedication of the temple or a home in Deuteronomy 20:5, 1 Kings 8:63 and 2 Chronicles 7:5. "Dedicate" or "commit" would therefore be fitting replacements for "train." The two Hebrew words that are translated "in the way he should go" literally mean road or journey (*derek*) and mouth (*peh*). The whole phrase is, "dedicate child journey mouth." Of course, these words communicate more complex ideas. The journey or road speaks of the path of life. The term *peh* is translated "commandment" 37 times in the KJV (second only to the literal translation "mouth"). Perhaps Proverbs 22:6 could be translated this way: "Dedicate a child to the narrow path of life that comes from the commandments of God, and when he is old he will not leave it." The verse speaks of a commitment to the commands of God and the long-term benefits to a child, and that is the point. The verse serves to encourage parents to search the pages of the entire Bible to understand how to show children the right road. Parents should follow God's instruction, example and Spirit specifically.

Proverbs 22:6 implores parents to present an experience to their children that will carry them safely to the grave. Letting children watch shows or play video games may keep them from getting in trouble at home, but it does not solve the long-term problem. Parents have to pay the price and take the time to discover and teach lasting lessons. Nothing else will do.

The Goals

One reason for articulating biblical goals is to make sure that the aims we perceive to be "good" and "better" do not replace those that are the "best." This chapter explored the best goals for children—biblical goals. Parents should hope their children display godly character, which is only truly attainable when a person considers himself to be a dependent slave of God. While in the house, children should develop a lifelong desire to obey God's commandments and should be taught to love and honor others with action. Between children and parents, friendship should be a goal. In addition, children should be taught to embrace self-control to the point of self-evaluation and welcoming correction. Parents should be preparing children to be godly parents who, in turn, will raise godly parents who will also raise godly parents. In the day to day, God wants moms and dads to delight in their children, which is possible when they are determined to correct bad behavior. Inasmuch as family members can live out God's will in these ways, they can be truly blessed to bless others.

Finally, parents should be aware that setting goals is not the same as learning how to accomplish them. Zeal with the wrong strategy is not what we want. I have known misguided zeal. In my desire to help my children respect God and others, I have been anxious and angry with them. I have also been the unkind drill-sergeant-type, believing that if I were the bad guy, I could eliminate my children's bad behavior once and for all. I have also trusted in moral training rather than pointing to the love of God and the power of his Spirit. Frankly, I have been inconsiderate about my children's struggle with sin. I have had to cry out, "God help me!" I needed and still need the power of his Spirit and the insight of his Word.

For Discussion

1. Which of the goals outlined in this chapter is most surprising to you?
2. Which goal speaks loudest to you?
3. How are you doing with each of the goals outlined in this chapter?
4. If you had to name your top three goals for your children, what would they be?
5. How could your family's schedule be improved to promote your top goals?
6. What are some good ways to communicate your goals to your children?

Chapter 3

GOD THE PARENT

Although this book cites verses throughout the Bible, it has a special focus on 137 chapters—the books of Exodus, Leviticus, Numbers and Deuteronomy. These books are full of information about parenting well.

After the lives of Abraham, Isaac, Jacob and after four centuries in Egypt, the family group that was to be the light of the world, Israel, grew quite large. God determined to bring them out of slavery in order to be his people in a new land, the Promised Land.[5] In this situation, God chose to deal with the people group in a remarkable fashion. He chose to treat the nation as a father treats his *son*. Deuteronomy 1:31 reflects on God's treatment of Israel these forty years: "the LORD your God carried you, as a father carries his son" (NIV). If God treated Israel as a son, we can see the way in which God would parent. Deuteronomy also says, "Remember today that your children were not the ones who saw and experienced the discipline of the LORD your God" (11:2, NIV). This means that someone did see and experience the discipline of the Lord, and, fortunately, we have a record of it.

God adopted Israel and treated the nation as a child: "Theirs is the adoption to sonship" (Romans 9:4, NIV). This New Testament verse refers to an Old Testament truth that Israel was "to be the people of his inheritance, as you [Israel] now are." (Deuteronomy 4:20, NIV, see also Numbers 6:27). A son or daughter receives an inheritance and parental instruction:

---

5. Leviticus chapters 18 and 20 tell us why the people in the Promised Land were to be driven out. They sacrificed their children to Molech and consulted mediums. They also practiced homosexuality, bestiality and incest.

From heaven he made you hear his voice to discipline you. On earth he showed you his great fire, and you heard his words from out of the fire.

Deuteronomy 4:36, NIV

Truly, God was taking Israel under his parental wing.

Some verses, such as Leviticus 26:12, strongly imply the relationship between a Father and his *son* without stating it explicitly: "I will walk among you and be your God, and you will be my people." The verse is in the context of the Father explaining what good things would come to Israel if they obeyed and what trouble they would have if they disobeyed, and it suggests a very special relationship. In Deuteronomy 8:5, the relationship is explicit: "Know then in your heart that as a man disciplines his son, so the LORD your God disciplines you." (NIV). For someone who wants help with parenting, this truth is a major breakthrough.

How should a parent treat his child? The 137 chapters of Exodus, Leviticus, Numbers and Deuteronomy show us. The Exodus was a unique time in history, a time when God acted in a unique way toward a unique nation, and we can learn from it.

The List

Needing to present my observations about God the parent in a coherent fashion, I resolved, with some hesitation, to provide a list of God's seven parenting principles as I saw them in Exodus, Leviticus, Numbers and Deuteronomy. I was hesitant because I questioned whether presenting seven points on parenting was fair to God Almighty. Was I oversimplifying his wisdom? Would my list encourage people to go to the Bible for parenting advice on their own or would it tend to replace the need for personal Bible study? Would my list of principles encourage someone to fellowship with the Holy Spirit on a day-to-day basis or would my list replace that kind of fellowship for some? My desire is that the reader continue to search the Scriptures for parenting wisdom and keep in mind that God has said that he is willing to live in us. We should relate to and worship him, not lists.

When I took an account of how a loving God *parented* Israel, I noticed the following recurring themes:

1. **Trust:** The observable process from the Exodus to the Promised Land started with a focus of building trust. God's actions gave the nation of Israel reason to be confident in him.
2. **Judging:** In Israel, God was king and he utilized judges to uphold his rules. This simple system helped Israelites trust and respect God and his laws.
3. **Heart:** Compliance gained by behavior modification did not interest God. He looked at the heart. When Israel obeyed, it was because the people's hearts were set on him. When Israel proved they were not willing to trust or obey, it revealed a collective heart problem. The heart problem would require a heart solution.
4. **Rules:** God made rules about how Israel should act and established them with repetition.
5. **Discipline:** When Israel broke the rules, God used loss or hardship to help bring about a change of heart (also referred to here as correction or consequences).
6. **Testing:** God tested Israel to see if the nation would obey. He gave commands and created circumstances that brought unexposed heart issues to the surface.
7. **Reasoning:** Deuteronomy, especially, is a book dedicated to thinking sensibly about right and wrong. God reasoned with Israel so that they would be careful to obey him. He prepared them for the future by reminding them not to repeat past mistakes. He also painted a very clear picture of what good things would come to the nation if they obeyed and what bad things would come if the people did not.

If God's example does indeed confirm the observations I have made here, it would be worthwhile to carefully consider these seven points and, even, to memorize them. The key to this concept is thinking about how to imitate God the parent.

Many of us don't think about parenting as a process of imitating God. Instead, we are looking for results. We want our children to stay out of trouble and, ultimately, to be successful; but that is the incorrect way to think about parenting. If our motive is results based and kid-centered, we are emphasizing the wrong ideas.

Popular parenting models seek to gain results by focusing either on the will of the child or the will of the parents. Some who give advice about parenting suggest that parents devote themselves to helping draw out the child's feelings to develop emotional intelligence and self-discovery. This requires that the control go to the child which, in effect, is child-centered parenting. Others advise parents to think of children as welcomed members of the family who are an addition to the central unit, the husband and the wife. Children are loved but expected to toe the line, which could be thought of as parent-centered parenting.

The best way to be a truly successful parent is to adore, admire, obey and imitate God and to consider his examples of parenting. Today we can say, "I am going to act like you, Father. I am going to try to imitate the way you are with your children." This mindset is absolutely necessary because it is the only attitude that leads to God-centered parenting. In the end, we should want to parent well, not for results, but because it honors God to imitate him. "Be imitators of God, therefore, as dearly loved children" (Ephesians 5:1, NIV).

Understanding Correctly

I need to do a little housekeeping before presenting my findings about imitating God the parent in detail in the remainder of this book. Most importantly, I need to explain that there are many biblical references that do not fall into God's parenting example. A parent could do harm if he were to try to copy everything God has done. God is the holy, all-powerful, all-knowing Creator. What he did through history was not done exclusively from a parental perspective. He was showing his greatness and righteousness, and he was preparing the way for sins to be forgiven and for the relationship with him to be restored. He was (and is) also preparing to destroy the earth, judge every person and condemn many to eternal punishment. Just as it is important to find ways to imitate God, it is also important to identify what parents should not imitate because their role is not to be God, but to be moms and dads.

Parents would be mistaken to attempt to duplicate something like the Exodus agreement because it was not indicative of a father-child relationship. If Israel broke the covenant, God had every right to sever his relationship with the nation (e.g., Exodus 32:9-10, Deuteronomy 9:11-29).

Also, the "you" in verses like Deuteronomy 1:31, 4:20, 8:5, 11:2 and Leviticus 26:12 is not "each one of you," but "all of you" as a group of people, the nation of Israel. God was treating the nation as a child, not individuals as children. This is an important distinction; and if we don't pay attention to it, we will end up with strange conclusions from our study. Consider Exodus 20:5-6 (NIV, see also Deuteronomy 5:9-10).

> You shall not bow down to them [idols] or worship them; for I, the Lord your God, am a jealous God, punishing the children for the sin of the parents to the third and fourth generation of those who hate me, but showing love to a thousand generations of those who love me and keep my commandments.

If "you" was meant to apply to each individual, then it goes against God's own instructions that children should not die for their parents' lawlessness (Deuteronomy 24:16, Ezekiel chapter 18). The interpretation "each one of you" in Exodus 20:5-6 does damage to the reputation of God (making him appear unfair) and to the lives of those who believe it (causing them to wonder what punishment they will be getting for their matriarch and patriarch's sins). On the other hand, the passage makes sense when we read it in light of the fact that God was treating one nation—"all of you"— as a father would treat his own child. If the people were to serve God, they would never receive painful discipline; however, if they disobeyed, the nation would receive discipline for several generations. Why several generations? Because God knew how long it would take for a society to change and to humbly seek him (Deuteronomy 30:1-3). We can note that very often, hardship came to Israel for many years at a time (e.g., Judges 3:14, 13:1, Jeremiah 25:11, Daniel 9:2). God's example of parenting is specific to the nation of Israel as a whole, not to each person who was part of the Exodus (e.g., Numbers 25:8, 26:10). This distinction is very important. We must look at the nation as if it were a single person to understand how to imitate God.

Certain rules that God gave the nation would not be fitting in our search for fatherly examples, either. "Tooth for tooth," for example, does not work in parenting or even in one's personal life, as Jesus points out in Matthew 5:38-44 (see Leviticus 24:20). The "tooth for tooth" rule was meant to punish an individual who acted violently (and the punishment exactly matched the crime). The individual suffered loss and society benefited because such crimes against others were less likely to happen in the future. This is not how parental discipline works. A parent's discipline should always be designed with the best for the one who did the wrong (his child) in mind. Thus, commands like Leviticus 24:20 would not apply to parenting.

In order to gain insight from the records of the Old Testament, we must realize the fact that God did not show parenting in every situation. Also, God made some rules and consequences that were not the kind a father would make, and he did not treat individuals or other nations as children. With these things in mind, we can better investigate the actions of God to understand good parenting.

One more thing. I primarily use three words to refer to loss or hardship meant to help a child refrain from disobedience—discipline, correction and consequence. All of these require some clarification. First, the word *correction* may be thought of by some to refer only to verbal correction, but I mean something more. Second, the *consequence* to which I refer is a parent's well thought out choice meant for the benefit of the child, not a consequence a child would suffer because his parents act foolishly. Finally, *discipline* in this context is accurate in English, but as I explained in chapter 1 while making observations from the book of Proverbs, the biblical concept of discipline includes other components like teaching, preparing and developing a self-controlled life. It is a holistic approach. Whether I use the word consequence, discipline or correction to refer to hardship or loss that a parent administers to a child after disobedience, one should always keep in mind that biblical parenting has many facets.

A Unique Case

Another issue to note about God's fathering of the nation of Israel was that if Israel were a "child," it would be a unique case. When we think about everything God did for Israel, we might think that they were an especially decent people group who made a few mistakes, but that is not the case. In fact, they were consistently stubborn and thoroughly unworthy of all of God's goodness (Deuteronomy 9:4-6). Rather than deserving the Promised Land, they deserved the description "a stiff-necked" and "rebellious" people (Deuteronomy 31:27, NIV). The nation came out of Egypt with lusts and strange beliefs. The people were idolaters and seemed to enjoy that lifestyle (Ezekiel 20:6-8, Acts 7:42-54). Recall that when they made the golden calf, they had some sort of immoral party (Exodus 32:6, 17; 1 Corinthians 10:7, 20). To add to this point, we can observe that when they were near the Midianites they worshiped Midianite idols, and Israeli men hired Midianite women for immorality (Numbers 25:1, 8; 1 Corinthians 10:8). The society God claimed to treat as a "child" was made up of millions of people who were experienced in the ways of the pagan world, which made it a unique *parenting* situation. It took quite a bit of time, grief and reason to bring a degree of civility to this rogue civilization.

I do not believe that it is helpful for parents to expect the worst, bemoaning that they have "stiff-necked" and "rebellious" children. Children may occasionally be challenging, but they are not like Israel. They come to us small and needy (usually). By God's design, they are made to receive guidance from parents year after year as they grow. Heartaches may come from time to time, but much of a parent's experience with their children will likely be warm and friendly.

Personal Bias

I am firmly committed to expound on the seven lessons I derived from God's parenting example; but the simple fact remains that for a person to learn, he must want to learn. Almost everyone has established ideas about how to parent. Some have looked to extra-biblical sources for parenting help, and some of these ideas contradict God's teaching. All of us have had our own childhood experiences which are well engrained in our way of thinking and our actions. For better or worse, these ideas create a bias in our minds toward certain concepts. If we approach the Bible with biases, it may spoil our ability to see and live out God's parenting example. We may not accept his ideas because we are so entrenched in our own.

People sometimes protect their biases and write off the Bible by saying things like, "These things are personal decisions because the Bible doesn't give us enough direction." "Christians need to stick to the essential truths." "This topic is just mentioned a couple of times." "What you decide is right for you, and what I decide is right for me." Instead of grasping for statements like these, we must trust the Word and its Author.

Another way people allow their biases to ruin God's plan to help them is by picking and choosing verses to support their point of view. Picking and choosing will, at the very least, leave our understanding incomplete. Looking hard through the Bible and being open to whatever we find is the very best way to learn what pleases God most.

Though biases are personal, humans sometimes avoid people who would challenge their views. This can further inhibit one's ability to see the truth. Overcoming any biases takes humility and commitment, and it is a necessary first step in truly understanding God's inspired words. It is fine to consider our feelings, experience, habits, traditions and book learning, but we should make sure that priority in our understanding always defers to the wisdom found in the Bible.

Using the Whole Bible

The seven topics discussed in the rest of this book are based on findings from the Old Testament, so it is important that the reader does not have a bias against it. One should trust that the principles God gave us in the Old Covenant still instruct today.

When Paul taught about Jesus, he taught out of the Old Testament. There was no New Testament at that time, yet Paul "reasoned with them from the Scriptures explaining and demonstrating that the Christ had to suffer and rise again from the dead, and saying, 'This Jesus whom I *declare* to you is the Christ.'" (Acts 17:2-3, NKJV, see also Acts 17:11). Those "Scriptures" were the Old Testament. Paul also concluded that "the law is holy, and the commandment is holy, righteous and good." (Romans 7:12, NIV). According to 2 Timothy 3:16-17, the Old Testament "*is* given by inspiration of God, and *is* profitable for doctrine, for reproof, for correction, for instruction in righteousness, that the man of God may be complete, thoroughly equipped for every good work." (NKJV).

The Old Testament has remarkable value and its teachings can lead our children to Christ. Second Timothy 3:15 says the Old Testament is "able to make you wise for salvation through faith which is in Christ Jesus" (NKJV, see also Romans 7:7, Galatians 3:24). The teaching principles of the law help develop a child's conscience, the historical record gives him a context for understanding God's ways and purposes, and the prophetic elements point him to Jesus (see Luke 24:27, 44-47).

Some imagine life in Old Testament times to be liturgical and spiritually empty, but following God wasn't rote ritual. Actually, what they were doing was the opposite in many ways. In animal sacrifice, for example, they were taking something that they owned and knew well to be put to death for their sin, reminding them that because of sin, they would "surely die" (Genesis 2:17, NKJV). Forgiveness was experiential and relational, not ceremonial and liturgical. "The wages of sin *is* death" would have been real to them (Romans 6:23, NKJV).

Some biases against the Old Testament may come from modern living. For example, if a person is put off by the fact that sacrifices were bloody, he is not likely to appreciate the lesson of those sacrifices. We are among the first generations who don't regularly catch, kill, bleed, skin or pluck animals to be eaten. All these things are usually done for us. Watching animals die, whether in sacrifice or for dinner, was a way of life for people throughout history.[6] Those experiences communicated a spiritual truth.

> For the life of a creature is in the blood, and I have given it to you to make atonement for yourselves on the altar; it is the blood that makes atonement for one's life.
>
> Leviticus 17:11, NIV

God intended for all people to learn from observing these Old Testament processes. In sin is death, and in blood is life. The life-blood of God's Son was necessary to set us free from sin.

Our lives are insulated from reality, not just in the fact that we don't have to kill the animals we eat. Few of us stay outside in prolonged exposure to the power of nature—wind, heat, snow, hail, lightning, rain, wild animals, etc. Most of us don't live the demanding lives of un-modernized agrarians. If life lessons for those who lived in Old Testament times were derived from experiences we no longer have, perhaps some of us may be disinterested in understanding these lessons. Perhaps we are too quick to ask, "What does the passage say about me and my life?" Instead, we need to do our best to understand what any particular part of the Bible was meant to communicate to the original hearers. This is how we learn its true meaning.

Believers need to understand what was taught in the Old Testament to understand God. They should not brush it off as something foreign to them. They should take time to understand it rightly because in it is wisdom.

Not Exasperated

Bias against the Old Testament will cause us to misunderstand verses in the New Testament. For example, for a long time I misunderstood

---

6. Most of the remains of sacrificed animals were eaten by the priests. It was God's provision for them (Deuteronomy 18:1).

Ephesians 6:4 because I didn't think about how it might reference the Old Testament (NIV).

> Fathers, do not exasperate your children; instead, bring them up in the training and instruction of the Lord.

When I thought about the verse without considering the Old Testament, I was asking questions like, "Was I doing something that exasperated? Did my expectations or my discipline exasperate? Were my rules exasperating? Was it permissiveness or rigidity that exasperated a child?" I was completely missing the point of the verse, which does not try to tell us what exasperates, but what does not exasperate. According to the verse, there is only one thing that does not exasperate, and that is "the training and instruction of the Lord," which was already disclosed in the Old Testament. I didn't get it because I didn't think seriously about how much information on parenting the beginning of the Bible would provide. I had a bias that kept me from searching rigorously through the whole Bible.

The Old Testament is extremely helpful to those without a bias against it. When a person treats it as the reliable Word of God, he can more accurately understand the New Testament. That person can also better learn about the character and plans of God.

The Rest of This Book

One might wish that the Bible provided specific how-to steps in every conceivable circumstance a parent will face, but that is not the way it is. What we do have, though, is more than sufficient. Whether one has teens or toddlers, strong-willed or compliant children, the teachings in the Bible apply. A reasonable expectation from God would be, "Show me your example and your ways and walk with me." The answers to questions about specific circumstances will follow.

This does not mean that parenting is a lonely proposition, or that it should be. Parents should seek encouragement, prayer and advice from other believers. Primarily, though, our parenting framework should come from the Bible.

How did God train his "child," Israel, during the Exodus? He built trust. He understood what it would take to change Israel's heart. He made rules and required that Israel obey them. He used judges. He knew that discipline hurt the nation for a while, yet he was willing to do it anyway for their sake. He tested Israel to see if they would obey, even in tough situations. He also taught, prepared and reasoned with them. The Bible recorded him doing these things consistently with mercy, love and blessing.

When I started studying the Bible to write about parenting, I didn't think, "There are seven points I want to make, and I can find a little of each in Exodus, Leviticus, Numbers and Deuteronomy." Instead, I studied and took notes on each book, asking, "What do my notes show that is common throughout?" I seriously considered presenting the information the way I found it, one Bible chapter at a time. I wanted to share the process of biblical discovery, but I also realized that the reader would be better served with topical organization.

The remainder of this book pursues the seven ideas on the list. One chapter considers ways to build trust, one explains judicial parenting, two explore the heart, two address making rules, two deal with discipline, one explains testing and one considers reasoning about important issues of life.

For Discussion

1. Are you comfortable with the idea that God would apply good parenting concepts in order to care for a nation? Can parents imitate him in this?
2. Of the seven parenting concepts listed in this chapter, what do you think interests you most right now? Which do you think will help your parenting the most?
3. Do you have any personal bias that may affect your Bible study or application of biblical principles in parenting?

Chapter 4

TRUST

One generation shall praise Your works to another, And shall declare Your mighty acts.

Psalm 145:4, NKJV

God's relationship with the people of Israel in the Exodus started with trust. I considered using the word "love" for the first observation about God's parenting style, but "trust" better describes the historic record.

According to Abraham Maslow's hierarchy of human needs, people generally choose to be safe (a trusted situation) before they choose to be loved.[7] If Maslow is right, the newly-adopted *child*, Israel, would first seek to know that it could have confidence in God. If Israel were afraid of the Egyptians and the dangers of the wilderness, believing God could deliver them safely would be their primary concern. However, it wasn't just that Israel needed to be able to trust God, but that God wished to be trusted. In fact, it is impossible to please God without finding him worthy of trust (Hebrews 11:6).

Trust is not better than love or *vice versa*. They are different and trust stands out in certain circumstances. If a child said, "I love you, Mom," a mom would find it endearing. If a child said, "Mom, I trust you," a mom would feel a duty to maintain that trust. God calls us to love people regardless of character, but to say that we trust someone speaks of their integrity and reputation. It feels good to be loved, but it is honorable to be trusted. Trust is a very powerful notion, and it is the right way to approach God.

7. Abraham H. Maslow, "A Theory of Human Motivation," *Psychological Review* 50, (1943): 370-396. http://psychclassics.yorku.ca/Maslow/motivation.htm

In the wilderness, Israel might have debated whether God was lovable, but his record would prove that he was trustworthy. When dealing with a temperamental nation, trustworthiness would last through the up-and-down emotions of the day better than the human perception of love.

God Built Trust

As we read about the great Exodus, the years in the desert and the preparation for the Promised Land, it is clear that God was not only a rule giver. He constantly presented himself as the one with "the mighty hand and outstretched arm" (Deuteronomy 7:19, NIV). By his power, he proved himself trustworthy in the plagues on Egypt, in his presence in the cloud by day and fire by night, in the destruction of Egypt's army and on many other occasions (Exodus 7-10, 13:21-22, 14:22-30).

Right before his death, Moses spoke these words to Israel:

> The LORD himself goes before you and will be with you; he will never leave you nor forsake you. Do not be afraid; do not be discouraged.
>
> Deuteronomy 31:8, NIV

After forty years of service (and one hundred and twenty years of life), Moses knew the Almighty's character. God was faithful to the Israelites.

God is trustworthy, which is why we can speak of him to our children confidently today. "God will provide." "God will show us." "God intends to bless us." "God will use us for his purposes." "God loved us enough to die for us." "I have made many mistakes, but he has forgiven me and taken care of me anyway." "God can be trusted."

Trusted Parents

There is a big difference between God's trustworthiness (having the power to save) and what parents can do (try not to mess up). Although parents should be the kind of moms and dads their children can rely on, they should point to God when they speak about trusting someone. Only God is qualified to be trusted with one's life. Children need to put their trust in him.

That said, children are much better off when parents are reliable. Listening, playing, being involved and working together are all part of developing relationships. Showing love and having fun help endear a child to his parents. Trust required for a relationship is broken when parents disobey God's rules, act carelessly, disengage, show pride, focus on trivial issues, become anxious or act out in anger. Being consistent, thorough and logical are important for keeping trust. One of the most important ways to maintain trust is to be fair and judicial with children, which I will address at length in the next chapter. Good discipline also builds trust.

> Moreover, we have all had human fathers who disciplined us and we respected them for it. How much more should we submit to the Father of our spirits and live!
>
> Hebrews 12:9, NIV

Many parents have been led to believe that their children will respect them less if they use discipline. That idea is completely turned around. The better the discipline, the more children can trust their parents.

Rather than trying to convince their children to trust them, parents should focus on what God requires. If parents honor God with their actions, they will maintain the trust needed for good relationships with their children, and it helps create an atmosphere in which their children can experience the One with "the mighty hand and outstretched arm."

Experiencing God in the Family

There are many life pursuits from which to choose, but only the pursuit of Jesus brings life to the fullest. Parents need to pursue and introduce their children to him. They need to help children understand who God truly is. His power is unthinkable. His knowledge pierces the most hidden thoughts of the human heart. This life isn't a game or a pastime, and knowing this ought to help children know him. This is why the Bible advises people to fear God (e.g., Deuteronomy 6:2). True fear of God shows absolute respect for him and the commands he gave us. Faith must lead to obedience. We shouldn't just fear God, but we should also love him (e.g., Deuteronomy 6:5). How do we show our love for him? We obey him (John 14:15).

Parents must share the Good News, which starts with understanding that we are all going to be judged according to God's good rules. If we have disobeyed or sinned, then we will be condemned. We have earned death. The Good News is that Jesus has died to pay our penalty. If we trust him enough to turn from our sin and to be filled with his Holy Spirit, we will get his reward, living with him, rather than the just penalty. Parents shouldn't explain this once and consider it done, but rather continue to find different ways and new opportunities to share the Good News. They might consider using simple, clear explanations like the Romans Road, the Four Spiritual Laws and The Bridge to Life™.

Children also need to understand how water immersion relates to the Good News. In immersion, a person acts out being buried in a watery grave and then coming out of the water to new life. It is about being born again by believing in Jesus.

Experiencing the Bible

In order to mature in God, children must experience the living words of the Bible. Parents and children should read and discuss it together. Parents might utilize a helpful Bible study. Or, they could make the learning fun and engaging by reading and narrating while children act out biblical events. There is also an abundance of video and audio lessons that help families think about God and his ways.

Studying together is great, but children should experience the Word of God all on their own, too. One idea is to have children listen to the Bible for 20 or 30 minutes a day. By doing this, children have firsthand experience with the entire Bible at a young age. It is possible to listen from beginning to end several times before the teen years.

Memorization is a good way to meditate on the Bible and retain its truths for life. Families can memorize verses, chapters or even whole books of the Bible together.

Although the following passage was advice for a king about studying the Bible, it seems appropriate for us, too.

> When he [the king] takes the throne of his kingdom, he is to write for himself on a scroll a copy of this law, taken from that of the Levitical priests. It is to be with him, and he is to read it all the days of his life so that he may learn to revere the LORD his God and follow carefully all the words of this law and these decrees and not consider himself better than his fellow Israelites and turn from the law to the right or to the left. Then he and his descendants will reign a long time over his kingdom in Israel.
>
> Deuteronomy 17:18-20, NIV

The king's Bible study was a means of redirecting his focus from temptation to healthy thoughts. For the same reason, parents and children should be in the Word daily, which should help to foster a deep appreciation for God.

Experiencing Worship

Parents should teach their children how to turn their appreciation for God into authentic praise. God's presence, worship and prayer are necessary for an individual's edification, and parents should pursue such experiences with their families.

Worship requires that we take time to remember and appreciate who God is and what he has done, which leads to thankfulness. Consider how the Bible emphasizes remembering. Deuteronomy 7:18 says, "… remember well what the LORD your God did to Pharaoh and to all Egypt" (NIV). God also told Israel to keep a serving of manna so that the people in future generations would remember how he provided on a daily basis (Exodus 16:32-33). Jesus told the disciples to let the unleavened bread and the wine be reminders of him (Luke 22:19, 1 Corinthians 11:24-25). Washing each other's feet was also meant to help them remember (John 13:3-17). These memories were to lead to appreciating God.

Since worship is directly tied to remembering and appreciating, it can take on different forms than a worship meeting. For example, in Exodus 17, Moses worshiped by building an altar for remembrance called "The Lord is my Banner" (v. 15, NIV). Families can worship in unique ways as well. For instance, family pictures or videos can be used to stir up thankfulness and to remember that "God has loved us." Memories of God's work in our lives can be written, related to certain objects or in pictures. Families can also worship God for what he has done for others whom they know. They can even remember and appreciate what he did long ago (consider Psalm 77, 105, 1 Chronicles 16:7-36).

Often, worship does mean meeting together to sing praise and proclaim the goodness of God. The First century worship meetings were an encounter that could cause a person to exclaim, "God is really among you!" (1 Corinthians 14:25, NIV). A key feature of these meetings was that everyone was encouraged to participate (1 Corinthians 11-14). These kinds of meetings were, and still are, important for children and adults.

In fact, meetings in which everyone may share a song, verse or word that God has spoken to their spirit "must be done so that [those assembling] may be built up" (1 Corinthians 14:26, NIV). Finding a meeting in which all worshipers are able to participate may prove difficult. It might mean inviting people to such a meeting.

Splitting up the family and separating children into groups by age may be counterproductive to the goal of helping them become mature disciples of Jesus. God should be worshiped and experienced with the spiritually mature, most of whom will be older. Families should think about how they can worship with other families and with individuals of various ages.

Remembering, being thankful, and worshiping together in a way that allows all to participate according to the Spirit's leading, builds a child's faith in our worship-worthy God. Parents should maintain a steady pursuit of these types of experiences with their families.

Experiencing His Spirit

Parents should tell their children of their relationship with the Spirit of Jesus (John 16:1-15). On a regular basis, they should talk about how God is working in their lives, about how they love him and about how good it is to be loved by him. Children need an example, not only of sticking to a moral code, but of actually knowing and trusting God.

In Numbers 11, Joshua was concerned that the Spirit of God had fallen on a few people in the camp and he beseeched Moses to stop them, but Moses disagreed.

> Then Moses said to him [Joshua], 'Are you zealous for my sake? Oh, that all the LORD's people were prophets *and* that the LORD would put His Spirit upon them!'
>
> Numbers 11:29, NKJV

In the same way, God's Spirit wants to immerse our children and work beyond the confines of normal human capabilities (Acts 19:6). For this reason, parents should teach their children about the Holy Spirit and his gifts (1 Corinthians 12:31, 14:1). All gifts of the Spirit can be understood by studying the Bible to see how God moved in or upon people to do what was beyond their power or insight. For example, Jesus knew that Nathanael was sitting under a tree before they met (John 1:48). This is a gift of knowledge, that is, something supernaturally known (1 Corinthians

12:8). A person who has studied for many years obtains knowledge and the one who loves to learn will seek knowledge, but a gift of knowledge is supernatural. God wants children and adults to seek these types of gifts for his glory's sake—"that the LORD would put His Spirit upon them!"

Prayer

The idea that God lives with and in us is no small matter. It is a big deal, yet he asked us to speak to him in simple terms about all that we need. Supernatural living starts with and relies on straightforward requests. So, families should talk to God together often.

Almost every time we leave the house to go somewhere, one of our children will ask if we can talk to God. It was not our idea but theirs. They have seen that God is close and that he gives to those who ask, so they petition him.

Are any verses more pointed about the need and motive for prayer than James 4:2-3 (NIV)?

> You desire but do not have, so you kill. You covet but you cannot get what you want, so you quarrel and fight. You do not have because you do not ask God. When you ask, you do not receive, because you ask with wrong motives, that you may spend what you get on your pleasures.

This speaks of opportunity to me. We can line our hearts up with God's plan, ask, and get what we need. This is faith.

At times, the ones perceived to be most spiritual among us don't take Jesus' advice: "And when you pray, do not keep on babbling like pagans, for they think they will be heard because of their many words." (Matthew 6:7, NIV). Long, elaborate prayers can be motivated by the superstitious belief that God is more likely to respond if we talk to him about what we need at great length. Instead, a family should simply ask and be thankful. Also, parents should help their children think beyond their own needs to the needs of others and to God's plan in the world—"your kingdom come, your will be done, on earth as it is in heaven." (Matthew 6:10, NIV).

When we seek his provision for the right reasons, we can take steps of faith. Our job is to follow God to places where he will show himself faithful. Watching TV, gaming or wasting time on the Internet is not going to be that place. For Israel, it was the experience of slavery in Egypt, being set free, and following the fire and the cloud. We get to know God in situations that give him the opportunity to show his ability and reliability. This is where a genuine trust in and love for God develops, and we internalize the fact that we are his adopted children.

Our daughter, Meredith, reminds us that God was faithful to lead us in a move to Florida. While we were asking him about whether we should move, my wife, Ginny, was impressed that the baby we were expecting should be called Meredith. We soon found out that the name likely means "of the sea." She was born a month after we moved, and her name is another testimony to God's faithfulness in our lives. Many good experiences and challenges have come since the move, including the writing of this book. God wants us to ask him first, to experience his plan and then to remember what he has done in order to be grateful. That is why it is so important that we and our children speak to him.

Serving

Parents should also give children opportunities to love and serve others, especially those unlikely to return the favor. Jesus said, "But if you love those who love you, what credit is that to you? For even sinners love those who love them. And if you do good to those who do good to you, what credit is that to you? For even sinners do the same." (Luke 6:32-33, NKJV). Jesus' words are a convicting challenge to find ways to care for strangers and neighbors. "It is more blessed to give than to receive," but that is something that is realized only by experience (Acts 20:35, NKJV).

Christian biographies are a great way to ponder the lives of people who have served. This type of book can help children identify with those who have pursued God and loved others.

Blessing Children

One day one of our boys asked me a question about a verse he had read.

> Then all the people left, each for his own home, and David returned home to bless his family.
>
> 1 Chronicles 16:43 (see also 2 Samuel 6:20)

My son asked, "Did that mean that they were blessed to see him again?" I said, with my arms stretched wide and my voice deep as if to be David,

"You are now blessed with my presence again." He laughed, realizing how ridiculous I sounded. Then I explained that David came in to speak the blessings of God to his family. By his words, he was going to convey some good thing of God to them.

Much was and is still accomplished in the Kingdom of God by speaking a blessing (In Hebrew, *barak*, literally "to kneel") over another person. It acknowledges that God first spoke things into existence. Now we can imitate him by speaking his principles and will. Blessing is, in some sense, saying, "I consider you worthwhile and get on my knees to intercede so that God will make you successful in the things that matter." Blessing communicates adoration and worth. It builds faith and imparts the good things that come from a good God. If we hope for our children to experience God's goodness, we should say it out loud to them. We might say, "God bless you with peace" and "I bless you to know God." We can ask them, "How do you want to be blessed by God?" We can also encourage our children to bless one another. This does not have to be a formal affair. One could simply ask a child how he would bless another.

One idea for blessing children or grandchildren would be to read Colossians 1:9-14 as if it was to them (NIV).

> For this reason, since the day we heard about you, we have not stopped praying for you and asking God to fill you with the knowledge of his will through all spiritual wisdom and understanding. And we pray this in order that you may live a life worthy of the Lord and may please him in every way: bearing fruit in every good work, growing in the knowledge of God, being strengthened with all power according to his glorious might so that you may have great endurance and patience, and joyfully giving thanks to the Father, who has qualified you to share in the inheritance of the saints in the kingdom of light. For he has rescued us from the dominion of darkness and brought us into the kingdom of the Son he loves, in whom we have redemption, the forgiveness of sins.

Or, a parent or grandparent could speak Ephesians 3:14-19 or Numbers 6:22-27 to them (NKJV).

> For this reason I bow my knees to the Father of our Lord Jesus Christ, from whom the whole family in heaven and earth is named, that He would grant you, according to the riches of His glory, to

be strengthened with might through His Spirit in the inner man, that Christ may dwell in your hearts through faith; that you, being rooted and grounded in love, may be able to comprehend with all the saints what *is* the width and length and depth and height—to know the love of Christ which passes knowledge; that you may be filled with all the fullness of God.

And the LORD spoke to Moses, saying: "Speak to Aaron and his sons, saying, 'This is the way you shall bless the children of Israel. Say to them: "The LORD bless you and keep you; The LORD make His face shine upon you, And be gracious to you; The LORD lift up His countenance upon you, And give you peace."' "So they shall put My name on the children of Israel, and I will bless them.'"

The Bible has many such blessings (e.g., Exodus 23:25-26, Deuteronomy 1:11, 33:1-29, Jeremiah 29:11-13, 2 Corinthians 13:9-11, 2 Thessalonians 1:11-12), and parents could say these to their children to bring the blessings and build faith in God.

God Intervenes

If God exists, and he does, then he will not only prove himself in our children's lives, but he will enjoy doing so. If parents obey God, he will have opportunity to reveal his good work in both subtle and spectacular ways.

In Numbers 16, Israel was complaining about the fact that Aaron and his family had a special job in the tent of God. In Numbers 17, Moses placed the staffs of each of the perceived-to-be leaders of the tribes of Israel in the tent of meeting. The matter would be settled by God. The next day, Aaron's staff had buds, blossoms and ripe almonds growing out of it. The other people's staffs were duds. In verse 12 of Chapter 17, Israel agreed with God's appointment of Aaron to special, holy work in the tent of meeting. God made his plan clear. Aaron's staff was kept as a reminder that Israel should not grumble about such things. God performed a miracle to set his *child* on the right path.

We should ask God to use his power as he did for Israel in Numbers 17. I am not suggesting a repeat of the buds and the staff, but that we should ask God to be uniquely involved in our family. We should let him solve problems and provide for our needs and wants.

I believe that God wants to make himself known even in little things. For a time, our daughter was really pressing us for some cowboy boots. I wanted her to have some, and she had been given money to buy them; but when we went to order them, I sensed a resounding, "No," in my spirit, but I could not tell her why. Her patience was beginning to stretch thin when, unsolicited, an acquaintance gave her a pair of boots that had been "just sitting in the closet" still new in the box. They were the right size and were high quality. We were all encouraged by this nice gift and provision from the Lord. In the process, our daughter was learning how to trust Jesus. Although cowboy boots aren't a big deal, showing a child that God really does want to be involved in our lives is.

Faith

Trusting God in our thoughts and actions is the solution to life's problems. For example, if we have faith to see our life on earth as relatively short-lived, like a vapor, a mist (James 4:14), then jealousy, covetousness and strong desire lose their grip. Faith in action is also being thankful to God in everything. We know "that in all things God works for the good of those who love him" (Romans 8:28, NIV), but capitalizing on that truth in a tough situation requires thankfulness. If parents endear these truths to their own hearts, they will be able to teach them to their children.

When a child cheats, lies, refuses to obey, speaks negatively about another person, eats too much, takes a toy from someone, is lazy or does any other unacceptable-to-God behavior, it is, in part, for lack of trust in a good God. Disobedience is a symptom of independence from God. When parents see it, they should be reminded to return to the fundamentals of experiencing the Almighty. Parents should help children grasp that our Heavenly Father is close and reliable. They should share the Good News. They should study the Bible, worship and pursue the Holy Spirit with their children. Parents should be open about what God is doing day to day in their lives and help their families remember how he has been faithful to them. Families should speak to God together and should go where God calls them to go and do what God calls them to do.

It is necessary to add that, for children to trust God, parents must combat lies. Evolution between the species isn't fact. Satisfaction can't be found in something or someone. Parents should not be afraid when children debate issues like these. Such reasoning is necessary for trusting

God in a world full of lies. When possible, parents should consider persuading by asking questions that help lead a child to a good conclusion rather than by telling him what the conclusion ought to be.

To introduce God our Father and his ways to children it will take time, the right priorities and true intention. If parents are not willing to design their lives to pursue God together with their family, they are unlikely to end up with good results. Every day presents decisions—easy, convenient, and fun decisions. Parents need to have the gumption to say *yes* to some activities and *no* to others.

One night we joined several families to worship in a living room. Some verses about Passover and the Lord's Supper came up, so we decided to stop the meeting and make unleavened flat bread. While we were eating it, we talked about how the bread had substance. For the Israelites, it was good energy food for the next day's hike out of Egypt. We also talked about how Jesus is the same for us. He is not a small morsel, but one who can fill a person up and stick with him during the day. We should gratefully get our daily energy from him. It was a faith-building night for all of us. The families who met had made the priority to get together and were blessed because of it. If parents are willing to lay down their lives so that their children can take up their lives in Jesus Christ, God will meet them there.

For Discussion

1. Do you look for opportunities for your children to have rich experiences with God? Where do you find them?
2. Are your children introduced to the living, loving God, or to ritual?
3. Are you providing your children with reasonable responses to the arguments of skeptics? What issues have come up?
4. Does God have your children's trust?
5. What would you want to say to bless your children?
6. Are you seeking to submit yourself to God? Are you a trustworthy parent?
7. Have you experienced a time when you asked God for a need and have seen his provision? How do you share that experience with your children? Have your children had first hand experiences with answered prayers?
8. How do you explain to your children the power of the Holy Spirit?
9. What are some options for serving others with your children?
10. What have you found to be beneficial in terms of helping your children to know the Bible?

Chapter 5

JUDICIAL PARENTING

God prefers a certain style of human authority. He likes judges. Learning about his preference and applying it in our family was a major breakthrough in our parenting, and perhaps it will be in yours, too. Those whose zeal turns to anger or who deal with conflict with over-sensitivity or people-pleasing will find this chapter helpful. If a parent struggles to discipline consistently because he feels sorry for his child because he is worried about what others think or because he ends up yelling, this chapter will be freeing.

My belief used to be that I would have my children for a while and then pass them on to God. My thought was that children had to learn to submit to their parents so that they would later submit to him. The pressure was on because I only had a brief time to get them right. They were mine, a reflection of my plan, skill and authority. If my children behaved well, they were for me. If they behaved badly, they were against me. I felt as though others evaluated my merits as a Christian parent by how well my children behaved, and I looked at other parents in the same manner. In time, it became clear to me that my job was simpler. I needed to execute beneficial judgment of my children's behavior according to the principles of God. With this change, I had much more hope of helping my children trust God and me.

Acting as a judge is as it sounds. In response to apparent disobedience, the judicial parent asks a bunch of questions, gathers facts, listens to appeals. He also explains why the rules matter to the King and assigns consequences if necessary. It might go like this:

Dad: What are you doing?

Son: Watching a mountain biking video. I want to learn a new skill.
Dad: Did you ask your mom or me for permission?
Son: I asked mom.
Dad: When?
Son: I don't know what time it was.
Dad: Well, about what time was it?
Son: When I finished my math.
Dad: Which was?
Son: Before lunch.
Dad: Did she give you permission to watch videos any time today?
Son: No.
Dad: So, she gave you permission to watch a video several hours ago, but you did not have permission to watch the video you are watching now.
Son: I guess not, but she let me watch more than one video this morning.
Dad: So you don't have permission to watch the video you were just watching, right?
Son: I did not.
Dad: So, you broke our rule that we want you to ask before watching videos?
Son: Yes.
Dad: Why didn't you ask permission?
Son: I don't know.
Dad: Do you think there should be a consequence?
Son: Probably.
Dad: Do you know why we have the rule to ask permission?
Son: So I will do my school work instead of watching videos?
Dad: That is part of it. If Mom were to have to constantly check on you and the other kids to make sure you are doing what you are supposed to do, that would be tiring. It also matters to God. He does not want us doing whatever we want. He wants us to get his permission and to stay focused on what we are supposed to be doing. It is the same for me as it is for you. There is something else I want to ask you. When you told me that mom gave you permission, were you trying to deceive me?
Son: I don't know.

Dad: When did you decide you would use the excuse that Mom gave you permission to justify watching the video? Was it before you started? Did you think of it while you were watching?

Son: I think it was right when you asked me.

Dad: What did you hope would happen when you said that Mom gave you permission?

Son: I wouldn't get in trouble.

Dad: But she had not given you permission?

Son: No, she didn't.

Dad: So, you told me something that was not true in order to try to get to do what you wanted to do, right?

Son: To try to get out of trouble, I guess.

Dad: What commandment is "Do not lie?"

Son: Number 9.

Dad: When we try to deceive someone, we lie, and we know that telling the truth is very important to God. When you responded to me with something that was not true, it was because, in your heart, you were ready and willing to try to trick me. I think that trying to deceive me should have a consequence, too. I am going to think for a little bit about what the consequences should be for watching videos without permission and for not being honest when I asked you questions about it.

Son: Sorry, Dad. Will you please forgive me?

Dad: I will, but you also need to ask God to forgive you. It is a big deal to sneak and to lie.

When parents are judicial, children can take comfort in the fact that Mom and Dad are consistent and, like good judges, deal in facts, logic and rules. Consistency builds confidence. The main benefit, though, is not that the parent is trusted, but that the judicial arrangement stops a parent's scramble for dominion and puts God in his proper place as Lord. Judging is the system that facilitates trust in God.

Before explaining how to be a judicial parent, we should consider the concept as it is seen in the Bible. The principle is introduced in the Exodus.

Judges or Kings

Authority is a tricky word because its meaning is so broad. For example, the ruler of a totalitarian government may have the power to demand a person's life, while the person directing traffic in a parking lot can only implore a person to put his car next to the last vehicle. Both could be said to have authority, but their authority is vastly different. So, if one says, "a parent has authority," it offers little clarity because the statement does not tell us what power the parent is supposed to have.

The best way to look at parental power is to step back and see what God thinks of human authority in general. We find his opinion presented well during the Exodus and in the first years in the Promised Land, and it challenges many popular views of a parent's role. Authoritarianism and permissiveness don't match up with the principles from the Bible.

Not too long after Israel left Egypt, Moses began to settle grievances between the people. When managing it became too much for one man, Jethro, Moses' father-in-law, encouraged him to delegate.

> Listen now to me and I will give you some advice, and may God be with you. You must be the people's representative before God and bring their disputes to him. ...But select capable men from all the people—men who fear God, trustworthy men who hate dishonest gain—and appoint them as officials over thousands, hundreds, fifties and tens. Have them serve as judges for the people at all times, but have them bring every difficult case to you; the simple cases they can decide themselves. That will make your load lighter, because they will share it with you. If you do this and God so commands, you will be able to stand the strain, and all these people will go home satisfied.
>
> Exodus 18:19, 21-23, NIV

Moses did as Jethro suggested. While recalling the four decades in the wilderness, Moses said,

> "And I charged your judges at that time, 'Hear the disputes between your people and judge fairly, whether the case is between two Israelites or between an Israelite and a foreigner residing among you. Do not show partiality in judging; hear both small and great alike. Do not be afraid of anyone, for judgment belongs to God. Bring me any case too hard for you, and I will hear it.'"
>
> Deuteronomy 1:16-17, NIV

Judges were the plan for ongoing authority in the Exodus, and the only plan. To be thorough, Israel's system included army commanders

(Deuteronomy 1:15), but they were only active in times of war. The priests and Levites were in charge of sacrifices, but this was more a duty than a role of leadership. Even if we consider Moses, we still don't find a boss of the people. The dynamic of having God right there in the camp at the tent of meeting meant Moses' main job was to follow simple instructions like, "Tell the children of Israel to go forward." (Exodus 14:15, NKJV). Moses pretty much just repeated what God said. It was not Moses, but God who provided the leadership.

Understanding why judges were appointed instead of leaders is crucial. Having leaders would not take into account the reality that God was there.

> Moses took his tent and pitched it outside the camp, far from the camp, and called it the tabernacle of meeting. And it came to pass *that* everyone who sought the LORD went out to the tabernacle of meeting which *was* outside the camp.
>
> Exodus 33:7, NKJV

> And let them make Me a sanctuary, that I may dwell among them.
>
> Exodus 25:8, NKJV

God was with them. What person could have competed with the leadership of God? How many more leaders would they need? None, God was sufficient.

Israel enjoyed God as king with a simplistic judicial system throughout the books of Exodus, Leviticus, Numbers, Deuteronomy, Joshua, Judges, Ruth and the first eight chapters of 1 Samuel. "Appoint judges and officials for each of your tribes in every town the Lord your God is giving you, and they shall judge the people fairly," was the standard (Deuteronomy 16:18, NIV). This was the golden age of God as the king in Israel and should be our guide for understanding all things related to authority.

The most distinctive aspect of the structure that started in Exodus is its lack of moving parts. It appeared more like a wispy skeleton than a body of leaders. The nation of Israel, a group of millions, had almost no human governance at all; but they didn't really need it so long as they were willing to follow their King. God wanted to be the one in authority. Judges met a need to uphold the rules, and that is all.

During this season of Israel's history, judging was within clans (Deuteronomy 1:15-16), and, at times, prophetic (e.g., Judges 4:4, 1 Samuel 7:15), meaning that God was actually the Judge with a human as the conduit. These judges should not make us think of black robes, bailiffs and limestone buildings. For the most part, these were people living ordinary lives who could, when needed, compare God's law to what was done. Judges did not make up rules or tell people what to do. God gave the rules and prescribed consequences for breaking them.

Judging did take integrity.

> Do not pervert justice or show partiality. Do not accept a bribe, for a bribe blinds the eyes of the wise and twists the words of the innocent. Follow justice and justice alone, so that you may live and possess the land the LORD your God is giving you.
>
> Deuteronomy 16:19-20, NIV

Judges could pervert justice in many ways. In these verses, if a judge showed partiality or did favors for a person, then he was a derelict in his duty. Good judging took, and still takes, veracity.

The judicial system was in place until Israel, against God's will, demanded a king. Sadly, the entire history of aristocracy in Israel began when the people "rejected me [God] as their king" (1 Samuel 8:7, NIV).

Jesus and Authority

Jesus' teaching on authority harmonized with the principles of the judicial system of the Exodus. The right response of a leader was to be less visible, more humble and to uphold God as the authority of all things.

Circa 30 AD, Jesus ushered in the Kingdom of God in which God was to be king to those who would be his people. At that time, a Roman king was in control, and that system was certainly one that would "lord it over them" (Matthew 20:25, NKJV). Jesus had more to say about the power grab of the religious leaders, however. In Matthew 23:4, he spoke very directly about the scribes and Pharisees (NKJV, consider also Colossians 3:21).

> For they bind heavy burdens, hard to bear, and lay *them* on men's shoulders; but they *themselves* will not move them with one of their fingers.

The way of the Pharisees was to give too many rules and no help. Jesus taught this:

"They [scribes and Pharisees] love the best places at feasts, the best seats in the synagogues, greetings in the marketplaces, and to be called by men, 'Rabbi, Rabbi.' But you, do not be called 'Rabbi'; for One is your Teacher, the Christ, and you are all brethren. Do not call anyone on earth your father; for One is your Father, He who is in heaven. And do not be called teachers; for One is your Teacher, the Christ. But he who is greatest among you shall be your servant. And whoever exalts himself will be humbled, and he who humbles himself will be exalted."

Matthew 23:6-12, NKJV

With these words, Jesus brought authoritarian hierarchies down. At the same time, he brought God and what he had to say up. The only proper response to this new kingdom would be to serve in such a way that all actions pointed specifically to God and his righteousness. There would be no pyramid of power. Those who would have been authorities were to first reject special treatment and recognition. Second, they were to realize that all of us are brothers and sisters. Third, they were to focus on God being in charge. Finally, they were to carry out duties as one willing to serve. These principles work for parents, too.

Now that the Kingdom of God is here, God is the one in charge. Being a dominating authority does not make sense. Instead, the focus should be on helping those we serve be successful at obedience. So, parents, "Let your gentleness be evident to all. The Lord is near." (Philippians 4:5, NIV). In the family, gentle, just judging is needed.

Kingly Parents

Much of what we read in biblical history involves the great power structures of kings—Hebrew, Babylonian, Assyrian, Roman, etc. In nearly all of the books of the Bible, a human authority is a king. Some people read about those kings and assume because it is the dominant record in the history of Israel, that God is looking for a point man. That is not true. God's planned governance for Israel was judicial, and when Israel wanted it another way he said, "They have rejected me."

A person does not have to don a crown in order to take on the attitude of a king. "Follow God's appointed leader" communicates something similar. Also, "God has put him in charge of making decisions for us." This is king- and queen-style leadership, and it very often, if not always, ends up squeezing Jesus Christ out of his role as King. In the family, the father is not the king, and the mother is not the queen.

There are varying degrees of king-like authority, but any idea that denies God's constant presence falls short of God-as-King. Avoiding the royalty trap is not so much a matter of stating, "I am not going to act like a king or queen," but a matter of acting like there is already a king here. God says we must believe he is with us, and that changes the dynamic.

Some parents might think of themselves as a steward or a manager of the family. These do not necessarily contradict the judicial style of parenting, but they can. For example, if someone believes that God left parents to be stewards of his possessions until he returns, his understanding falls short. If the result is, "God is the King, but I make all the decisions since he left me in charge," then one has become, *de facto*, king. If parents are stewards or managers, or even servants or slaves, they are not the kind whose master is absent.

The part of parenting that is leadership or authority is best expressed as judicial. Parents should act judicially for the sake of a king who is present. One's children already belong to God and are his subjects. He rules their lives as he rules ours. This attitude is necessary for building trust with each other and with God.

Benefits of Being Judicial

A parent could respond in several ways to conflict with his child. He could take the permissive stance, perhaps seeking to understand on an emotional level why the child is going to do what the parent does not want. In this case, the parent and child will agree to disagree and they may, ultimately, go down different paths: "You have to do what you feel." Alternately, a parent could take the authoritarian perspective and say, "Because I said so." In this case, conflict becomes *us* versus *them*. Of all of the possibilities, the best option is judicial, which actually draws parents and children toward God rather than parting ways or setting one against another. With good rules and reasonable consequences, parents and children can work together to put into action God's good ways. Judicial parenting is unifying. This is one of its most important benefits.

Another benefit is that stereotypical, negative parenting is not necessary. Certain familiar sayings can and should be eliminated from a parent's experience with jurisprudence. There is no need for parents to use phrases of inconsistency: "Finally, I just caved in." "You have pushed me too far." Nor is there a need for threats like, "Don't make me." Sarcasm has no place in the judicial parenting process either: "Do you think I work for you?" "So you finally decided to do what I asked." "Let's see if you can actually obey for once." Judging takes the place of anger, rudeness and melodrama, too. "Don't talk back to me," "Both of you, shut up," "That's it. I've had it," "You are ruining this" and "Don't ever do that again," are all unnecessary. A parent focused on judging can skip general criticism like, "You are so lazy." "You don't care about anyone but you. Think of someone else for a change." Instead of, "I am pulling my hair out. You have done this 100 times," judicial parenting combines persistence and patience, by comparing behavior to God's ways.

Similarly, in a home with good judicial parenting, a child has no logical reason to fire off statements like, "Why do I have to?" "That is stupid." "You aren't fair." "You're an idiot." Why not? With the elements of jurisprudence (rules and questioning), a child is encouraged to wrestle with moral rules rather than with parents. With judicial parenting, moms and dads have a mechanism for introducing their zeal for thinking rightly. Children may not always welcome having their behavior questioned. They may complain that the parent is mean, but a parent can refocus the child on the issue that needs to be evaluated and the principles that come from the Good King.

Another benefit of judicial parenting is that the strategy is not age specific. Because it is concerned about what is right and is also respectful of the person who may have done wrong, it does not need to change much with time. At all ages, a parent can ask, "Do you think you did something wrong?" "How would you handle it next time?" In fact, a parent could ask similar questions of an adult friend. Or, a child could ask his parents the same kinds of questions. Judicial questioning is a lifestyle that does not end at a certain age. The habit of questioning is part of the process of encouraging one another to do what pleases God. Therefore, the judicial parenting process offers a natural and healthy transition from toddler to adult.

Acting as a judge when necessary will also strengthen friendships. As Proverbs says, "Whoever rebukes a person will in the end gain favor rather than one who has a flattering tongue." (28:23, NIV).

Parenting should be relaxed and enjoyable. Because we have ten children, people often say to us, "You have your hands full." When I watch other families, I realize why they think we must be overwhelmed. They wrangle back and forth with only a few children. Biblical principles, starting with trust and judicial parenting, make the experience different than what others have imagined or known.

Questioning

Central to fair judging is asking good questions. Deuteronomy 13:12-15 describes how an investigation was to be carried out when a town appeared to have started worshiping other gods: "inquire, probe and investigate it thoroughly" (v. 14, NIV). Those are good principles for parents to apply.

A judicial parent asks rational, poignant questions like, "What did you just do?" "How did it happen?" "Did you break a rule?" "Which rule did you break?" "How should you have handled this?" A parent should also seek to understand the more complicated dynamics of the situation because "The purposes of a person's heart are deep waters, but one who has insight draws them out." (Proverbs 20:5, NIV). A parent should ask questions that get to motive. Statements like, "I'll tell you what you were thinking," don't really get to motive. It is better to ask questions: "What motivated you to break the rule?" Or, "What were you thinking about before you did that to your brother?" Questioning should also encourage a child to consider solutions to problems: "Is there something we could talk about that would help you not repeat what you did?" A parent should also consider questions that would cause his children to reason with him. "Why do you think we have this rule?" "If you had a child, what would you think she should do?" "What would your friend think if you did that to him?" "What would happen if everyone did what you are doing right now?"

Not all questions are fair. For example, "How many times have I told you?" is almost always impossible to answer accurately. It would be okay to ask, "Approximately how many times do you think I have told you in the last month?" This might be valuable information for a child to consider, but it starts with the right question, not an impossible one.

A judicial parent focuses on moral issues, not menial ones. For example, he does not argue with a child about the right way to play: "Are you really going to put the red one on top of the green one?" Parents should reserve judgment for instances in which moral codes may have been broken.

A parent might see benefit in asking questions that recount what a child reported. For example, he might ask, "So, you decided to do it without permission because you saw that your sister was doing it, is that correct?" These questions show that the parent wants to understand the details, a practice that will help children think in details, also. Further, it gives a child time to add clarity in case a parent misunderstood. Children struggle with language, and it is good to confirm that what they seem to be saying is what they mean—"inquire, probe and investigate."

A parent should not jump to conclusions but should start with the assumption that a child may have meant well, that he may not have known better, that it may have been a mistake or that the situation may be different than the way it appeared. For example, it is possible that dad gave permission, and mom did not know it. Or, it is possible that a parent took pretending as reality. We say in the American judicial system, "innocent until proven guilty." The whole idea of judging is pursuing the truth.

> Acquitting the guilty and condemning the innocent—the LORD detests them both.
>
> Proverbs 17:15, NIV

Things are not always as they appear. Listening, understanding, talking about feelings and thoughts takes time and should be part of the process.

> To answer before listening— that is folly and shame.
>
> Proverbs 18:13, NIV

After questioning to gather information and to insure that a child understands what he did wrong, a parent can say, "Here is how you could handle it next time." As always, it is helpful to point a child back to the heart. For example, a parent can say, "You had an attitude in your heart that caused you to do it the wrong way. If you had started with the right heart attitude you would have reacted the right way."

Here are a few practical suggestions for questioning: ask judicial questions face to face, eye to eye. Bend a knee and draw up close. This posture is helpful when applied to all important communication with children. A child should not be allowed to keep playing during the questioning. Also, in certain situations it is thoughtful to judge in private (a principle of Matthew 18:15). Quiet your voice rather than raise it. Speak slowly, so children have a moment to think about what you are saying. Take time to think about the questions you will ask and consider carefully the answers given. Don't be in a hurry. Consider taking at least one minute to question with every incident, whether you need the time or not. If it is a big or more complicated incident, take five or ten minutes or longer if necessary. Even if you saw and heard the event, ask questions. This is not only for the sake of good judgment but so that the child can meditate on the events that unfolded. He is learning as questions are being asked, and questions often teach better than speeches.

> The one who has knowledge uses words with restraint, and whoever has understanding is even-tempered.
>
> •   Proverbs 17:27, NIV

Parents will find great benefit in avoiding what are known as logical fallacies when they are trying to understand what happened. (Our own children study them as part of their schoolwork, and more than once the phrase, "Dad, that is a logical fallacy," has been heard in our house during judicial conversations.) One common logical fallacy is the false dilemma, when a person gives too few options:

Dad: "Did you hit him or pull his hair?"
Child: "Neither, he tripped over his own shoe."

Similarly, a parent might jump to conclusions, especially about a child's motives. Or, a parent might appeal to probability, saying something like, "You probably broke it because kids your age are always breaking stuff." *Ad Hominem* attacks criticize the arguer rather than his argument: "Since you are a liar, I know your sister must be telling the truth, not you." An argument from silence would be, "Since Mrs. Jones did not mention how polite you were, you must not have said 'please' and 'thank you.'" The best way to avoid most logical fallacies is to ask questions rather than to make statements.

A parent should be keen to find contradictions in what is said when a child is explaining an incident, showing that he is committed to getting to the truth. For example, a parent might question whether "I don't know" means "I don't want to tell you." If a child "forgot" what happened, a parent could ask why he did not treat the activities more thoughtfully. Whenever a parent hears that an inanimate item seemed to do something on its own (known as a pathetic fallacy), he should wonder if his child is telling the whole story. For example, since cups have no innate power, they seldom fall off the counter unassisted. Details like, "I hit the wiffle ball across the living room, which hit the refrigerator and came back across the room and knocked the cup off," may be left out. A judicious parent should not be naive but should watch for concealed information, exaggeration and flat-out lying.

A child might try to avoid the question, too. For example, a mom might inquire, "Did you hear me ask you to do it?" The child might respond, "Well, she said she would do it," which is not really answering the question. One way to deal with children who are avoiding the question is to keep repeating the query until it is answered.

Any criticism a parent offers during the judicial process should be about specific action in a specific instance. "You did it again. You do not care about your sister," will not do. On the other hand, "In this situation, you did not consider her to be important," does not criticize the child personally, but addresses her specific action. Saying, "You are just annoying," is damaging, but pointing to a principle of God that has been violated is constructive evaluation. A parent should always give specifics.

Sometimes children don't want to answer questions quickly and to the point. Something as simple as having the child stand without leaning on a piece of furniture or a wall can help her engage in the conversation. Also, when a child is hesitant, a parent might put off the questioning for a bit. He might say, "Please go empty the dishwasher; it needs to be done anyway. While you are working, think about what happened and think about how to most accurately answer my questions." Emptying the dishwasher would not be a consequence, but a duty, distraction and test. The child might as well do something productive while stepping away from the emotion of the situation. It is vital that the parent resume the questioning after the dishwasher is emptied, though.

Parents and children should think about excuses. Most excuses actually end up being an admission of greater folly than what would have been otherwise assumed. For example;

> Mom: "Did you run into your sister."
> Daughter: "I didn't see her."
> Mom: "Doesn't that mean that you were running without looking where you were going?"

Now, which sounds more ridiculous, for a child to be excited and therefore careless about a sister who is in the way or for her to be willing to run with no concept of what she will run into? As is often the case, the excuse meant to defend oneself actually makes that person look worse.

After questioning, a parent may decide that a consequence is appropriate, but before a consequence, a child should have the opportunity to politely object to conclusions a parent has made. If children are not permitted to object, then they may be wrongly accused, or they may not understand fully what they have done wrong. What good is the judgment to them if they don't comprehend the moral deficit in their actions? After children do get it, parents might also ask them for advice in assigning a consequence: "What do you think the consequence ought to be?" After the discipline, a parent can ask questions to review. "What did you do wrong?" "Why were you disciplined?" This is a good time for teaching.

From time to time, a child will do something immoral that is not governed by a family rule. Asking questions about the situation is still valuable, but consequences are only fitting when expectations are known. It is better to let it go and introduce a new rule than to discipline for a rule that does not exist. Rules need to be established well to be enforced.

How often should parents judge? As much as is needed. The amount of judging is determined by a child's behavior. Parents should ask judicial questions every time a rule may have been broken. Some children will require quite a bit of questioning while others will require less. If parents engage children in a judicial manner 2% of the time but are not involved in their lives the other 98% of the time, then all of their experience will be with a judge. Parents should make sure to spend time with their children when judicial questioning is not necessary.

With every conflict and with every chance to be judicial, parents should see the opportunity to teach principles that would be important to our King. When rendering their judgment, parents who discover a child has done wrong might explain exactly how the child's behavior dishonors God and that the consequence is going to help the child be sensitive to God's principles the next time the issue comes up. Parents might also explain how life is better when one obeys God and they might return to the source of behavior, the heart.

Questioning and Family Life

When questioning is necessary, siblings should provide any helpful facts they know about the situation, but they should not be questioning with mom or dad, ganging up on the child whose actions are being judged. Also, parents should watch out for a kick-him-when-he's-down attitude toward a sibling who got in trouble because that is what sometimes comes naturally to children.

> Now instead, you ought to forgive and comfort [the one who was corrected], so that he will not be overwhelmed by excessive sorrow. I urge you, therefore, to reaffirm your love for him.
>
> 2 Corinthians 2:7-8, NIV

All family members should have a restorative attitude toward those who have disobeyed.

To say that a child should not join in the questioning does not mean that he should never question a sibling on his own. In fact, children should be encouraged to gently correct one another. A good way for a child to correct while facilitating respect for his sibling would be to ask judicial questions.

> If your brother or sister sins, go and point out their fault, just between the two of you. If they listen to you, you have won them over.
>
> Matthew 18:15, NIV

> My brothers and sisters, if one of you should wander from the truth and someone should bring that person back, remember this: Whoever turns a sinner from the error of their way will save them from death and cover over a multitude of sins.
>
> James 5:19-20, NIV

Siblings should "spur one another on toward love and good deeds" (Hebrews 10:24, NIV).

When potential disobedience also involves sibling conflict, a parent might begin with some conversational ground rules like, "Okay, each of you will have a chance to tell me what happened. Don't interrupt one another." If a child does interrupt, a parent would do well to take a break from the original issue, and deal with the disobedience of interrupting. It will be a better discussion if children are willing to listen.

In a large family, parents may at times feel like they are doing a lot of judging. They might feel like the only clerk in a small store. The clerk must help one customer make a decision and check out as the next customer comes in the door needing help. A parent might think, "Okay, which child may I help next?" It is fine if judging happens this way at times. Other times won't require such an intense focus.

Whether he has many children or a few, a judicial parent does not leave it up to others, like youth workers, teachers or government employees, to correct or persuade his child. Being judicial should be understood as a lifestyle job that must be maintained by parents, and every conflict should be seen as an opportunity for teaching.

Unresolved Dilemmas

Parents should not accuse children of wrongdoing on scant evidence or on a hunch. Deuteronomy 19:15 says that it is necessary to have multiple witnesses for criminal convictions. Such a stiff requirement may not be needed for coming to a conclusion about the behavior of a child who has broken a rule and for whom the consequences will be relatively mild. Still, it is important to have reasonable evidence. So, after a parent has thoroughly probed with questions, he might have to say to his child, "I don't know what happened, so I can't do anything about it right now. God does know what happened and perhaps he will reveal it. We will have to leave it between you and God."

A parent can talk to God with his child and ask for help. Numbers 5:12-31 (help for jealous husbands and acquittal for faithful wives), Deuteronomy 17:8-11 (hard cases that require a prophetic resolution), and Acts 5:1-11 (the exposure of the lies of Ananias and Sapphira) tell of situations in which God intervened. However, God does not always choose to provide new information, and so long as parents are consistent when what children have done is obvious, letting an instance pass without a conclusion is not a big deal.

Feelings

Judicial questions should focus more on deeds done rather than feelings felt. Behavior is concrete while the expression of emotion is subjective. This is not to say that parents should ignore feelings. Children are independent, reasoning, spiritual beings. Emotions help them express how they perceive the world. Also, children will need to learn to consider feelings so that they can respond to them appropriately. A feeling in line with what is right can alert a child that he should take action (e.g., caring for someone who needs care). Also, if a feeling contradicts the truth, a child who identifies it can dispel its power by adjusting to what is true.

I don't think dealing with feelings has to be complicated. It can be as simple as asking, "Can you tell me how you feel and why you feel that way?" It is best to avoid questions that assume a conclusion about how a child feels, like "Why are you mad?" By answering general questions about emotion, a child has more leeway to share what is really going on in his mind. Responses to emotions like, "Well, you are just going to have to get over it," "Stop. Everything will be fine," or "Get a hold of yourself" are harmful to the judicial process. Even worse is a statement like, "I'll give you something to cry about."

In some cases, actions that seem to be related to emotion can be judged. When a child throws a temper tantrum, he is not only showing emotion but also intending to manipulate his parents. Most often, this type of manipulation happens between the ages of two and five. Discerning between the temper tantrum and the frustrated child is important, so parents should be cautious. If a child screams out while trying to put a toy together, it probably isn't because he is attempting to gain control of his mom or dad. A parent could say, "Would you like me to help? If you feel frustrated, use your words and ask for help. I like to help you." On the other hand, if the child is asked to go do something and a tirade ensues, a different response from a parent is necessary if a rule against such behavior has been established.

When emotions are strong, parents will do well to postpone the conversation. Often, time changes the way one feels. People can be very upset one moment and hours later be completely indifferent or unemotional about a situation.

It is important to note that parents should not let feelings be the trump card when there is a disagreement but rather focus on the pursuit of righteousness. If the choice has to be between the two, seeking to honor God is far more important than how a person feels at the moment.

Cities of Refuge

Cities of refuge were established to help judges make fair decisions.

Then Moses set aside three cities east of the Jordan, to which anyone who had killed a person could flee if he had unintentionally killed his neighbor without malice aforethought. He could flee into one of these cities and save his life.

Deuteronomy 4:41-42, NIV

Deuteronomy 19:2-10 offers an example:

> For instance, a man may go into the forest with his neighbor to cut wood, and as he swings his ax to fell a tree, the head may fly off and hit his neighbor and kill him. That man may flee to one of these cities and save his life. Otherwise, the avenger of blood might pursue him in a rage, overtake him if the distance is too great, and kill him even though he is not deserving of death, since he did it to his neighbor without malice aforethought.

Verses 5 and 6, NIV

Parents can take note of what God has done here and learn. The cities of refuge allowed for time to pass, anger to abate and facts to be fully heard. Why would parents not offer their children the same privilege when they feel angry or frustrated? Parents who always make decisions right away may be too lenient—"let's just move on"—or too harsh, acting in anger. There is no good reason to be in such a hurry.

When temper, whether a parent's or a child's, is a hindrance to good judgment, a parent should put it off for a bit. In other words, a mom or dad can say, "I am going to set a timer, and in ten minutes we are going to talk about this." Once the dust has settled, the parent can ask questions and listen to learn what happened.

The idea of delaying judgment is helpful in some situations that don't involve anger, too. For example, a parent should not judge when one of his children is hurt. He should first care for the injured child (perhaps picking him up and taking him for a short walk). Good judgment will not occur if questions are asked while an injured child is screaming in pain. How tempting it is to yell, "What happened?"

Time can be taken after questioning and before assigning a consequence. "Let me think and pray about this for a while. I am not sure if there should be a consequence, and if so, what that consequence should be. I would like for you to think about it, too." This is a good response, but a parent must come back to the issue in a timely manner to make a decision. Failure to return to the subject in situations like these may teach children that they do not have to think about it, but that it will likely be dropped.

Israel's cities of refuge functioned as part of the judicial system by protecting a person from hasty judgments motivated by anger. Likewise, parents should try to find practical ways to make sure that judgments of their children's behavior are fair. When questions need to be asked, parents should be free to slow down in every step. They should take time to calm down, to inquire, to determine consequences, to explain their decisions and teach about why the moral lessons matter.

Moses' Anger

A parent's awe of God should exceed his frustration with his children. He ought to deal in facts rather than in emotional outbursts. This is the lesson for parents from Numbers 20-21. Israel was in the wilderness and without potable water; it had been in this predicament at least twice before (Exodus 15 and 17). God's instructions for solving the problem were similar to those given in Exodus 17.

> "Take the staff, and you [Moses] and your brother Aaron gather the assembly together. Speak to that rock before their eyes and it will pour out its water. You will bring water out of the rock for the community so they and their livestock can drink."
>
> Numbers 20:8, NIV

Moses made a mistake when bringing water from the rock, and it seems like the type of mistake parents could make. (Aaron was also guilty, see Numbers 20:12.)

> He [Moses] and Aaron gathered the assembly together in front of the rock and Moses said to them, "Listen, you rebels, must we bring you water out of this rock?" Then Moses raised his arm and struck the rock twice with his staff. Water gushed out, and the community and their livestock drank.
>
> Numbers 20:10-11, NIV

Many have tried to parse these verses to find out what Moses did wrong. Perhaps the most popular conclusion is that God said to "speak to the rock," and, instead, Moses struck the rock twice. Although this is true, the Bible emphasizes Moses' underlying attitude when Moses "rebelled against my [God's] command" (Numbers 20:24, NIV, also 27:14). Psalm 106:33 says that "...rash words came from Moses' lips" (NIV). Simply put, Moses was fed up. His words, "Listen, you rebels," were indicative of his attitude. God told Moses, "…you did not trust in me enough to honor me as holy in the sight of the Israelites" (Numbers 20:12, NIV). God did not expect a level of faith that simply acknowledged his existence. He required a type of faith that brought about reverence in every situation, even the frustrating ones. God said that Moses failed, "…to honor me as holy at the waters before their eyes", and he said, "…you broke faith with me in the presence of the Israelites" (Deuteronomy 32:51, Numbers 27:14, NIV).

As part of the royal family, Moses had everything in Egypt, but he traded it in to follow God and adopt his customs (Hebrews 11:24-28). In the Exodus, he had been faithful to God and had not participated in the rebellions. Eventually, the fact that Israel kept messing up made Moses' spirit bitter, and that was the source of his sin. Anger was stirred, resulting in rash speech. Moses was becoming more consumed with his frustration than he was with his need to fully respect the Almighty. Moses who, in his anger, literally broke the law by throwing down the tablets on which the Ten Commandments were written, also struck the rock, which represented the stricken Christ, in anger (Exodus 32:19, 1 Corinthians 10:4). One could say that these situations spoke of the Messiah's death. Those with the law (who had also broken the law) struck Jesus, and his death brought forth springs of living water that leave a person satisfied forever (John 4:14, 7:38-39). Yet, God expected Moses to trust and honor him rather than to become angry.

In Numbers 20 and 21, there is a rock that appears to be like all the others, but out of this Rock flow the waters of new life. A parent's job is to introduce his family to this Rock. Moms and dads are ambassadors year after year, and they should not do anything in the process to tarnish the experience with anger, indifference or busyness—"honor me as holy … before their eyes." God calls parents to uphold him as holy, never squandering the opportunity. So, if a parent starts to feel irritated or upset, he should gain control: "In your anger do not sin" (Ephesians 4:26, NIV).

> My dear brothers and sisters, take note of this: Everyone should be quick to listen, slow to speak and slow to become angry, because human anger does not produce the righteousness that God desires.
> James 1:19-20, NIV

Parents shouldn't rebuke their children in their anger, but take control of their emotions for the sake of their children.

I am aware that Bible translations say that misbehavior would "provoke [God] to anger", (Deuteronomy 4:25, NKJV), but I don't think that people should imagine that what they feel or experience is so-called "godly anger." In English, the word "angry" suggests a degree of self-pity and vulnerability. For many, the word also conveys a feeling of wanting vengeance: "I'm mad and I want to hurt someone." When Bible translations use the word "angry," it is not as though God had steam coming out of his ears and was looking for revenge. The phrase translated "provoke [God] to anger" is one word, *ka`ac*, in Hebrew. The emphasis is not as much on the emotion of anger but on the provocation to action. *Ka`ac* communicates that God was disappointed and, more importantly, that he had reached the point at which something would have to be done. Because of the modern emphasis on emotions, parents should not even bother using the word anger when they speak of their response to disobedience. The word is too loaded. They would do much better to be provoked and in need of taking some loving action.

There is no need for anger to be a step in the process of parenting. Too often feelings of anger come from a parent who is personally offended, frustrated or afraid that a child might ruin his family's reputation. In reality, God is the one who has the right to be offended, frustrated or afraid that his reputation will be tarnished, not us. When a parent starts to feel the emotion of anger, he should remember that he is a representative of the king, not the king. Often, a parent can explain to his child, "You have not wronged me, but God. He made you. He has a purpose for you. What you did goes against his ways. You really need to apologize to him, not to me."

Usually I feel angry easiest when I believe I have to get something done in a hurry. I also feel angry with the repeat offender. I have to remind myself that my life is hidden in Christ. What happens to me does not matter. If I have this perspective, the feeling of anger abates and I can focus on being faithfully judicial. When do you feel angry? What do you need to do in order to put the situation into the proper perspective so that you do not act out in anger? Let's encourage one another to keep our attitude toward our children holy.

Bad Judging

The system of judges, ironically, had largely fallen apart by the time of the events recorded in the book of Judges. Israel lost interest in God and his rules. The people sought false gods and, as promised in Deuteronomy 28, Israel was subject to the people around them. From time to time, God used a single person to set them free from oppression, and this person was sometimes said to have "judged Israel" (Judges 3:10, 10:2-3, 12:7-14, 15:20, 16:31, 1 Samuel 4:18, 7:15-17, NKJV). The terms *leader, ruler* or *king* were not used because God was to be Leader, Ruler and King. That principle was set in Gideon's heart.

> Then the men of Israel said to Gideon, Rule over us, both you and your son, and your grandson also; for you have delivered us from the hand of Midian." But Gideon said to them, "I will not rule over you, nor shall my son rule over you; the LORD shall rule over you."
>
> Judges 8:22-23, NKJV

Gideon understood that God was King, but others had lost sight of God's plan. Parents need to make sure they don't follow Israel's example here. They need to keep God as king and remain judicial.

In many ways, the most common problems in families are similar to the mistakes Israel made in its failure to uphold a robust judicial system. Is there a concern for what God wants? Do parents care what their children are doing? Are they going to let bad behavior pass? Are desires for possessions or a certain lifestyle stronger than the desire for obedience to God? Will they be consumed with the worries and cares of this world rather than focused on the things that truly matter? If any of these are true, parents are denying God as king and will lose interest in upholding his righteous ways.

Judicial parenting must be performed in the midst of eating, playing, cleaning, working, packing up, shopping, socializing and other activities. That is no excuse for poor performance, but it is an admission of reality. In that reality, sometimes parents might ask too few questions, ask the wrong questions, be drawn in by a child's bad excuse or make up rules after the fact. Parents might jump to conclusions when judging. Or, they might be impatient, wishing to get on with life when a rule appears to have been broken. Certainly good judgment and values lapse when parents are anxious. If they are in a hurry to get out the door, have a project that must be finished or are worried about money, their parenting will be less than what would be desired. Instead, we should obey Jesus' command not to worry and take comfort in his words, "Each day has enough trouble of its own" (Matthew 6:34, NIV). Parents must be faithful to question children when necessary without distraction from the worries and cares of this life.

In order to judge well, parents have to be generally attentive. If they choose to be oblivious when children are yelling at each other or when the house is chaotic and messy, they are probably not going to do a good job parenting. Good judges must choose to be observant.

Parents who cannot stick with discipline when a rule is broken will not make good judges, either. Generally, they shouldn't cave in, drop the issue or withdraw consequences.

Finally, moms and dads should judge their own actions. If one is willing to say, "This is business, and it has to get done, right or wrong," or is willing to gossip and write it off saying, "I just like to talk," then he is neglecting the mindset that helps a parent teach a child God's ways. Parents should have a wholehearted commitment to the King's rules in their own lives. They should deal with their own issues swiftly. They should set the standard very high for their own behavior. These are the principles of Matthew 7:5 (NIV): "first take the plank out of your own eye, and then you will see clearly to remove the speck from your brother's eye." Parents are obligated to give children whatever help they can, whether they act perfectly or not, but certainly it helps to be clean-eyed. To see bad behavior, parents have to know and long for good deeds, which starts with knowing and revering God. We all pursue what we love, and judicial parents should feel compelled to pursue their children's hearts and God's good ways at the same time.

Judicial Parenting

In the family parents have some level of authority. The question is, what should it look like? When God is present, certain types of leadership don't make sense. For example, a controlling or bossy parent would be out of place. Judicial-style authority is appropriate, as it was in Israel when God was with them and when judges upheld rules that represented the King's holiness. Seeing the wisdom behind God's system of judges is not first a matter of embracing judging but rather of identifying that God is King and that he is here with us. Parents should draw from the principles of the judicial system, upholding rules, questioning with persistence, assigning beneficial consequences and explaining the right way. Parents should take the time needed to avoid feelings of anger and make sure they get it right. Judicial parenting should lead to calm parents and a family that is quick to forgive and restore its members.

The greatest benefit of using rules, judging and consequences is that they help children become aware of heart problems, motivating them to pursue a heart solution. We are saved by grace but only when we realize how badly we need grace; and that is, foremost, why children need judicial parents.

An entire chapter on God as King and the parent as his judicial agent is by no means meant to suggest that our children should only know their parents as judges. In fact, judging is not always mandatory and is not always the highest principle. For example, when our oldest son was two, he crawled into bed with his four-year-old sister. He broke our specific rule to stay in bed. I walked in to see them smiling and cuddling together as close friends. I felt happy because my children liked each other, and they were delightful when they showed it. In this case, there was no judging, and there were no consequences. Judging is not the end goal but the means of getting to love. It is the kindest way to present the truth about a son's or daughter's life, but it, alone, will not bring righteousness.

There are differences between the role of the judges of the Exodus and a parent's role. For the judges, the rules and consequences were defined, but parents make up family rules based on the principles of God's ways. Further, parenting is far more complex than judging alone. Parents direct, teach, nurture, encourage, love, hold, provide, etc. Parents are not judges. They are parents; however, thinking like a judge is a mindset and philosophy that will help them best relate to children in times of conflict. Moms and dads, knowing they have such a solid, yet simple system of rules and consequences in place can savor and take pleasure in the times when judging is not necessary. They can enjoy their children as friends.

For Discussion

1. Do you think people respond better to questions about their behavior or to statements about their behavior? Please explain your answer.
2. What are some ways you applied or could have applied judicial principles in parenting recently?
3. What are some good ways to remind yourself to be judicial throughout the day?
4. How could you use judicial principles to help adult friends in your life?
5. How would you help your children think about how to live with God as king?
6. Do you live in such a way that God is the King of your life?

Chapter 6

HEART PROBLEM

After the flood, God said something that parents would be wise to observe.

> "Never again will I curse the ground because of humans, even though every inclination of the human heart is evil from childhood."
>
> Genesis 8:21, NIV

I love the ages of two to five. Children are learning so much and saying so much at this age. My eyes soak in their cuteness, and I enjoy frequent laughter with them. Every day offers a chance to make a new memory. Of course, there is another side of ages two to five. Many parents know that children don't need to be taught to disobey, to whine, to throw temper tantrums, to take other children's toys, to lie and so on. It is a mistake to think that children are little angels. They have hearts that defy good rules—"every inclination of the human heart is evil from childhood."

"Heart" in this context refers not to the organ that pumps blood but to another heart, the core of a person's being, where we find will, desire and conscience. The heart harbors deep thoughts, hidden plans and affections. If you have ever been in love, you know what it is like to have your heart feel like it wants to jump out of your body to be with the one you love. If you have ever been sad, really sad, you know what it is like to have a broken heart. We also learn best when we take something to heart. True obedience is heart-centered as well, as is true disobedience. Actions always follow the heart. This is by God's design, and the Bible repeatedly confirms the importance of this other heart. Deuteronomy, especially, connects obedience, understanding and true devotion to the heart. It also speaks of the need for a heart made new (Deuteronomy 10:16, 29:4, 30:6).

The Need for a Second Birth

Jesus was not exaggerating when he said, "…unless one is born again, he cannot see the kingdom of God." (John 3:3, NKJV). Parents are left with children who are only born the first time (that is, born of the flesh). They must have a second birth. Let's consider why.

In the beginning of creation, before sin entered the picture, a man and a woman were friends with God and shared in his image and likeness. The leader of the demons, Satan, persuaded Adam and Eve to eat fruit that changed them. They ate from the tree of the knowledge of good and evil, no longer knowing only good. When they displeased God, they didn't just sin. They became sin-producing individuals, having the will to do evil living in them.

To describe the sin living in us, the Bible uses the Greek word *sarx*, or flesh.[8] *Sarx* primarily refers to the soft tissue of any living thing, but it can also refer to the whole body or a group of people who descended from one couple (e.g., Romans 11:14). I believe that *sarx* was chosen because the problem with mankind is expressed in all three of these meanings. It is the soft tissue, the whole body and the offspring. First, the satisfaction of disobedience is often felt in the skin or is seen in the outward appearance. Second, the corruption takes residence in the body. It can't be separated except by death. Third, this is the way life is because we all are fleshly descendants of the ones who swallowed the knowledge of good and evil (Genesis 2:17, 3:6).

Like a genetic disease, sin is passed on from one generation to the next. Jesus confirmed this when speaking about the need for a second birth, saying, "That which is born of the flesh is flesh." (John 3:6, NKJV). Romans 5:12 says, "…through one man sin entered the world, and death through sin, and thus death spread to all men, because all sinned" (NKJV). If one has children, then his children have this condition, and it is deadly. They are stuck with this reality. The sin living in them will come out. This inescapable propensity to do wrong has caused a great chasm between God and man.

---

8. Translating the word *sarx* as "sinful nature" is not just translating, but coming to an interpretive conclusion that is not in the original Greek. *Flesh* would be the preferred translation.

Once you were alienated from God and were enemies in your minds because of your evil behavior.

Colossians 1:21, NIV

Those who know the depth of the problem of the flesh know the significance of Jesus' commitment to save us.

But God demonstrates His own love toward us, in that while we were still sinners, Christ died for us.

Romans 5:8, NKJV

The heart problem has been resolved by God's love in action, but it requires that one be born again at his core.

Apparent Good

Many believe that, although people do bad things, humans are generally good, compassionate and caring. Some might hypothesize that, were we truly at enmity with God, the world would look much worse than it does.

First, it is important to note that mankind didn't just consume the fruit of evil, but the fruit of the knowledge of both good and evil. Humans have a conscience, and it seems that the world is made more livable by it. Sometimes this conscience shows up in non-biblical worldviews. These promote some sort of morality but deny Jesus. This is rebellion against God, though society may not see it as such.

We also must consider that people do so-called good because of the order that God has provided through family, society and government. It is hard to imagine life without these controls, since we all have been immersed in them. These institutions outside of a person incentivize him to behave contrary to his flesh and are relatively effective. Because God designed us to live together in society, we learn that being nice increases the likelihood of having friends and gaining success. We are rewarded for good behavior, but such behavior does not make us good people. Also by the grace of God, laws and government restrain evil (Romans 13:1-7). How would people act if there were no police service? Although laws vary and governments are all, to some degree, corrupt, their overall effect is to make the planet generally livable. One of the most powerful sin-taming forces is the God-made institution of the family. By God's design, children spend a lot of time with their parents, providing opportunity to pass morality on to the next generation.

Mankind is not innately noble. Society, government and family limit bad behavior, but these can't fully do the job.

Bad from Within

Understanding that "every inclination of the human heart is evil from childhood" is difficult without God's perspective.

> Every way of a man *is* right in his own eyes, But the LORD weighs the hearts.
>
> Proverbs 21:2, NKJV

The delusions that make one think he is moral are strong.

> The heart is deceitful above all *things*, And desperately wicked; Who can know it?
>
> Jeremiah 17:9, NKJV

Even when doing the wrong thing, one can be convinced that his way is the right way. To sort out right and wrong, who we are and the inclination of the heart, we need God's perspective.

Jesus gave us a glimpse into his view of mankind when he said to the crowds of people who wanted to hear him, "If you then, being evil, know how to give good gifts to your children..." (Matthew 7:11, NKJV, see also Matthew 5:1-2, Luke 6:32-36, 11:13). If a person can still give good gifts to those he loves and, at the same time, be evil, then maybe the so-called good that humans do could be criticized by someone outside of humanity. If we were able to evaluate the good we do from a heavenly perspective, would we find that it is ultimately driven by vanity? This seems to be what Jesus thought.

Jesus also asked, "Why do you call Me good? No one *is* good but One, *that is*, God," (Matthew 19:17, NKJV). His synopsis was that no person should be called good. Of course, he was no ordinary person. He was good because he was God.

In Matthew 7:11, Jesus called people "evil." In Matthew 19:17, he said, "No one is good." In John 2, the people believed in him and wished to support him, "But Jesus did not commit Himself to them, because He knew all *men*, and had no need that anyone should testify of man, for He knew what was in man." (v. 24-25, NKJV). What was in people such that Jesus did not even trust them when they wished to lend their support?

Except for those who have been born again, "the whole world is under the control of the evil one." (1 John 5:19, NIV). This is why the only hope for children (and parents) is to be born again.

> And you *He made alive*, who were dead in trespasses and sins, in which you once walked according to the course of this world, according to the prince of the power of the air, the spirit who now works in the sons of disobedience, among whom also we all once conducted ourselves in the lusts of our flesh, fulfilling the desires of the flesh and of the mind, and were by nature children of wrath, just as the others.
>
> Ephesians 2:1-3, NKJV

It is the sin living inside that makes us utterly distasteful to God, and, as he says, makes us "by nature children of wrath." Because of the way things are now (that is, "by nature"), we ought to be thrown out. We are of no moral usefulness unless we are born again—"made alive."

The sin problem is so complete that people share the fate of the demons. In Matthew 25:31-46, Jesus explains what will happen when all of the people of the world come before him in judgment. He will say to those who do not know him, "Depart from me, you who are cursed, into the eternal fire prepared for the devil and his angels." (v. 41, NKJV). Why would mankind deserve a place designed for the demons? Because humans and demons have both rebelled against our Maker. Mankind is in cahoots with the demonic, and, therefore, our destiny is the same. The idea that we are good is a man-made mirage.

Eventually, the flesh, helped out by the world, the devil and his demons, comes up with all sorts of ideas, responses and reactions contrary to the ways of God. The flesh is the enemy of obedience. Our poor children are stuck in this condition, and we should have compassion for them while being serious about the problem.

The fact that our children are sinners should not be misunderstood. Sin refers not only to an evil act, but also to the force in a person that causes him or her to do evil. Before we are saved, our problem is not that we sinned in the past, but that we, from the inside, produced sin. Paul speaks of this state of being when he says, "For I know that in me (that is, in my flesh) nothing good dwells" (Romans 7:18, NKJV). In fact, if one reads through the book of Romans, Paul clearly talks about "sin" (those things done in the past) and "sin" (that which lives inside a person that compels him to commit sins). Listing sins that we have done at some point in time in our lives—lust, greed, pride, theft, hate, etc.—only touches the surface of the evil. We grasp the concept of "sin" when we realize that these things come from within.

For some time, I was confused on this issue. I heard about what Jesus did on the cross and believed that I had sinned, but it wasn't until I started to read the New Testament on my own that I realized committing sins in the past wasn't my biggest problem. My biggest problem was the fact that I was producing sin every day. Not only did I produce it, but I seemed to strive for it, each day wanting more (Romans 6:19). I was devising new ways of sinning (Romans 1:30). I thought, "If my heart is so full of filth, then what good is in me at all?" I realized that my heart was the center of my being and that if it was evil, I was evil. By a new birth, I was born spiritually. Instead of desiring to sin, I wanted to please God.

> And because you are sons, God has sent forth the Spirit of His Son into your hearts, crying out, "Abba, Father!"
>
> Galatians 4:6, NKJV

This is ultimately the hope for children. No amount of coaching and discipline is going to set them free from the flesh's hunger for sin. Only the Spirit of Jesus is able to do this.

Moms and dads must remember that without God, the heart of a child is not positive or neutral but tends toward selfishness, greed and evil. It is the flesh. Biblical parenting must wisely respond to these certainties.

With the knowledge of the sin problem, parents can be ready and expect conflict. Rather than seeing a child's behavior as overwhelming, exhausting or scary, it can be seen as ordinary and can be handled calmly by following God's example. Also, the understanding that children are born of the flesh should lead a parent to be careful and wise with his child's heart, evaluating the world through the prism of truth and making decisions about life accordingly. Finally, acknowledging the heart problem should lead us to seek a heart solution, which is beyond what a parent could ever provide, but it is available. The first two of these topics—compassion and wisdom—will be addressed in this chapter, and the heart solution will enjoy a chapter of its own.

Calm and Compassionate

Mothers and fathers should make sure they don't lose sight of the need to present God in the very best light possible, which is what he fully deserves. Parents should reflect the goodness of God to their children. With that in mind, the reasonable response to a child's flesh problem is to remain calm and compassionate. There will be repeated conflicts between parents who wish to impart godliness and their children. Why should we be surprised? Children are born of the flesh. Like their parents were, they will be creative sinners and repeat offenders. Knowing what to expect should be very freeing to a parent, who can say with confidence, "We will work through this."

So often, parents choose to respond to a child's misbehavior with, "How dare you?" instead of thinking, "How can I help you?" The parent who says, "I can't believe you would do that," is not speaking as if he believes the Bible. He actually should think, "This is something I would believe you would do." With this attitude, a parent should provide steady, judicial responses to disobedience.

If a parent thinks less of his children in the fleshly condition, he is caught in the folly of self-righteousness. Did we make ourselves good and reasonable? How long was God patient with us? Isn't he still patient? Those who would be hardliners when it comes to children's bad behavior should remember that Jesus unequivocally had compassion for us in that condition. How could we not do the same?

Parents can be completely empathetic. Our children are truly stuck, and we know what that is like. Parents may catch, discipline and coach thousands of times over the course of a decade. It is not a hard or terribly inconvenient job. It is life and, fortunately, God gives moms and dads plenty of time with their growing children to work through it. Thus, knowing of the flesh problem should not make parents bitter, grumpy or rude, but full of grace and hope for their children's freedom. Parents should be kind and understanding, not prideful and impatient.

Compassionate does not mean ignorant or naive. It should not cause parents to close their eyes to disobedience or to become less consistent in their discipline. That would make matters worse.

Parents have to be content with the idea that their children's hearts will oppose what is right and good in some way. Until children acknowledge the problem and accept and apply the solution, it will be ongoing. A child's struggle with sin is not going to be an easy one, and moms and dads should love and care for their children in the process.

Attitudes Accompanying Disobedience

What can a parent expect from his children in the flesh? At different ages, the flesh pulls out different stops to try to derail God's purposes. One could study lists of age-appropriate misbehavior, but such lists have limitations. For one thing, each child is different. A child may be like most or like none. Also, what is predicted may change with the parenting strategy employed. I suggest a different approach. When a parent sees a new misbehavior, he should realize that it is at least typical for his or her child. He shouldn't be surprised, but should temper expectations accordingly. He must be willing to correct inappropriate behavior consistently over time. That said, the Bible does provide insights into the tactics employed by the disobedient. Here, we will consider several scenarios from Israel's time in the wilderness that show us how the nation that God treated as "child" disobeyed.

When the Ten Commandments were given, Israel was making an unsound claim, "...we have seen that a man can live even if God speaks with him. But now, why should we die? This great fire will consume us, and we will die if we hear the voice of the LORD our God any longer." (Deuteronomy 5:24-25, NIV). Which is it? Did people die when they heard the voice of God or not? Was this proclamation legitimate, or were they trying to push back God and his rules? Moses observed this about Israel:

> They are a nation without sense, there is no discernment in them. If only they were wise and would understand this and discern what their end will be!
>
> Deuteronomy 32:28-29, NIV

Moses observed that Israel was illogical when they were not following God.

Disobedience is not a head problem. It is a heart problem, and when the heart takes over, sometimes the brain goes loco. We should expect it. A wise parent will see how his own children lose their minds in order to satisfy a desire. Thus, a parent should reason, remind, explain and discipline like God.

Forty-seven days after ten basic rules had been given, the people of Israel pursued their inner desires. Israel's overt disobedience started when they justified what they would do by concluding that Moses was dead or gone and that the whole thing had come to an end (Exodus 32:1). It didn't make sense. They were eating miracle-manna the very day they worshipped the cow and committed other immoral acts. To them, all that they had seen, heard and experienced seemed to mean nothing. The people were comfortable with the gods of the Egyptians, and they stopped thinking reasonably in order to get a golden cow and all that went with it.

More examples of Israel's behavior can be seen in the events of Numbers 13 and 14. God asked Israel to go into the Promised Land, and they showed signs of hesitation.

> Then all of you [Israel] came to me [Moses] and said, "Let us send men ahead to spy out the land for us and bring back a report about the route we are to take and the towns we will come to." The idea seemed good to me; so I selected twelve of you, one man from each tribe.
>
> Deuteronomy 1:22-23, NIV

Instead of obeying God, the people showed hesitation by requesting that spies be sent in first and that specific plans be made. God accepted the plan: "The Lord spoke to Moses, saying, 'Send men to spy out the land of Canaan, which I am giving to the people of Israel'" (Numbers 13:1-2). The spies came back, and ten of the twelve gave a bad report. Israel had to decide whether it would obey God's instruction or not. "That night all the members of the community raised their voices and wept aloud" because, compared to the people of the land, Israel said that they were like grasshoppers (Numbers 13:33, 14:1, NIV). They were concerned for the safety of their families (Numbers 14:3). In fact, they wanted to go back into slavery in Egypt (Numbers 14:4). They even said that it would be better to have died in the past than to die now: "If only we had died in Egypt! Or in this wilderness!" (Numbers 14:2, NIV).

All of that was untenable logic. In the end, Israel decided it would not do what God asked. We should note that the disobedience was accompanied by a convoluted thought process. Similarly, for children, hesitation, emotional outburst, exaggeration and confused thoughts are likely to occur when they don't want to obey. When we see it, we can remember that the nation God treated as a child acted similarly.

To see common flesh behavior, we can also go to Numbers 11, 16, 20 and 21. We find high drama, complaining, and discontentment, attempt to control, deception and ungratefulness.

In Numbers 11, the stubbornly hardhearted in Israel, the "rabble," had a strong desire for meat. They roused the people, who then began to weep on account of the craving (v. 4, NIV). That led to exaggerated claims about the benefits of living in Egypt: "We remember the fish we ate in Egypt at no cost—also the cucumbers, melons, leeks, onions and garlic." (v. 5, NIV). They also claimed that they were "wasting away" because they only had manna to "look at" (v. 6, NIV). Maybe they lost their appetite for manna, but certainly the "bread of angels" would have fully nourished (Psalm 76:25, NIV). In the end, God provided quail to eat but also sent a plague on those who had craved meat and complained.

The scenario in Numbers 16 is similar to that of Numbers 11 in that the offense started with a small group and spread to others. In Numbers 16, three men convinced 250 influential men (likely judges, v. 2) to question Aaron's priesthood. The 253 contentious Israelites said to Moses and Aaron, "You have gone too far! The whole community is holy, every one of them, and the LORD is with them. Why then do you set yourselves above the LORD's assembly?" (Numbers 16:3, NIV). In other words, "You need to stop acting like you are special." On top of this, two of the leaders complained, "...you have brought us up out of a land flowing with milk and honey." They continued, "Moreover, you have not brought us into a land flowing with milk and honey, nor given us inheritance of fields and vineyards" (Numbers 16:14, NIV). Of course, this statement completely ignores the fact that the people had refused to go to the Promised Land. Eventually, the whole nation was coming to take part. Again, deception and exaggeration accompanied rebellion. The event showed Israel's willingness to whine, but God patiently dealt with it until the Israelite society was ready to comply.

Finally, we should consider Numbers 20, in which Israel protested that there was no water. The people also grumbled that there was no fruit and said that they wished they'd died sooner (20:4-5). The latter was particularly odd because it appears that they wished to stay alive at the time when they wanted water. It was melodrama.

Fallen human beings can display a curiously delusional intellect. Remember all that God had done for Israel—miracle after miracle after miracle. The Israelites had been disciplined repeatedly by fire, wanderings, plagues and their enemies. Still, human folly was overwhelmingly powerful. Israel was a repeat offender. Logic, reason and even awesome experiences couldn't depose the trouble of the flesh.

When a parent hears melodrama or griping, it should signal that something is wrong. When a child complains, it shows his discontentment. When he exaggerates, it shows he is willing to manipulate in order to get what he wants. Being practiced at disobedience means being practiced at creating the lies that make it possible. In other words, if people want to do the wrong things, they get good at justifying their behavior. This is not a virtuous habit or an advantageous life skill. Parents who hold the expectation of obedience grant their children a better start in life, yet cool heads must prevail.

Being Careful and Wise

Parents should design family life to meet the reality of the flesh and all its manipulations. Opening the door wide for the influences of the world can make resisting the flesh more difficult for a child. In fact, it is mean. A child may not see it this way, but a parent who understands the inclination of a child's heart and how it will be affected by messages from others should know better. Children battle the flesh. Why should parents put fuel on that fire?

Parents need to be discerning about what influences their children in areas such as movies, music, friendships and pop culture. Almost every parent affirms this idea to some degree, but the application varies significantly. One parent permits almost anything, while another restricts almost everything. The Bible provides us with good rules of thumb when it comes to these types of decisions. For example, we can consider some of the instructions given during the Exodus meant to eliminate negative influences in that context. Before Israel entered the Promised Land, God instructed the Israelites not to marry the people there because they would not be strong enough to endure their temptations.

> Do not intermarry with them. Do not give your daughters to their sons or take their daughters for your sons, for they will turn your children away from following me to serve other gods.
>
> Deuteronomy 7:3-4, NIV

The passage goes on to explain how the temptations of the gods were to be removed.

> This is what you are to do to them: Break down their altars, smash their sacred stones, cut down their Asherah poles and burn their idols in the fire. For you are a people holy to the LORD your God. The LORD your God has chosen you out of all the peoples on the face of the earth to be his people, his treasured possession.
>
> Deuteronomy 7:5-6, NIV

Theoretically, the people could have intermarried (there was nothing otherwise wrong with intermarrying) and left all of the idols in place ("an idol *is* nothing in the world", 1 Corinthians 8:4, NKJV) and not worshipped them. Israel did not live in theory, however. They lived in reality, and God knew what they should do in order to have the best chance of following him. It was to remove temptations.

Our children live in reality, too. Why should we want to increase the power of the flesh by letting the world pack their heads with bad ideas? Surely, some of these things are going to come, but why invite them in? Why consume them?

Consider another warning from the Exodus that was meant to curb temptation. Should Israel have foolishly desired a king (Deuteronomy 17:14), God had instructions that were meant to keep that king from becoming corrupt.

> The king, moreover, must not acquire great numbers of horses for himself or make the people return to Egypt to get more of them, for the LORD has told you, "You are not to go back that way again." He must not take many wives, or his heart will be led astray. He must not accumulate large amounts of silver and gold.
>
> Deuteronomy 17:16-17, NIV

These prohibitions were meant to limit sources of temptation, keeping the king from becoming proud, self-reliant or otherwise foolish. (Even though God's design was one husband and one wife (Matthew 19:4-6, 1 Timothy 3:2, 12, Titus 1:6 and Ephesians 5:22-33), 1 Samuel 8:13 showed that kings would do whatever they wanted.)

Our children are not likely to be influenced by a spouse who worships at the Asherah pole. In their youth, they are unlikely to accumulate large quantities of wealth in which to hope. We should not disregard these verses, though, because the principles absolutely apply. God provides good reason to opt out of activities that could "turn your children away from following me." Knowing of the inclination of the heart, parents should seek God's wisdom in order to reduce temptations because the wrong influence may lead children away from God.

Romans 6:19 describes wickedness as "ever-increasing" (NIV), which must mean that it starts as less wicked and progressively gets worse. Parents need to be able to think about how a certain path or idea is going to end up. For example, when I first started listening to rock music as a child, the songs I chose were fun and mostly about romance. Over time, the music I chose grew darker. The cute songs no longer satisfied, and the world provided new material for my maturing flesh. Sin was ever-increasing.

Knowing the weakness of the human heart and reality of ever increasing sin, how does a parent help his child? First, parents must accept that, in light of eternity, there are only two kingdoms—the kingdom of the world and the kingdom of God. The subjects of each kingdom, to some degree or another, will promote the kingdom in which they live. Jesus said this about people who were of the opposing kingdom:

> "He who is not with me is against me, and he who does not gather with me scatters."
>
> Matthew 12:30, NIV (see also Luke 11:23)

Every person has a drive, and every person either ends up scattering or gathering as far as Jesus is concerned. Parents who do not want their children to be those who are scattered must act with wisdom.

Media, pop culture and friendships are all similar in that they are the expressions of the individuals involved. When we think about a movie's influence, for example, we can ask simple questions: "What is the maker of the media like?" "Is he on Jesus' side, or does he promote something else?" "Do his ideas gather people to Jesus or send them headed in another direction?"

Wise About Media

There is good reason not to read most books or watch most TV, web shows and movies. People who produce the media have flesh, and that flesh has desires that will be, in some way, unrestrained. They will introduce ideas that have not occurred to a child yet, and will thereby make that child a little more experienced in the ways of rebellion. So, parents have to ask, "Would we want the story writer, producer or director to influence our children in an entertaining, emotionally compelling presentation?" Can a person welcome messages motivated by the flesh and then effectively communicate to his child, "...only be careful, and watch yourselves closely" (Deuteronomy 4:9, NIV)? Are the creators of the programming for God or against him? Do they scatter or gather? Should we let their thoughts fill our house?

One should seriously consider whether technology that edits out scenes or language is sufficient. While using this technology, a family is still financially supporting the kind of program that needs editing. Further, movies' problems go deeper than a few bad scenes or words. Can electronics filter scenes that feed the desire for greed, fear, lust, fame, revenge, gossip, humanism, selfish ambitions, worthless pursuits, etc.? Almost every show glamorizes some kind of wrong desire. There is no technology, nor will there ever be, to clear the flesh out of a movie produced by people in the flesh. The person who believes that eliminating language will clean the movie up is in a delusion.

We might consider a practical question like whether it is beneficial for a Christian boy or girl to read or watch a series like Harry Potter that introduces witchcraft as fun, interesting and exciting. A parent has to ask, "What should I do, Lord?" God loathes witchcraft. No doubt, some people have started meddling in witchcraft because of the Harry Potter series. Even if parents were to predict that their children would not be harmed in any way by the enticement, would it still be best for families to call such a message entertainment?

Certainly, if a family does engage in popular media, they should talk about it afterward, interpreting the message from a biblical perspective. For example, a parent could parse a televised sporting event, discussing the commercials (many of which should be skipped), the hysteria around trivial activities and the cheering of good performance rather than good character. While these types of discussions can have some value, a parent should not justify watching shows in order to discuss the ways of the world. That is not the kind of education children really need. They need to learn about God's kingdom, not the counterfeit.

I believe that regular exposure to media produced by people in the flesh will cause serious problems in a family. More secular books and shows equals more trouble, and there are better things to do. The TV is an active thief, stealing lives away by distracting people from what matters most. The Internet can be an equally efficient time-waster. When a child's life is full of entertainment, he will replace opportunities for growth with hours of self-absorption. Entertainment also distracts parents from their duties. Instead, families should engage one another in conversation, make music, play games, gain knowledge, create something, exercise or enjoy edifying media. If you don't have better things to do than watch whatever show is on TV tonight, I challenge you to re-evaluate. Following Jesus is not a matter of only avoiding certain indecencies. We are given a great commission to know God and make him known; and it seems that regular consumption of secular books, movies or shows would be an obvious denial of our calling. Whether for the purpose of avoiding messages that promote the flesh or for the sake of choosing a better alternative, parents would do well to avoid almost all secular media.

Wise About Sensuality

How are the moral messages of some of today's styles, shows and ads different than the adulterous women referred to in Proverbs? They are not. They are visually suggesting immorality.

> Then out came a woman to meet him, dressed like a prostitute and with crafty intent.
>
> Proverbs 7:10, NIV

The seduction of the women in a provocative scene in a show or a magazine's "swimsuit issue" are on par with the mindset of the woman described in Proverbs, inciting covetous and adulterous desires.

> Many are the victims she has brought down; her slain are a mighty throng. Her house is a highway to the grave, leading down to the chambers of death.
>
> Proverbs 7:26-27, NIV, see also Matthew 5:27-28

Pop culture sensuality aims to elicit lustful thoughts. As my college advertising professor said, with seemingly no moral bias on the issue, "sex sells." Don't buy their version.

How could a person maintain his concern for righteousness if he were to identify with and purchase products primarily sold through an appeal to lust? Wouldn't it be better to shun the brand and teach children about the advertiser's techniques? Similarly, styles that clothing makers promote often appear to be something an immoral woman might don in order to attract a man. Wouldn't it be better to teach children how some of the latest styles are designed to gain the attention of lustful men? Shows also use sensuality in order to gain viewers. I am not just referring to overt immorality, but suggestive immorality as well. Children and adults are enticed by and imitate what they see (or sort of see).

I am afraid to imagine what some parents watch after their children go to bed. Married people are free to be intimate, but it should only be the two of them. This seems obvious. So why would a husband and wife's evening plans include watching another couple be intimate? Isn't the married couple emotionally, mentally and visually participating? Also, do these programs show the consequences one would expect from such immoral behavior in real life? It is unlikely. They are selling a lifestyle that opposes God's plan. Certainly, we should not be entertained by such a movie (or book). These scenes should grieve us to the point of being repulsed by the entire presentation.

When one meditates on God's rules, seeing how others are being encouraged to break these rules causes grief.

> I gain understanding from your precepts; therefore I hate every wrong path.
>
> Psalm 119:104, NIV

If a person is indifferent to those encouraging others to run to sin, he has not embraced God's precepts. Knowing God and his ways must result in a strong distaste for the paths that lead people to destruction. One who calls himself a Christian can't care for people and, at the same time, be okay with the paths of life that lead those people to Hell.

Keep in mind, when it comes to sensuality, that the body is not the enemy. There is a way of thinking about the body that is for good and for family. The threat is the perverted, sensational way of looking at the body. The Devil, the world and the flesh know this way.

Our culture is, in many ways, a desensitizing machine. People seem to be willing to say, "Oh, that is the way it is, okay." The truth is that the world's sensuality is not "art" but an opportunity to inflate emotions related to immorality. It awakens unhealthy desires. Once seen, the burden of these ideas may be carried for years.

Parents should be wise and make efforts to limit their family's exposure to the debased sensuality presented by the world. The dress and the behavior of the world are attempts to emulate the wayward woman or the perverted man. These are great embarrassments to the people who pursue them. Parents should call that sensuality what it is. At the very least, a home should provide some reprieve from the messages children will likely receive elsewhere.

Wise About Friendships

Children can become tempted by friends who share ambitions, stories and descriptions related to their own sinful desires. Even very young children can persuade a friend to break family rules. Family principles should aim to put those relationships into proper perspective. For example, for several thoughtful reasons, a parent might ask his children not to label another person a "best friend." First, "best friend" raises the potential for emotional or behavioral trouble. What if there is a disagreement? What if the best friend wants to do things that she shouldn't? What if someone finds another best friend? How does one handle the drama of "You're not my best friend anymore"? All of this is unnecessary. More than that, however, Jesus tells us that no one should come before him, and we want to be equally kind and loving to all people rather than having tunnel vision toward one who satisfies us the most. It is thoughtful to consider the use of the term "best friend," and it is fair to evaluate all sorts of other friend issues. Are sleepovers a good idea? How does a child choose friends? What is a child to do about people who need a good influence in their lives, but who are a bad influence on others? How do parents put relationships into the proper perspective?

There are different types of relationships and each has its own batch of issues. Although the practical solutions that limit temptations from friends are different from one age (and type of relationship) to another, the principles applied don't change that much. Here, I have decided to reason about the relationship between a young single man and a young single woman. My hope is that the ideas brought up will help parents teach children to be careful in other relationships, too.

For young adults, here is a good starting principle: until a person is ready to be married and have children, the concepts of "dating," being "interested," having a "girlfriend" or "boyfriend," or anything of the sort, are premature and inappropriate. Song of Solomon says that love should wait to be awakened until it is time (2:7, 8:4). There is no reason to play around beforehand. Those parents who encourage what they believe to be cute little romances need to heed these warnings. Parents should not set their children up for years of unsatisfied desires. Many children are looking for acceptance. The flesh's simplistic solution is often, "I hope he likes me." This kind of hope frequently leads to greater disappointment and leaves children, particularly girls, in a frightening, emotionally fragile situation. Instead, parents should acknowledge the wisdom of Ecclesiastes, which informs us that life has seasons (Chapter 3). For many years, boys prefer spending time with boys, and girls prefer spending time with girls. The season of life for romance between men and women will come in due time.

How can a parent help a child prepare for a healthy romantic relationship? Jesus tells us that greater responsibility should come with evidence that one has been faithful with smaller issues (Luke 16:10). The way to prepare to be a good husband or wife is not by playing boyfriend or girlfriend, but rather by focusing on growing mature and responsible as a single person.

Convincing a child to become mature and wait for the right time to look for a spouse will not be done by harping only on the temptations. A parent should promote what is good in life. Persuading a child to look forward to his marriage as a source of life-long joy will help him. Children feel comfortable with parents who are committed to teach them to do all things well, including finding a mate and preparing for marriage. A child can understand that a parent has her best interests in mind and can use the Bible as a guide. For example, we might think of Proverbs 31 as instructions to a noble woman, but these words were originally for a young man who was seeking a wife. His mom was describing the kind of woman he should try to find, and the chapter is a great starting point for parents today.

I think it would be wise for young women and men to build two lists: "Who I should be" and "Who the right marriage partner should be." Young adults should seriously consider what it will take to be a good spouse and parent. There should also be expectations for potential spouses. How is his or her work ethic? How are relationships with his or her parents and siblings? Is he or she into purity or willing to cheat some? Is he or she evaluating what is right and wrong or going with the crowd on most issues? Is he or she a student of the Bible? Does he or she walk after the

Spirit of God or the flesh? Does he or she speak with God? Is he or she looking forward to caring for children within a year of the wedding? Are there any time- consuming hobbies with which he or she is not willing to part? What are his or her long term goals?

Once ready for marriage, I would encourage young adults to be intentional, but not embarrassingly so. In the midst of it, they should be thankful for being single (1 Corinthians 7:8). Finding a spouse is a noble pursuit, but it should not be all-consuming. Our Father is looking for "godly offspring", and he certainly wants to bless the process (Malachi 2:15, NKJV). At the same time, we should consider 1 Corinthians 7:25-39 for a realistic way of looking at marriage in light of our relationship with God.

The activity of finding a spouse should be handled with thoughtfulness on every level. If a grown child has the right objectives and understands how to minimize the temptations and potential heartaches associated with finding a partner for life, good decisions will follow; however, parents should help young adults set up rules for accountability. Parents may recall that these are exciting times for young people, and excitement sometimes clouds judgment. It is an important time for coaching.

Above is a brief application of God's wisdom in a hard-to-navigate relationship situation from dating to marriage. God's wisdom in taking friendships seriously, at times limiting them and considering potential temptations, applies to friendships between neighbors, teammates, teenagers, etc. Relationships are important to God and appreciating people is enjoyable and natural, but relationships require wisdom in a world in which people's hearts tend toward evil. The goal for friendships should not be selfish—"What can I get out of this?" Instead, children should help their friends pursue God. When temptations come through these friendships, it can be especially confusing to children, and it may be difficult for them to identify sin as sin because feelings can cloud the truth. Parents who understand the heart problem will have a greater ability to provide wise coaching at these times.

Wise Parents

Parents need to be wise about the world in which their children reside and careful not to feed the taunting flesh. They should do what they can to keep their children's lives free of unnecessary temptations so they can get more enjoyment out of growing up. Also, if possible, parents should deal with the flesh in the more innocent circumstances of life, rather than having to tackle flesh that has experience with more perverse desires. For these reasons, parents should restrict some outside influences. Moms and dads may have to restrain themselves as well. For example, parents can incite temptation when sharing tales of their sinful pasts. A child might even decide that the way to really appreciate God is to first follow in his parents' footsteps. Remember, the flesh does not necessarily need logic in its justifications. For this reason, I encourage parents not to tell sin-filled stories about their life before Jesus. Sometimes this is true of a parent's past: "For it is shameful even to speak of those things which are done by them in secret." (Ephesians 5:12, NKJV).

What about other circumstances in which a parent might be liberal about what he says and does? If a parent were to make an inappropriate comment about how a lady looks, to talk about how he loves food or shopping, to drive dangerously, or to suggest, even in jest, some illegal activity, is he cautionary? The will of God should permeate every area of our lives, and every action should be considered in the light of his plan.

Parents should spend more time talking about the right way to do life than they do talking about the wrong way to do it (Philippians 4:8). Joy and thanksgiving will be more helpful for a child than pessimism about the sin that surrounds him. So, when necessary, sin should be pointed out as sin, but God's alternative should be spoken of highly and often. Romans 16:9 says, "I [Paul] want you to be wise about what is good, and innocent about what is evil" (NKJV).

It is not unheard of for parents to believe that children need time to explore different lifestyles to "get it out of their system." Such a suggestion should never be considered biblical or wise. Only one full and abundant life exists, and it is the one provided by fully submitting to the will of Jesus. Those who believe their children would do well to "live it up" for a while do not know the abundant life.

Parents who want their children to live in a home where the abundant life is experienced will need wisdom about limiting what a child sees, hears and does. I am not saying that parents can remove their children completely from the world, or that they should: isolation is not the goal. Wisdom is the goal, and it says that light has nothing in common with darkness (2 Corinthians 6:14). This is why a family should not run after the world and its entertainment. Why incite the flesh? The heart problem means that parents need to take things very seriously, being aware of those who scatter instead of gather. Exposure to sinful ideas places an extra burden on children. That burden is going to come, but it does not have to come quickly or in full force. Parents should give the gift of innocence to their children because innocence is freeing.

Let me say again, I do not mean that families should remove themselves from society. I am not talking about forming a group with a standardized response to the world. Fear that every exposure to the world will somehow whisk a child away from his family is not healthy. Parents should not be constantly shocked about what the world says or does. Instead, parents should be confident in the power of God to save, possessing the ability to calmly explain the world around them and having the good judgment to eschew unnecessary temptations when they can be so easily avoided.

Searching for a Heart Solution

The very nature of the situation—"every inclination of the human heart is evil"—demands that parents be ready. For example, parents might expect their children to act as the Israelites did at times. They doubted, complained, and shunned God. Logic was replaced with ideas that didn't make sense. Wise parents understand this condition and make decisions for the family that will make navigating these waters more likely to end in success.

When moms and dads talk about behavior, they should refer back to the heart because, "As water reflects the face, so one's life reflects the heart" (Proverbs 27:19, NIV). So, a mom could say, "When you disobeyed, we found out what you had put in your heart;" and, "What you put in your heart will always come out eventually, whether good or bad;" and, "Trials show what was already in your heart. They bring out what you had there, and if it was bad, it was sin in your heart."

In the end, knowing about the heart problem should leave us optimistic. Imagine a family in which each person can consider the current condition of his or her heart and turn that heart to the ways and ideas of the one who brings life.

God's desire is not to change people's behavior alone but to change them at the core of their being. In fact, one can't know Jesus without a heart made new. The Good News is that a child can receive the Holy Spirit and experience the kingdom of God. In fact, Jesus said that in order to take hold of the kingdom, we must become like a child (Matthew 18:3, Luke 10:21). If a child is born again, he or she may actually be one step ahead of a born-again adult. Children have little concern about social reputation and are used to trusting in others. These are significant advantages when Jesus is King.

For Discussion

1. Children have a heart problem that will lead them away from God. What can a parent do to stop this?
2. What can you do to help protect your child from outside temptations?
3. Discuss examples of people whose influence has scattered and compare them to people whose efforts have gathered.
4. How does knowing about the heart problem change your parenting? How will it affect your parenting as your children grow older?
5. Do you tend to focus more on the heart or on behavior? Do you relate behavior to the heart?

Chapter 7

HEART SOLUTION

Those who belong to Jesus should earnestly seek to obey God because it is the way we show love to him. The pursuit of righteousness is not old-fashioned, nor should Christians be content with mediocre living. Unfortunately, not all see it this way. Maybe some think we should go on sinning so that grace will increase (Romans 6:1) or have decided it is easier to give up than face the potential disappointment of disobeying God again. Maybe some believe that God is going to get rid of their vices one at a time. It is his job, not theirs. Maybe some have decided that God's goal is their happiness rather than their purity or that, since they have stopped doing most bad things, their life has changed enough already. None of these will do. A parent is responsible to live in and teach his children God's holiness.

When it comes to obeying God, we might think of biblical commands first. One example would be the Sermon on the Mount in Matthew chapter 5. Another example is the command to "*Be* hospitable to one another without grumbling" (1 Peter 4:9, NKJV). These types of verses explain what a person is supposed to do and not supposed to do.

Next, one might observe messages about the necessity of obedience: "But why do you call Me 'Lord, Lord,' and not do the things which I say?" And "...work out your own salvation with fear and trembling" (Luke 6:46, Philippians 2:12, NKJV). Hebrews 12 goes so far as to compare a believer's willingness to resist sin to Jesus' commitment to defeat it: "In your struggle against sin, you have not yet resisted to the point of shedding your blood." (v. 4, NKJV). The most powerful driving force for obedience is a heart which is fully satisfied with God. The one whose affection is set on Jesus will no longer thirst for sin. The one who loves God will have a compelling reason to obey (John 14:15, 23-24).

Parents would be right to teach their children what to obey and the motive to obey, but they must also teach important how-to-obey instructions from the Bible. To experience life change, there must be a new birth, an eternal perspective, the experience of worship, the words of Jesus, the knowledge of sin-living-in and the Spirit's power. Parenting must point children to a heart solution.

The Paradigm of the Flesh, and the Spirit

In the first century, when people believed in Jesus and were spiritually born, they were taught a paradigm meant to facilitate righteous living. It was the way for any follower and still is. It was, and still should be, a first-order lesson.

The New Testament tells us that we are to put off the flesh and walk in the Spirit, which is what I refer to as the flesh and Spirit paradigm. In other words, we are to consider the old person dead and to live as a new person who is made alive by Jesus' Spirit. If this is the only hope for adults (and it is), it is also the only hope for children. There is no other way to truly obey, and there is no higher standard for morality.

Parenting should include the flesh and Spirit paradigm, and I will do my best to explain it. Fortunately, these truths show up all over the New Testament. This chapter is a result of studying Romans 6, 7, 8, 12:1-2, 13:12-14; 2 Corinthians 4:11, 5:16, 10:2-7; Galatians 2:20, 3:3, 5:16-26, 6:8; Ephesians 2:1-19, 4:17-5:21; Philippians 2:12-18; Colossians 2:6-3:17; Hebrews 9:13-15, 10:14-17; 1 Peter 4:1-6 and 1 John 2:16-17. Unless otherwise noted, all Scripture quotes in this chapter are from the NKJV.

Included in the Basics

The lesson of the flesh and Spirit paradigm was one of the first things taught to new Jesus-followers. For example, Romans 6:3 says that the message was to be taught along with immersion. In fact, teaching this paradigm accompanied conversion—the "form of doctrine to which you were delivered" (Romans 6:17).

When letters were written to the believers in a certain city, it was not the first time the paradigm of the flesh and Spirit had been explained to them. For example, Colossians 2:7 says, concerning the flesh and the Spirit, "as you have been taught". Also, when believers in Ephesus failed to function in the flesh and Spirit paradigm, they were corrected: "But you have not so learned Christ" (Ephesians 4:20). The passages about the paradigm are reminders of lessons previously explained as a necessary truth.

Because the New Testament letters to the fellowships were meant for reviewing the topic of the flesh and the Spirit, the comments of any one passage may leave some questions unanswered. We can gain rich understanding of the original message when we look at several passages at the same time that cover the same topic.

The Flesh and the Spirit

From God and those in whom he produces fruit, one can expect "love, joy, peace, longsuffering, kindness, goodness, faithfulness, gentleness, self-control", "righteousness, and truth" (Galatians 5:22 and Ephesians 5:9). This is what a parent should want to see produced in his child as well.

What is to be expected from people without God is quite different, and as I explained in the previous chapter, the "flesh" is the source of the trouble. Consider its deeds—"adultery, fornication, uncleanness, lewdness, idolatry, sorcery, hatred, contentions, jealousies, outbursts of wrath, selfish ambitions, dissensions, heresies, envy, murders," "to work all uncleanness with greediness," "passion, evil desire, and covetousness, which is idolatry, …anger, wrath, malice, blasphemy, filthy language," "strife", "lusts, drunkenness, revelries, drinking parties" (Galatians 5:19-21, Ephesians 4:19, Colossians 3:5, 3:8 Romans 13:13, 1 Peter 4:3). The flesh's deeds also include "filthiness," "foolish talking" and "coarse jesting" (Ephesians 5:4). These are "the lust of the flesh, the lust of the eyes, and the pride of life" (1 John 2:16). These are issues of the heart. In the words of Jesus, "What comes out of a man, that defiles a man. For from within, out of the heart of men, proceed evil thoughts, adulteries, fornications, murders, thefts, covetousness, wickedness, deceit, lewdness, an evil eye, blasphemy, pride, foolishness. All these evil things come from within and defile a man." (Mark 7:20-23). Further, these lists of fleshly behavior may not have been complete—"and the like" (Galatians 5:21).

Some behavior, like committing murder, may seem obviously wrong while other actions, like jealousy, may seem more innocent. It is all the same flesh however. Furthermore, these passages describe an adult's flesh. A child's deeds of the flesh will generally be more subtle—pushing, grabbing, ignoring, and delaying. Nevertheless, a child's selfishness, pride, laziness, sass, carelessness, etc. are disobedient to God and often cruel to others. Any one of these behaviors will confirm that a child (or an adult) is in the flesh.

Sometimes sin isn't for pleasure's sake. Since people oppose God, hearing one of God's rules can make one oppose that rule whether it makes sense to do so or not. If it is good not to cross a line, people will do it just to defy goodness. A good rule can cause "sinful passions" to be "aroused," just because it is a good rule. *"'You shall not covet.'...*produced in me [Paul] all *manner of evil* desire." (Romans 7:7-8). This is as true for children as it is for adults. Disobedience for disobedience's sake may be appealing at times.

Young people who are "dead in trespasses" and without the Spirit of Jesus, will produce "dead works" because there is a drive "at work in our members to bear fruit to death" (Ephesians 2:1, 5, Hebrews 9:14, Romans 7:5). In fact, people are not just in darkness. The Bible says that those who were born again "were once darkness," "sons of disobedience" (Ephesians 5:8, 2:2). It was not what they did, but who they were. Jesus said, "Most assuredly, I say to you, whoever commits sin is a slave of sin." (John 8:34; see also Romans 6:6, 17 and 20). Like slaves of sin, unsaved children and unsaved adults don't just sin but are mastered by it.

When a child begins to understand the power of the flesh, he might realize that not all is well with the world: "So, everyone else wants to get away with bad stuff, too?" Yes, that is correct. "O wretched man that I am! Who will deliver me from this body of death?" (Romans 7:24). Children would be blessed to come to this realization. Parents should teach their children about the flesh, so that what they feel inside makes more sense and they will search for the Savior.

The flesh is not a distant theological concept but a personal reality for us all. For example, one day our then four-year-old seemed hesitant to obey. I told him that I was going to hold on to his hand for a while. He was absolutely irritated by my grip and began to fight against me, squirming and complaining. In most other instances, he would not have been bothered that we were holding hands. This reaction of defiance was typical flesh, as far as I can tell from life and my study of the Word of God. Adults have similar feelings about different issues. Whether we are

CHAPTER 7 HEART SOLUTION

squirming at the idea of obeying the speed limit, wanting to snap back at someone we love, wishing we could live someone else's life or thinking of gorging ourselves on some favorite food, the flesh is present to stir up ideas that range from bad to awful.

These passages make it clear that the flesh produces some behaviors and the Spirit produces others. This is a biblical view of life. Our children need to know that obedience boils down to these two.

Believing in New Life

When a person sees that Jesus is God and that Jesus died on the cross to save him, he does so by first choosing to acknowledge that those events were historically true. By faith he repents and seeks to be filled with Jesus' Spirit. He would have "received Christ Jesus the Lord" by believing these facts. If he obeys the command to be immersed, he does so by faith. How, then would he walk out his Christ-following life? The Bible says, "As you therefore have received Christ Jesus the Lord, so walk in Him." (Colossians 2:6). His walk should be by faith. To "walk in him" he is to believe two main truths: First, he must believe that he has already died. Second, he must believe he has come to new life, eternal life. Thus, in order to teach children how to lead the Christian life, parents must first help them understand what the Bible says about this death and subsequent new life.

The passages that explain the flesh and Spirit paradigm say more than a dozen times that those who are in Jesus have died. It is central to understanding the how-to of pleasing God. "Our old man was crucified with *Him*," "for you died," "we died with Christ" and were "buried with Him through [immersion] into death" and, therefore, "have crucified the flesh" (Romans 6:4, 6, 8; Colossians 3:3; Galatians 5:24). Do you and your believing children consider yourselves dead? Do you believe these verses? Think about Paul's commitment to this truth: "I have been crucified with Christ; it is no longer I who live, but Christ lives in me; and the *life* which I now live in the flesh I live by faith in the Son of God, who loved me and gave Himself for me." (Galatians 2:20). This was not a mediocre or normal existence. This was supernatural, righteous living; and it was experienced by Paul through accepting some things "by faith", first that he had already died.

Perhaps a family portrait should have a bubble graphic next to each individual labeling them as "dead."

Or do you not know that as many of us as were [immersed] into
Christ Jesus were [immersed] into His death?

Romans 6:3

Object lessons can help children understand concepts that are true but not
seen. Immersion is one such object lesson. It is a pretend burial of the old
man and the resurrection of the new man, pointing to the idea that we are
to consider ourselves dead.

I get the impression when some Christians talk about "carrying their
cross" or "dying daily" that it is a heavy hardship or something that only
the spiritually mature are able to do. These ideas are not consistent with
the Bible. The verses that talk about this death are past tense, and the
implied instructions are to have faith. In other words, believers, whether
recently reborn or older in the Lord, are to accept something that has
already been done, that is, that they have already died with Jesus. It is
not by self-sacrifice that they are to die, but by faith they are to consider
themselves already dead. It isn't that they have to be tough enough to die,
but that Jesus let them die in him when he died (2 Corinthians 5:14).
Their job is to accept that they did die in Jesus and to let him live through
them moment by moment.

This type of believing revolutionizes life. When a born again person
believes that he died, "sin shall not have dominion over" him (Romans
6:14). The reason God did it this way was so that the "righteous
requirement of the law might be fulfilled in us" (Romans 8:4). Those who
believe, whether children or adults, have gone from one extreme to the
other not in the future, but in the present. Certainly, we still experience
the temptation to sin from inside, but amazingly, it is "no longer I who
do it, but sin that dwells in me" (Romans 7:20). God is telling those who
follow him to believe in something that cannot be seen or touched. They
have to believe they have been crucified and that those ideas that pop into
their heads are no longer theirs, but the flesh—"it is no longer I who do
it", which brings us to the next item of faith.

Those who are saved can say, "I know who I am now. I want only what
is good and right." What an amazing truth for the believer: "For in Him
[Jesus] dwells all the fullness of the Godhead bodily, and you are complete
in Him" (Colossians 2:9-10). True life is a matter of living in unison with
the Spirit of Jesus, as the power that raised Jesus from the dead strengthens
our spirit to do what is right (Romans 8:11).

Many things will change when believers go to heaven. They will be able to see God. There will be a new world, a new city, a new culture, new homes and we will have new bodies. The flesh will be done away with, as will sickness and sorrow; however, the new man will not be new. He or she has already been made new, alive with Christ. This is mind-blowing:

> Since you have purified your souls in obeying the truth through the Spirit in sincere love of the brethren, love one another fervently with a pure heart, having been born again, not of corruptible seed but incorruptible, through the word of God which lives and abides forever, because *'All flesh is as grass, And all the glory of man as the flower of the grass. The grass withers, And its flower falls away, But the word of the LORD endures forever.'* Now this is the word which by the [good news] was preached to you.
>
> 1 Peter 1:22-25

Those who have been born again do not need to be born again another time in paradise. The made-alive spirit we now have is sufficient for all eternity (non-perishable). This is what we are to believe about who we are now:

> ...and that you put on the new man which was created according to God, in true righteousness and holiness.
>
> Ephesians 4:24

> ...and have put on the new *man* who is renewed in knowledge according to the image of Him who created him...
>
> Colossians 3:10

Those who are saved are now created in "the image of Him," "in true righteousness and holiness." Therefore, parents can say to their saved children, "The new you says, 'I delight in the law of God'" because he said he "will put My laws into their hearts, and in their minds I will write them" (Romans 7:22, Jeremiah 31:33, see also Hebrews 8:10, 10:16, Isaiah 59:12). Out of the heart comes all behavior, and out of a Spirit-alive heart comes righteous behavior.

Parents create a problem for their born-again children when they teach them that all thoughts are theirs, all feelings are theirs and all desires are theirs. Malicious thoughts, feelings and desires do not come from them, but from the flesh: "You are not in the flesh but in the Spirit", "slaves of righteousness", "set free from sin", a "new creation; old things have passed away; behold, all things have become new" (Romans 8:9, 6:18 and 22, 2 Corinthians 5:17). When thinking of their saved children, parents are to "regard no one according to the flesh" (2 Corinthians 5:16). Parents should make certain that their language communicates who their heaven-bound children are in the Spirit, not who they might have been in the flesh. Certainly a parent should not say, "You are stubborn," or anything similar. If children are born again, parents should tell them who they are now.

If a saved child believes the flesh is him, he may determine that he is a wreck inside. He may be desperate for God's help, but it will seem that God only helps some of the time. Or, he may justify a lot of behavior as, "who I am" or "the way God made me." This sentiment is awful because what the flesh produces is disgusting, and it should be noted as such rather than accepted as normal or "distinctly me." For this reason, a parent should always consider carefully when he or she says, "I am" or "I like." Even identifying with cultural characteristics can be flesh identifications. Some cultures boast about being demanding, cold toward people, noisy, immodest, food-loving, drink-loving or quick tempered. If "I am" identifies with a certain cultural expectation, it may well be a flesh identification. People have personal flesh identifications, too: "I am ruthless: I don't like to lose." "I like to be the one in control." "I don't take instruction well: I like to figure it out on my own." "I am gay." "I like women—a variety of them." "I need a man to hold." "I am the type of person who has a little bit of a temper." In all of these cases, a person is embracing a behavior produced by the flesh and identifying it as who they are. This is very dangerous. How or why would a person get rid of a sinful desire if he has grown to appreciate it as part of who he is? Instead, parents need to teach their children how to respond to the temptations that come from within. They need to know how to say, "The flesh is tempting me to do something, but that is not my idea. That is the old me, and I don't want what he would want." It is not a mental exercise. Such a statement is a faith exercise.

How will our Spirit-filled children bear "fruit to holiness" (Romans 6:22)? The Spirit of God will "give life to your mortal bodies" (Romans 8:11). Each of them must say, "the *life* which I now live in the flesh I live by faith", "as being alive from the dead" (Galatians 2:20, Romans 6:13). It does not start with the mindset of pushing away sin. The starting point is to "reckon yourselves to be dead indeed to sin, but alive to God in Christ Jesus our Lord." (Romans 6:11). That is, Christ-following children have to believe that because they died with Jesus, who they are now is not who they once were. The temptations of the flesh are not evidence of who they are, but evidence of who they were and why they needed Jesus to die for them.

If we believe what God says about who he has remade us to be, we can be "light in the Lord" (Ephesians 5:8). It is "God who works in you both to will and to do for *His* good pleasure" (Philippians 2:13). These are the instructions for how we will "become blameless and harmless, children of God without fault in the midst of a crooked and perverse generation, among whom you shine as lights in the world" (Philippians 2:15). This is the very best hope for producing obedience to God. Believing children are truly "created in Christ Jesus for good works, which God prepared beforehand that we should walk in them" (Ephesians 2:10).

Living What God Says Is True

The fact that a child is born again in Jesus does not, alone, ensure that he will act right by any means. He clearly has a choice.

> Do you not know that to whom you present yourselves slaves to obey, you are that one's slaves whom you obey, whether of sin [leading] to death, or of obedience *leading* to righteousness?
>
> Romans 6:16

> Do not be deceived, God is not mocked; for whatever a man sows, that he will also reap. For he who sows to his flesh will of the flesh reap corruption, but he who sows to the Spirit will of the Spirit reap everlasting life.
>
> Galatians 6:7-8

It isn't, "live how you feel," but rather "work out your own salvation with fear and trembling" (Philippians 2:12).

The passages about the flesh and Spirit paradigm command that those in Jesus "walk in the Spirit", be "led by the Spirit", "be filled with the Spirit", "serve in the newness of the Spirit" and "by the Spirit you put to death the deeds of the body" (Galatians 5:16, 25, Romans 8:14, Galatians 5:18, Ephesians 5:18, Romans 7:6, 8:13). The only hope is that the "life of

Jesus also may be manifested in our body" (2 Corinthians 4:10). Whether child or adult, we have to "put on the Lord Jesus Christ" (Romans 13:14). To be his righteousness, Jesus-followers must be about "the things of the Spirit." (Romans 8:5)

The Christian life is not a matter of combining the old person with religious practices, but the members of our family who know Jesus are to "put on the new man" (Ephesians 4:24, Colossians 3:10). We are "alive together with Christ", and we "live together with Him" (Ephesians 2:5, 1 Thessalonians 5:10). Since this is who we are, we should "walk in newness of life", "as children of light" and "put on the armor of light" (Romans 6:4, Ephesians 5:8, Romans 13:12). Each of us who believe must be united with Jesus constantly, asking to know his will.

We must put off other philosophies, "bringing every thought into captivity to the obedience of Christ" (2 Corinthians 10:5). The Word of God says we should, "be transformed by the renewing of your mind" and "be renewed in the spirit of your mind." (Romans 12:2, Ephesians 4:23). One can know that his mind is free because being "spiritually minded *is* life and peace" (Romans 8:6). That is, if we died and are made new, then when we fellowship with the Spirit of Jesus we have "life and peace."

"Here I am, Lord," must also be the mindset. The Bible says: "… present yourselves to God as being alive from the dead, and your members *as* instruments of righteousness to God"; "present your members *as* slaves *of* righteousness for holiness"; "present your bodies a living sacrifice, holy, acceptable to God" and "serve the living God" (Romans 6:13, 19, 12:1; Hebrews 9:14). This is "your reasonable service" (Romans 12:1).

Wake up, children and parents, "Awake, you who sleep, arise from the dead, and Christ will give you light." (Ephesians 5:14). "…do not walk according to the flesh" (Romans 8:1, 4). "…put to death your members which are on the earth" (Colossians 3:5). "do not let sin reign in your mortal body," "do not present your members as instruments of unrighteousness to sin," "cast off the works of darkness" and "put off the old man with his deeds" (Romans 6:12,13, 13:12 Colossians 3:9). If the truth be told, the old person must be despised, or its desires will, by default, be embraced. Letting go of the old person is absolutely the only way children can live a life following Jesus.

Parents should hope that their children realize the old person can produce nothing good but is contrary to love, the will of God and gentleness. They should advise their children not to "set their minds on the things of the flesh" or "on things on the earth" (Romans 8:5, Colossians 3:2). Instead, we are to "seek those things which are above" and focus our minds "on things above" (Colossians 3:1-2). In regard to sin and the world, saved children should "not run with *them* [the unsaved] in the same flood of dissipation" and should "not grieve the Holy Spirit" (1 Peter 4:4, Ephesians 4:30). To live the new life, our children must believe it, remember it and enact it.

These passages about the flesh and the Spirit paradigm also include specific commands about how to live. For example, a person should "*speak truth with his neighbor*" (Ephesians 4:25). A believer should work, so "that he may have something to give him who has need" (Ephesians 4:28).

Many times the passages about the flesh and the Spirit remind us to be thankful (Romans 6:17, Ephesians 5:4, 20, Colossians 2:7, 3:15).

> And whatever you do in word or deed, *do* all in the name of the Lord Jesus, giving thanks to God the Father through Him.
>
> Colossians 3:17

> Rejoice in the Lord always. Again I will say, rejoice!
>
> Philippians 4:4

One can't walk in the Spirit without being thankful. Thankfulness can be in the form of song as well, "speaking to one another in psalms and hymns and spiritual songs, singing and making melody in your heart to the Lord, giving thanks always for all things to God the Father in the name of our Lord Jesus Christ" (Ephesians 5:19-20). If parents or children are thankful, they can sing it and encourage everyone else to join in.

Additionally, children and parents are to "put on tender mercies, kindness, humility, meekness, longsuffering; bearing with one another, and forgiving one another," "submitting to one another in the fear of God." (Colossians 3:12-13, Ephesians 5:21). Said again elsewhere, we are to "be kind to one another, tenderhearted, forgiving one another" (Ephesians 4:32). So, when a child makes a mistake, parents should correct, but should be quick to hug and accept that family member, too.

The passages that refer to the flesh and Spirit also invoke wisdom in phrases like, "walk circumspectly, ...redeeming the time", "Do all things without complaining and disputing," "holding fast the word of life" (Ephesians 5:15-16; Philippians 2:14, 16; also Colossians 4:5). They say, "Let no corrupt word proceed out of your mouth, but what is good for necessary edification" and "Let the word of Christ dwell in you richly in all wisdom" (Ephesians 4:29, Colossians 3:16).

To walk out the flesh and Spirit paradigm, it is necessary to know what God wants, as expressed in statements like, "finding out what is acceptable to the Lord," "*do* all in the name of the Lord Jesus" and "for the will of God" (Ephesians 5:10, Colossians 3:17, 1 Peter 4:2). Following his ways will lead us to "prove what *is* that good and acceptable and perfect will of God" (Romans 12:2). The end, of course, is to love God and others.

> But above all these things put on love, which is the bond of perfection. And let the peace of God rule in your hearts, to which also you were called in one body; and be thankful.
>
> Colossians 3:14-15

Missing Grace

Grace is not only the idea that God overlooks bad deeds, but that he grants the power to escape from the old self (the "old man," Ephesians 4:22, Romans 6:6). The only truly grace-based parenting is the kind that shows children that Jesus died, not only to forgive sin, but also to set them free from themselves. Grace-based parenting aims to show children that their sole hope for being truly alive is walking in the presence of the Spirit, relating to him—the ever-present helper. How might a family miss this grace?

Obviously, if children do not know the Spirit of God, they can't live according to the Spirit. Children have to repent, believe in Jesus and be born again by the Spirit of Jesus, not just learn about Christianity. They must accept the Good News, or they will certainly miss grace.

Christian parents will also miss grace if they present life as a matter of obtaining the right rules in hopes of getting the right behavior. Since the problem and the solution are heart issues, parents can't accomplish their goals by behavioral training, traditional parenting or some other parenting invention. They have to teach the flesh and Spirit paradigm. Righteousness will not be achieved with the "basic principles of the world", "self-imposed religion, *false* humility, and neglect of the body". These "*are* of no value against the indulgence of the flesh." (Colossians 2:8, 20 and 23). Parents must teach that there is only one liberator for their children, only one who is powerful against the "indulgence of the flesh."

Parents will also miss grace if they dumb down the verses about living a life with Christ. For example, if they teach that the flesh and Spirit passages are metaphors or only a matter of heady theology and not practical application, then they will likely miss grace. Or, the message could be skewed. For example, a parent could incorrectly teach that walking in the Spirit is a matter of feeling great about oneself or about positive thinking while enjoying the things that once pleased the flesh. If worldly, selfish pursuits consume one's life, is he living as though he were dead? It is not enough for parents to use the language of the flesh and Spirit paradigm, but they must hold to the full message as presented in the Bible. The Bible teaches that life in the Spirit requires humility and analysis and that it will yield righteousness.

Parents and children will also miss grace if they are not using God's Word correctly. Liberal interpretation or hunting and pecking for the verses that support a personal desire or wrong theology will taint life, sometimes horribly. Parents who fail to be thorough in their understanding of the Bible may end up misrepresenting God, his character, his goals and the power he wishes to be manifest in us.

God wants children to experience the full power of his grace. If parents understand and teach the flesh and Spirit paradigm well, their children will benefit. If they don't, their children may be in danger of missing grace.

Teaching These Truths

Parents should think about what they would say to answer the questions "How do I live in the Spirit?" and "How do I not live in the flesh?" They can help children properly analyze thoughts, ideas and emotions. They can refer to their own personal experience and can help children take note when the Spirit of God is at work in their lives. Parents can also encourage faith and practice thankfulness.

To teach about the flesh and the Spirit, a parent can say, "Ideas, thoughts and feelings flow from one of two sources inside a born-again person. There is the flesh, which feels like you, but is not, and the Spirit of God, who makes you alive. Your job is to listen only to God." While teaching the flesh and Spirit paradigm, a parent could say to his seventeen-year-old, "If you were walking in the Spirit, you could be trusted anywhere, but if you were in the flesh, you could not be trusted at all. That is how good the Spirit is and how bad the flesh is." Or, to a thirteen-year-old, a parent could say, "It seems as though you want something. You seem agitated and busy. Make sure that you are walking in the Spirit because whatever the flesh might want right now would be selfish, and you may end up in trouble." Or, to an eleven-year-old, "When you started to play, there was also a strong desire to win. The flesh felt that you would be satisfied by beating your six-year-old brother, but that won't satisfy. You hurt him. Don't be fooled when the flesh wants to rise up and try to show how important it is. Instead, love your brother."

Concerning being dead, a parent could say, "When someone shows us what we did wrong and we are defensive, it is a sure sign that the flesh is fighting for something. If we are dead, walking with Jesus, then we will be humble and teachable and can learn. If we are defensive, then we can't learn."

Concerning the made-alive spirit, a parent could say, "You are made new, and your spirit wants to do the right thing here, so follow God in it. Aim to please him." A parent can say, "Trust God and follow the Spirit of God. Put the right thing in your heart so that the new-you can be seen." Since a saved child's heart has been made new, a parent can say, "Let love for others well up in your heart."

Children should be encouraged to consider their thoughts, feelings and desires to ascertain when they have been sidetracked by the flesh. Obviously, if they are doing the wrong thing, they have been so distracted. The goal, however, is not for them to make this discovery after they have done something wrong, but to know the difference between the Spirit of Jesus and the flesh at the beginning of the day and to maintain that close-following relationship throughout the day.

When family rules are broken, a parent should discuss the motives of the flesh, so that the child can put off its deeds and seek the Spirit of Jesus. The conversation can start with, "What motivated you to do that?" A parent and child can discuss what the child might have put in his heart minutes or even hours before it came out as disobedience. "What was in here (pointing to the heart) that caused you to do what you did? When did you put it there?" It is prudent to teach a child that germinating seeds of sinful ambitions should be pulled as soon as they are noticed (James 1:14-15).

A child does not have to be saved in order to be taught about the misdeeds of the flesh or the feelings that accompany its desires. A parent could explain to a child, "That is what it feels like when the flesh is trying to take control." Or, "Whatever you put in your heart, that is what will come out."

To live the life God wants, a child might start by asking himself questions. For example, he might ask, "Am I living as though I have died right now?" If a child has decided that he has died, he is far more likely to experience the righteousness produced by the power of the Spirit of God. He might also ask himself, "Am I communicating with Jesus right now?" Or, "Am I doing what I am doing by faith, believing that God wants it done?" These are effective starting points.

Teaching the flesh and Spirit paradigm should be at the very center of parenting, and parents should implore their children to live as the verses referred to in this chapter teach. It is a life of dependence on Jesus and a life of disgust with the way humankind seeks its own glory.

Life-Giving Paradigm

Parents who know Jesus will wish for their children to obey God. These parents can identify with God's yearning in Deuteronomy 5:29.

> Oh, that they [Israel] had such a heart in them that they would fear Me and always keep all My commandments, that it might be well with them and with their children forever!

Parents should want their children to fear God in a good way, to learn to do what pleases him and to enjoy the benefits of doing so forever. The problem is that children do not naturally have the type of heart that will keep God's commands. The only viable solution is a heart made alive, which is available by God's provision.

Children would be blessed to be raised without the baggage, confusion and loss of flesh-living. Anyone who is not born again, who does not have Jesus living inside, is controlled by the flesh. Anyone who has Christ, but will not submit to him, is controlled by the flesh. Anyone who is not walking in the Spirit is controlled by the flesh. Walking in the flesh is easy and self-destructive, but the Spirit of Jesus is mighty to save us from who we were.

A parent's lesson for his or her children should be God's great revelation, which is "Christ in you, the hope of glory." The passage goes on to describe the commitment of those whom God sent to proclaim this great revelation: "He [Jesus] is the one we proclaim, admonishing and teaching everyone with all wisdom, so that we may present everyone fully mature in Christ. To this end I strenuously contend with all the energy Christ so powerfully works in me" (Colossians 1:28-29, NIV). Parents should have a similar commitment to help their children become "fully mature in Christ". They should try to relay the flesh and Spirit paradigm to their family every day. Have you taken to heart this way of understanding righteous living? If you have, then how do you communicate it to your children?

Finally, parents should also behave "devoutly and justly and blamelessly". Consider those who brought the Good News to the Thessalonians, how they "exhorted, and comforted, and charged every one of you." They taught the way of righteousness as a father should want to teach his children.

> You *are* witnesses, and God *also*, how devoutly and justly and blamelessly we behaved ourselves among you who believe; as you know how we exhorted, and comforted, and charged every one of you, as a father *does* his own children, that you would walk worthy of God who calls you into His own kingdom and glory.
>
> 1 Thessalonians 2:10-12

When children are grown, parents should be able to look back and say that they have done all they can to help their children "walk worthy of God."

Parents, don't forget the purpose of the ones to whom you hand the car keys or share a meal with. Consider carefully the one you read to, play catch with, tickle or hold in your arms in the evening. These are creations meant to reflect the likeness of God and are to be made alive by the fellowship of the Spirit of Jesus. Value and teach them appropriately.

For Discussion

1. Which section of this chapter is most helpful to you? Which section is most challenging?
2. Do you teach the good news of the new life in Jesus?
3. Do you teach that, in Jesus, we are to consider our old selves dead?
4. How would you explain to your child what it is like to walk in the Spirit?
5. Choose a scenario involving your children. How would you explain it in terms of the flesh and the Spirit paradigm?

Chapter 8

GOD'S EXAMPLE OF MAKING RULES

In the last chapter, I tried to make it clear that righteous living is not a matter of pursuing rules, but a matter of relating to the Holy Spirit in a certain way. That is not to say that rules are bad or inconsequential. Rules play extremely important roles, both spiritually and socially. For this reason, parents have to consider how to make rules for their family, following God's example of rule-making.

Family guidelines need to be sufficient to address behavior problems. If they are not, children may get away with bad conduct year after year. With rules, a parent forces her children to deal with desires of the flesh. The rules and discipline can't completely free them from it, though. Only being immersed in Christ's death and participating in his resurrection can do that. Rules, however, show children what is wrong and force them in the right direction, giving them experience handling the sin living within.

The book of Romans describes the mechanisms of salvation, explaining that people must first recognize right and wrong.

> What shall we say then? *Is* the law sin? Certainly not! On the contrary, I would not have known sin except through the law.
>
> Romans 7:7, NKJV

It is this realization that leads a person to need Jesus: "Therefore the law was our tutor to *bring us* to Christ, that we might be justified by faith." (Galatians 3:24, NKJV). The two greatest commands, the Ten Commandments, additional biblical rules, and any good rules that parents add serve to teach children right and wrong and who they are without Jesus. Standards lead children to God.

One would expect God's rules to convict, but he might wonder whether household guidelines could play a part in bringing a child to the Lord. Consider Romans 2:14-15 (NIV):

> Indeed, when Gentiles, who do not have the law, do by nature things required by the law, they are a law for themselves, even though they do not have the law, since they show that the requirements of the law are written on their hearts, their consciences also bearing witness, and *their* thoughts now accusing, now even defending *them*.

If people who don't have God's Law can come up with some decent personal and societal rules that would show that they are guilty, then certainly the good rules of a God-honoring parent could provide leverage for the Holy Spirit to convict a child, too.

Rules have benefits other than creating the knowledge of sin. For example, rules give a group of people a sense of stability. All participants willing to operate within the parameters of the rules can relate to one another with expected, good outcomes. In a family, a set of standards can make the home environment more stable. Also, without rules children can't get beyond heart issues to love one another. With rules and consequences, there is hope that a child's demeanor can change so that he will be able to have concern for others.

Some parents want to have as few requirements as possible. Perhaps they are concerned that rules will get in the way of relationships. Or, perhaps they don't like people telling them what to do, and so are generally opposed to all rules. Or, perhaps they think that God used to be interested in laws in Old Testament times, but they hold that now the role of rules should be greatly diminished. Disdain, disinterest, or carelessness about rules will not result in good parenting. Without rules, parents will not apply God's method for exposing the sin dwelling within and showing the need for a savior. Our Heavenly Father left an example of rule-making, and parents should follow suit.

No Rules Yet

One of the first and most surprising things about God and the nation he treated as a *child* in the wilderness is that he did not make rules for quite some time. He first focused on building trust. The Passover, when God took Israel out of Egypt, was introduced in Exodus chapter 12. Rules would not come until chapter 20, after Israel hiked at least 250 miles. A study of Exodus 15, 16 and 17 shows the people of Israel to be vocal in their complaints against God, but rules did not yet exist and consequences were not assigned.

After crossing through the Red Sea, Israel spent three days without finding water, according to Exodus 15. When they found water, it wasn't water they could drink. They grumbled. God responded to their lack of faith, not with discipline, but by making the water good to drink. Afterward, he added a "ruling and instruction."

> There the LORD issued a ruling and instruction for them and put them to the test. He said, "If you listen carefully to the LORD your God and do what is right in his eyes, if you pay attention to his commands and keep all his decrees, I will not bring on you any of the diseases I brought on the Egyptians, for I am the LORD, who heals you."
>
> v. 25-26, NIV

God warned the people that rules would be associated with blessings and consequences, but he did not yet give rules. Time passed.

In Exodus 16, Israel needed food. They complained. Israel was 2 million people or more at that time (Numbers 10:36 suggests 10 million), and they were in an arid and empty land. The situation was ominous. Still, God had set the precedent for the people in Exodus 15, not to mention all the miracles that were performed in Egypt. He would provide. In that situation Israel did not trust God and spoke against Moses and Aaron, but once again, there were no consequences for the nation (v. 2-3). God sent quail in the evening and manna in the morning to meet the people's needs.

In Exodus 17, Israel was without water altogether, so the nation complained (v. 2-4). God provided water for them through the rock.

Why didn't God have consequences for Israel's sniveling in Exodus 15, 16 and 17? I believe it was as if Israel were new to the *family*, and rules were not yet established. God's parenting example showed patience. He waited for the right time to introduce rules and consequences.

I think God's example of preparation and trust building especially apply to the toddler years. It is okay for a parent to say, "We haven't introduced that rule yet." Here is an example: A friend of ours looked surprised when she saw our nearly two-year-old son climb up on our coffee table. My explanation was, "He is a child full of climbing and jumping. We'll teach him eventually. The other children don't climb on the coffee table, and we would not let this one climb on your coffee table." Our toddler had rules to obey, but the coffee table rule was not one of them yet. At the right time parents should make rules, teach them repeatedly and then enforce them.

If parents were to take their family out to dinner with friends, and it did not go the way they hoped, instead of panicking, yelling or belittling, they could let their children know they are going to come up with some rules for the next time. Later, the children could practice these rules and when they have them down, the family could try going out to dinner again. This is the principle we can gain from God's example, that rules can be introduced patiently.

Even though rules and discipline are very important, and the goals that God lays down are ambitious, there is no reason to act as if all has to be perfect and in order by next Tuesday. I have felt that anxiety and acted out on it. I prefer to follow God's example by seeking to establish rules at the right time. In Exodus 15, 16 and 17, God was calm, collected and gracious. He knew he would have time to establish his rules, and parents should have similar confidence.

Establishing Rules

When God gave the Ten Commandments he did quite a bit to establish them in the people's minds. First, they were spoken (Exodus 20:1). When God spoke these ten new rules there was thunder, lightning, smoke and the sound of trumpets coming from Mount Sinai, and the people were scared they would die (Exodus 20:18-19). Moses responded to their concern.

> Moses said to the people, "Do not be afraid. God has come to test you, so that the fear of God will be with you to keep you from sinning."
>
> Exodus 20:20, NIV

The show of power surrounding the giving of the rules proved that the rules were from God and gave the people motive to obey. It helped establish the rules, but the rules were not just spoken. They were also written in the Book of the Covenant (Exodus 24:4, 7). The people accepted the rules by saying, "Everything the LORD has said we will do." (Exodus 24:3, NIV).

They also entered a covenant agreement to obey the rules (Exodus 24:4-8). Finally, God wrote the rules on stone (Exodus 31:18). He made sure that the nation he was caring for as a parent cares for a child knew the rules. Certainly Israel could not say, "We didn't know."

After God gave the Ten Commandments, he repeated, "...do not make for yourselves gods of silver or gods of gold" (Exodus 20:23, NIV). He made doubly certain they knew that rule. It was the first one Israel would break. Repetition helped establish the commandment.

More rules followed in the rest of Exodus, Leviticus, Numbers and Deuteronomy, and all were written down. God also assigned penalties for lawbreakers and the people agreed to the consequences. For example, "'The Levites shall recite to all the people of Israel in a loud voice: Cursed is the man who carves an image or casts an idol—a thing detestable to the Lord, the work of the craftsman's hands—and sets it up in secret.' Then all the people shall say, 'Amen!'" (Deuteronomy 27:14-15, NIV). God used agreement to make sure that the rules were established.

In an ongoing effort to keep the rules in people's minds, they were to be repeated regularly at home (Deuteronomy 6:4-9, 11:18-20). Commandments were also to be read at grand events, like the Feast of Booths (Deuteronomy 31:10-11).

Christian parents, as imitators of God, can glean from what God did with the people of Israel. Parents should consider ways to document their rules in order to establish them. They could post some of their most important rules on the refrigerator and get a journal book to write down the rest. For younger children, they might make picture lists or picture booklets showing the rules for different rooms of the house. Parents might ask their children to agree ahead of time about what the consequences should be for some offenses. They could also cover rules in family meetings.

One of the best ways for a family to become familiar with new rules is to work together to make them. A mom can say, "We have a problem," and the family can work out the solution.

Rules should be taught along with alternatives: "Instead of taking a toy from someone else's hands, you can come to me and ask for help or find something else to play with." Or, "Don't interrupt, but listen and wait for your turn." Or, "Instead of screaming, use your words."

It is important for both mom and dad to know what rules and instructions have been established. If not, one parent might allow a child to do something that the other has prohibited. Children should be expected to point it out when there is a conflict between the instructions: "Mom has us do it a different way. How would you like for me to do it?"

If a child does something that would not be obviously wrong to him, and no rule has yet been established, the situation should be shrugged off. For example, a child might hear and repeat a word that is inappropriate. Parents should not discipline a child who does not know better. Similarly, some rules might rarely be encountered in a family. Children should get a reminder and fair warning instead of consequences when rules are not well-known to them.

Freedom comes with confidence about the process of making, establishing and enforcing rules. Parents can relax about parenting because they know they can successfully solve problems, and children can enjoy living in a home with standards that protect them from being harmed or hurting others. The process does not need to be hurried but can be done in such a way that children fully understand the parents' expectations. This is judicial parenting; and it starts by following God's example in the Exodus, in which rules were spoken, written, repeated, agreed to and passed on.

Primary Rules

One way to think about rules in the Bible is to consider that some tackle sweeping topics while others address very specific situations. The Ten Commandments and the two greatest commandments are the types that cover a lot of ground.

> "Teacher, which is the greatest commandment in the Law?" Jesus replied: "'Love the Lord your God with all your heart and with all your soul and with all your mind.' This is the first and greatest commandment. And the second is like it: 'Love your neighbor as yourself.' All the Law and the Prophets hang on these two commandments."
>
> Matthew 22:36-40, NIV

The rules Jesus referred to can be found in Deuteronomy and Leviticus.

> Love the LORD your God with all your heart and with all your soul and with all your strength.
>
> Deuteronomy 6:5, NIV

Do not seek revenge or bear a grudge against anyone among your people, but love your neighbor as yourself. I am the LORD.

Leviticus 19:18, NIV

The foreigner residing among you must be treated as your native-born. Love them as yourself, for you were foreigners in Egypt. I am the LORD your God.

Leviticus 19:34, NIV

These rules to love God and others are the guiding principles for "all the law and the prophets." If someone were able to perfectly apply these two rules, he would have little need for any other rules. Out of necessity, rules build on one another.

Family rules should start with the two greatest and the Ten Commandments, the primary rules. Children should know these, and, as Deuteronomy points out, parents should discuss them often. These primary rules should act as the foundation for all other rules.

Secondary Rules

Secondary rules explain what to do in specific circumstances. For example, Deuteronomy 7:25-26 conveys specifics related to the Second Commandment, that no person is to cast an idol. An Israelite might have asked, "What if I find an idol that was made by someone else? In that case, I would not be forming it as the Second Commandment said. Can I keep it?" The secondary rule in Deuteronomy 7:25-26 provides more clarity to the primary rule. Israelites were instructed to destroy any idol they found in the land they were to inherit.

The fact that secondary rules have been needed throughout history implies that humankind needs to have details defined. If this is true, it is an important observation for parents. It would mean that parents need to discuss with their children how to apply the Two and the Ten in all sorts of situations.

Commands of the Moment

Primary and secondary rules are static. Once in place, they don't change unless they are repealed by the rule maker. There is another type of rule that is a one-off, a command meant only for the moment or occasion. One example is the challenge to move into the Promised Land (Numbers 13 and 14, Deuteronomy 1:19-45, Psalm 78:24-27). The event started with a command, "Go up and take possession of it [the Promised Land] as the LORD, the God of your ancestors, told you." (Deuteronomy 1:21, NIV). That particular command was given for a specific time, place and group of people. Many similar instructions were given in the Bible. For example, in Matthew 2:13, God told Joseph to take Mary and Jesus to Egypt. In Exodus 19:12, God told Israel, "do not approach the mountain or touch the foot of it" (NIV). These are what I refer to as commands of the moment.

Parents need to make commands of the moment often. Examples are, "Get in the car," "Go to the bathroom when you get inside the building," "Stay there," "Try again," "Put that down" and "Don't touch." This is rule-making on the fly, and these temporary instructions can be used to meet goals and solve problems. Some distinctive features of commands of the moment are: 1) Saying it once is enough. These don't need to be established over time. 2) Obedience is expected at a specific time, usually immediately. 3) The command is only for that occasion. If a parent says something like, "Stop playing with that toy and put your laundry away," the rule is mentioned only once, is expected to be obeyed right away, and is only necessary in this circumstance. After the laundry is put away, the child could play with the toy again.

Although commands of the moment seem simple enough, they can be bungled. For example, "Come in when it gets cold" and "Go to bed when you get tired," if they are meant to be commands are not good ones. They are too subjective. To know if a child obeyed, the instruction must be specific. "You should be completely ready and in bed by nine," would be an example.

Some of the nicest people avoid asking for what they really want. "Should we go to the store?" "Could you pick that up?" "Are you ready to leave now?" These are ways adults sometimes ask adults in order not to seem pushy. Parents should unlearn these niceties when it comes to giving commands of the moment. They should tell their children exactly what needs to be done.

Along the same lines, parents don't have to say "please" when giving a command of the moment. In fact, if a parent does say "please," it implies that a child has an option not to do what the parent is requesting. If parents want to say "please," they should be certain their children know that when they say "please," they are being polite and that the instruction is not optional.

When I say to my teenage son, "The shed needs to be cleaned out," he does not need to do it because the phrase communicates that I am thinking out loud. (Of course, I would want my child to ask for clarity, but as a matter of respect, not a matter of rules.) If I mean to communicate that I want him to do it, I should say, "Please go clean out the shed."

Instructions have to be specific, but instructions don't have to be harsh. A parent can say, "Come here" instead of "Get over here."

Parents shouldn't bribe, either. "Clean up and I'll give you ice cream" is enticement, and it could indicate that a parent is afraid of what would happen if he just asked, without compensation.

Since a lot of parents' rule-making is in commands of the moment, it is important to take time to get them right. One could think of it as sending a child on a mission. A mom or dad could call a child to a short one-on-one meeting, put an arm around him, look him in the eyes and give instructions in detail. Of course, not all commands of the moment can be delivered in this way, but when they are, it helps. The child and parent are focused and the instructions take on more importance. Extra focus is especially helpful for young children because they require more processing time. Also, parents would do well to require the young child to repeat the instructions: "Now, tell me what I asked you to do."

Children of all ages should be taught to acknowledge that they heard the command. The purpose would be to avoid excuses such as, "I didn't hear you" or "I thought you were talking to someone else." If responses like "Okay," "Yes, ma'am" or "Will do" are not required, children might also be tempted to come up with excuses to get out of following parents' commands of the moment.

For contentious young ones, it helps to break a command of the moment into its parts. Instead of "Go to the bedroom and put your dirty clothes in the basket," a parent might say, "Stand up" and "Hold my hand" and "Walk with me to your bedroom" and "Let go of my hand and reach down and pick up your clothes and put them in the basket." Younger children are more likely to obey in this type of scenario; and if they don't, their disobedience will become very clear.

A parent should mean what he says when he gives commands of the moment. For example, if a parent is in the habit of telling his children, "We are going to leave. Please, get in the car," but doesn't leave, the children will have reason to wonder if that parent means what he says.

A child should be expected to remember commands when given. For instance, if a child was told not to touch a certain item, he should not be touching it two minutes later. "I forgot," would not be an acceptable excuse.

Parents should be thoughtful about whether what they ask of a child is reasonable, but they should not always avoid asking a child to do a hard thing. As an example, consider that God expected Israel to do things the people thought were frightening. In Deuteronomy 3, Og, the king of Bashan, took up arms against Israel. In verse two, God commanded people not to be afraid: "The LORD said to me, 'Do not be afraid of him'". Or, consider Moses' charge to Joshua:

> Then Moses summoned Joshua and said to him in the presence of all Israel, "Be strong and courageous, for you must go with this people into the land that the Lord swore to their forefathers to give them, and you must divide it among them as their inheritance. The Lord himself goes before you and will be with you; he will never leave you nor forsake you. Do not be afraid; do not be discouraged."
> Deuteronomy 31:7-8, NIV

God's commands sometimes meant that those who followed him would have to be courageous. Similarly, parents should ask children to do things that take courage, but they should not throw children into just any situation. Obviously, it would be unfair to ask children to face a large water slide or ocean wave if they did not know how to swim. Instead, they should practice, prepare and build on past successful experiences. At the right age, and under safe circumstances, parents could command their children to try things that appear risky, but are not. Parents might also require children to pray out loud or speak to a group, even if it feels a little scary. Or, they could ask a child to negotiate or handle a purchase. Over time, children's willingness to try new things will become much less guarded, and their overall confidence will grow. Parents should be willing to give commands of the moment when children are a little bit afraid, provided that the demands are reasonable. The best way for parents to make these kinds of requests would be to first ask the Holy Spirit and to follow his lead.

Parents need to make commands of the moment, and they need to be specific about the instructions, taking time to say it as carefully as possible. Children should respond verbally to the request to show that they heard and understood. Also, they should be expected to remember the commands and should do what is asked, even if it is a little intimidating.

Making Rules

The Fifth Commandment says that a child must honor and obey his mother and father (Exodus 20:12; see also Colossians 3:20 and Ephesians 6:1-3). Thus, the mother and father's good rules and instructions, in a sense, become a subset of the Ten. The parent's role is unique and confirms, again, the preeminence of the family in the purposes of God. If parents are to be honored, and their rules obeyed on account of the Fifth Commandment, then they ought to give great thought to making rules for their children.

The verses of Proverbs also regularly refer to parents' rules with special regard: "My son, keep your father's command, And do not forsake the law of your mother." (Proverbs 6:20, NKJV). It is these family rules and instructions that provide hope.

> When you roam, they [your father's command and the law of your mother] will lead you; When you sleep, they will keep you; And *when* you awake, they will speak with you. For the commandment is a lamp, And the law a light; Reproofs of instruction *are* the way of life...
>
> Proverbs 6:22-23, NKJV

We may all think of the law of God providing hope, but perhaps we don't so value the parents' commands. Clearly, the parents of Proverbs felt their rules were an extension of the wisdom that came from fearing the Lord: "For I give you good doctrine: Do not forsake my law." (Proverbs 4:2, NKJV). Family rules should be similarly respected by those who make them and those who are to obey them.

The Bible does not specify all the rules a family should have. It would make sense for Christ-followers to share ideas with each other at times in an effort to engage the rule-making process, but they should not get together for the purpose of creating a unified code. Each family should make their own rules, trying to find out what pleases God and humbly submitting to him.

Where do parents find good rules? They spring from biblical principles, of course, but rules can also come from pragmatism. A parent might see a potential or existing problem and come up with a rule to discourage it from happening. Wherever a parent's rule comes from, it should be the kind of rule worth regarding.

The Bible First

Parents can read something in the Bible, realize that there is a good principle for their family in it, and then make a rule based on that principle. As we read from Exodus to Deuteronomy, we run into long passages or whole chapters devoted to rules. They were an important part of God's strategy for treating the nation of Israel like a *child* and were a means of maintaining an orderly society. Parents can look in Exodus, Leviticus, Numbers and Deuteronomy for rules for their own families.

The largest listing of rules in Exodus is in chapters 20-23. Rules are also recorded in 31:12-18 and 35:1-3. In Exodus 21 and 22, God established several practical rules for the nation of Israel. What happens if there is a fist fight? What if a bull gores someone? What if someone gets hurt falling into a pit that another person dug? What if someone steals an animal? Many of these rules were useful for maintaining a fair society. Though the rules in Exodus are not exactly what parents might need in their homes, they introduce concepts that can help parents maintain fairness daily.

Leviticus has a lot of rules. Leviticus 4:22-5:19 addresses unintentional sins (see also Numbers 15:22-31). Leviticus 11 speaks of dietary laws. Leviticus 12-15 concerns instructions and rituals regarding childbirth, diseases, rashes, molds and discharges. Leviticus 17 forbids unsanctioned sacrifices and eating meat with blood in it. Leviticus 18 outlaws certain intimate relationships. Leviticus 19 restates several of the Ten Commandments. This chapter also contains rules requiring a person to care for others who need help and rules prohibiting activities such as sorcery and tattooing one's body. Leviticus 20 lists the consequences for breaking certain commandments. Chapter 23 gives rules for festivals and feasts. Finally, chapter 25 introduces rules regarding special treatment of the 7th and 49th year, rest, freeing of slaves and redemption of property. (Slavery was entered into voluntarily and meant to be temporary for the Israelites (Leviticus 25:47, 54)).

Deuteronomy 5 repeats the Ten Commandments. Deuteronomy 6 speaks of loving God, and Chapter 7 gives instructions for driving the inhabitants out of the Promised Land. Deuteronomy 15 gives rules concerning canceling debts, freeing servants and eating firstborn animals. Chapters 22-25 contain rules on railings around roof decks, vineyards, accusations of impropriety, cross dressing and others. Finally, Deuteronomy 27 is a rule and consequence agreement.

When parents read the Bible and see a commandment or instruction, they might do some head scratching and ask God about how a principle in the passage will be beneficial to their family. For example, after reading Leviticus 5:1, parents might inform children that they are obligated to tell if another child does something wrong (NIV).

> If anyone sins because they do not speak up when they hear a public charge to testify regarding something they have seen or learned about, they will be held responsible.

This is not a verse about children or parenting, but it communicates a good principle that can be applied in the family. Telling isn't bad, provided the truth is told. Telling is ultimately the right thing to do and, in a family, a reasonable way to help a brother or sister overcome sin. Parents can say to children who tell, "Thank you, because telling me what your sister did will help her in the long run."

Moms and dads could also find good principles in Leviticus 12 through 15 when making rules. The rules in these chapters deal with leprosy, boils, bald spots, itches, nocturnal emissions, menstruation and other discharges. Israel was an enormous tent city meandering in the desert. We know that if a person has a contagious sickness it is considerate to stay away from others, and the rules in these chapters required that people with contagious diseases be separated. (Israelites would have housed and cared for the sick in that separate location. Being outside of the main camp would not mean that these people were without shelter or necessities.) Similarly, when a child washes his hands after using the restroom, he is showing concern for those around him. Parents might think through health and cleanliness issues in the family because of Leviticus 12 through 15, but many of those sent out of the camp did not have symptoms of a contagious disease, and there is another important principle from these chapters.

> You must keep the Israelites separate from things that make them unclean, so they will not die in their uncleanness for defiling my [God's] dwelling place, which is among them.
>
> Leviticus 15:31, NIV (see also Leviticus 26:11)

When God was around, they were to live in such a way as to make him satisfied with his "dwelling place." That was the etiquette they were to follow and was a means of showing love to God. (We do not need to understand the purpose behind each of these rules or how they affected the culture positively to understand this principle.) In a family, rules of etiquette express how one can honor those around him. Leviticus 12 through 15 is reason for teaching children to accept rules that accommodate others and to use these acts of courtesy to show love and concern.

A family should also look to the principles of the Ten Commandments in order to make up rules. When Jesus spoke of the command not to murder (Exodus 20:13), he said, "You have heard that it was said to those of old, '*You shall not murder*, and whoever murders will be in danger of the judgment.' But I say to you that whoever is angry with his brother without a cause shall be in danger of the judgment. And whoever says to his brother, 'Raca!' [similar to saying, "idiot"] shall be in danger of the council. But whoever says, 'You fool!' shall be in danger of hell fire." (Matthew 5:21-22, NKJV). There is a lot to think about in this passage (primary rules, secondary rules, principles derived from commands, words coming from the heart and judgment), but it is easy to see from these verses that, at the least, parents should not permit name calling or ridicule in their families.

When going to the Bible to develop family rules and practices, it is important that parents consider only ideas that carry a moral mandate. Sometimes, events that we read about in the Bible were not commandments but a record of how something happened, whether right, wrong or neither. For example, Abraham sent his chief servant to find a wife for Isaac among his own people. The passage should not be understood as a command to marry relatives, to have slaves, to place a hand under the thigh in order to make an oath or to arrange marriages (Genesis 24:2, 4, 37-38). Parents need to make sure that their biblical source for rules refers to a moral mandate, not simply a record of events.

Parents who meditate on God's Word go to a deep well. This is the best place for generating rules for the family, but it is not the only starting point for coming up with them.

The Problem First

We have a problem. When our children play together, they often want the same toy. To help solve the problem, we came up with a rule. We don't permit our children to take toys out of another child's hands, except in the case of imminent danger. Even if our child has had a toy taken from him, he is not to snatch it back. What does our child do if another took a toy from him? He goes to Ginny or me and says, "There is a problem."

In hindsight, we realized our rule that a child could not pull a toy out of another child's hands has some good biblical principles. Taking a toy shows discontentment and saving up treasures on earth. Also, taking a toy, stealing and envy are not too far separated when we consider the heart attitude behind the action. Our rule was a way for our children to respond without fighting with a neighbor, friend, brother or sister. Our regulation turned out to be necessary for keeping peace in the house (Proverbs 29:17). Finally, the rule helped our children learn to involve a third party to seek equity. This rule has done all sorts of good, and we did not make it as a direct result of studying the Bible. The problem came first, next the solution, and then we considered the biblical principles behind it.

To make rules this way, parents have to identify problems. Being regularly unaware of or indifferent to what children are doing would be detrimental to this type of rule making. On the other hand, wise parents will notice current problems and will anticipate future issues in order to make good rules.

Generally Expecting Obedience

Moses anticipated that Israel would try to change the original commands of God.

> Do not add to what I command you and do not subtract from it, but keep the commands of the LORD your God that I give you.
> Deuteronomy 4:2, NIV (see also 12:32)

This verse and many of Moses' exhortations, like "Observe them carefully" (Deuteronomy 4:6, NIV), leave us with the impression that there is more than one way to disobey. Careless, subtle or strategic disobedience is still disobedience.

Whether with creative disobedience or overt resistance, parents are responsible to find out if their children obey their rules. They must watch, which takes time and effort. Parents need to make sure that their children don't delay, complain, or do only part of what was asked. If parents have to ask again, the children did not obey the first time. If children start but do not finish all of what was asked, it is a type of defiance. If children add playing to the process and it hinders their progress, it should be considered disobedience. Lastly, parents should not think that their children are obedient if they complain about the instructions: "Do all things without complaining and disputing" (Philippians 2:14, NKJV).

Sometimes, complaining can be creative. A child might ask, "Are you sure that you want me to do that?" The difficult part for parents is that the same question can be asked in earnest and for good reason. Judging whether a child is complaining is subjective. Questioning and testing might be necessary to find out what the child really means when he seems to be complaining.

Moms and dads would do well to remember that God gave Israel only one opportunity to obey the command to enter the land (Numbers 14:39-45). God did not give them a second chance until the consequence for the initial disobedience was completed. Likewise, when children don't obey right away, parents should not make a habit of giving them more time to obey without a consequence. If they do, they will teach their children to disobey. Why? Because children will be learning from the experience that they can resist first, and then at the last minute comply. Children should not be taught to think to themselves, "I can get away with it a little bit longer." Similarly, when parents count, "one, two, three," waiting for their children to obey, they are teaching these children that obedience can be delayed, at least for a little bit. (Instead of using "one, two, three" to allow children's minds to catch up to the instruction, parents should ask slowly and carefully.) Parents must ask once and expect children to respond appropriately.

Some who may agree that true obedience is immediate, precise, complete, without complaining and without playing, may lower the bar as situations change. For example, parents may conclude that a tired child should not be held to the same standards. Behavior and attitude can get worse as bedtime approaches, there is no doubt about it, but children should develop the ability to control their behavior when circumstances are not ideal. It is a reasonable test, although testing should be brief if rest is needed. (A parent should not have the same expectations for a child who is exhausted, which is different than being a little worn out from the day.) For some parents, however, saying a child is tired is a cop out. In fact, when some see the first sign of disobedience, they conclude that their child must be tired and that discipline is not really necessary. Parents should avoid making these kinds of excuses for their children.

Moms and dads should not accept half-obedience, complaining or delay. Obedience should be willing, immediate and complete. The requirements for obedience put the onus on the parent to get the instructions right. Directives must be clear, rules well established and tasks should be age appropriate.

Finally, parents and children should remember that to be truly obedient, the desire has to be in a child's heart before the opportunity is presented because whatever is in the heart will be evident in a child's actions. A child can't let his heart wander off in one direction and, when a challenge is presented, expect to obey right away. Children should be encouraged to be ready for obedience.

Making Rules

When God treated Israel as a father treats a son, he showed that rules play an important role in the parenting process. His rules can be thought of as primary, secondary or commands of the moment. God gave parents their own rule-making rights in the Fifth Commandment. Day to day, parents will spend a lot of time enforcing their own rules. While doing so, they should help their children understand the connection between their rules and the Two, the Ten or some other significant biblical concept.

Parents should be careful when making rules. Bad rules can cause confusion and discord. If the reason for a rule can't be explained clearly and convincingly, it is a likely candidate for the bad rule pile. It would also be wise to carefully evaluate rules that seem to be popular, whether these rules seem liberal or strict. Parents should not let popularity be the enemy of thought, prayer and Bible study.

In a sense, making rules is also teaching. Rules teach what is right and wrong and give an opportunity to explain why it is right and wrong. Rules expose the sin that lives within and can cause a child to ask, "What is wrong with me that I am willing to break these rules?" That question can lead a child to dependence on God.

Rules should come at the right time and be established by being spoken, written and agreed to. Some might also have pre-assigned consequences. Rules can be made by applying principles from the Bible or by solving problems.

Parents won't have a rule to solve every problem. Life has too many problems. Also, some problems are not easily solved with a rule. For example, it may become clear to a parent that his teenage son has determined to do what it takes to be compliant and nothing more. He has no sense of responsibility but is obeying the rules. A parent could not make up a rule that objectively describes what more he would want from his teenager. With no rule to enforce, a parent might encourage, warn and teach.

If life is about rules, parents should be unbending and focused. The objective, however, is not for a family to live for rules, but for parents to use their rules to meet their children's needs. When children are unruly, careless, heartless or thoughtless, good rules are tools which parents can use to show love toward those children.

For Discussion

1. Why are rules so important to God?
2. Do you have some helpful rules that solve problems?
3. Do you have rules that relate to a specific Bible passage or principle?
4. Do you have any rules you think might be unnecessary or bad?
5. Do any of your rules need to be better established? If so, how would you do this?
6. How does a parent teach a child to obey right away and finish the instructions completely without complaint?
7. How do you teach the Two Greatest Commandments and the Ten Commandments?

Chapter 9

OUR FAMILY RULES

Beyond the two greatest commandments and the Ten Commandments, our family has many rules. My purpose in listing some of them is not to insist that you adopt them but rather to share how we have tried to make rules. Most of our rules came from problem solving with a biblical mindset. Studying the Bible influences what behavior we consider to be wide of the mark and what rules would be okay to solve the dilemma. Generally, rules in our house are enforced and full obedience is expected, meaning children should do what is asked completely, without complaint or delay.

Several of our rules have already been mentioned. To all the previous ones stated, we add the rules listed in this chapter, although this still does not list all of our rules.

Safety

We teach safety when our children do all sorts of activities. The Bible sets a precedent for such rules.

> When you build a new house, make a parapet around your roof so that you may not bring the guilt of bloodshed on your house if someone falls from the roof.
>
> Deuteronomy 22:8, NIV

It seems to me that the most likely person to fall off the top of an Israelite's roof deck would be his own family member. By installing a short wall a parent could provide a safer environment for his family.

We take reasonable steps to protect our children as well. For example, they have to wear closed-toed shoes and a helmet while riding a bike or skateboard. The flesh fights against the idea of wearing this kind of protective gear. It can be a little uncomfortable, inconvenient and uncool. Nevertheless, there is value in doing things safely, and failing to take reasonable precautions can end up costing those who have to care for the injured.

We have safety rules for coming and going in cars. Drivers have to look under and behind the car before pulling out of the driveway and a window must be open while reversing. Seat belts must always be worn. Little ones must be strapped in car seats properly. Other issues, like driving speed, phone use, limiting distractions and following cars too closely are more difficult to track. Siblings can help by letting us know how drivers are doing.

We have rules for handling and putting away dangerous tools, chemicals, knives and kitchen appliances. Our goal is to think carefully about how an item could be harmful and make good rules that foster a safe environment. For example, power tools should not be left where younger siblings could handle them unless they are depowered.

When we come upon a new situation, we try to take time to consider what could be dangerous. For example, if we go to a lake, we might make new rules. We might decide that the children can't go in the water or go on the dock without permission. We need new safety rules from time to time, and this is a great opportunity to ask our children for help in making up the rules. When children contribute to the rule-making process, it helps them understand the purposes for the stipulations. The discussion also helps establish new rules in children's minds. They come up with pretty good rules, too.

Accidental Harm

Obviously, we don't allow punching, kicking or biting. When a child hurts someone on purpose, discipline is needed, but these matters are seldom cut and dried. What does a parent do when it is difficult to figure out a child's intention? After giving it some thought, we decided that we would almost never accept the excuse, "It was an accident." Even if a child did not mean to hurt another, we realized that he usually still had some culpability. We have consistently discovered that "accidents" could have and should have been prevented. In our family, if a child hurts someone and makes him cry, we will very likely assign some sort of consequence.

Is it fair to discipline for accidents? We think so. Accidents are usually caused by carelessness, that is, "I care less about others than I do about myself at this moment." Accidents can be avoided by thinking something through beforehand or by asking a parent for safety advice. Consider what Exodus says about accidents involving a bull.

> If a bull gores a man or woman to death, the bull is to be stoned to death, and its meat must not be eaten. But the owner of the bull will not be held responsible. If, however, the bull has had the habit of goring and the owner has been warned but has not kept it penned up and it kills a man or woman, the bull is to be stoned and its owner also is to be put to death.
>
> Exodus 21:28-30, NIV

If the owner was not careful, he would be punished by society, either losing his bull or losing his bull and his own life. The principle is that one should be reasonably cautious. The owner of the bull should take charge of his animal to prevent accidents. I think the principle of the bull applies to two boys wrestling in the living room. If the boys' activity could be harmful, each child should play in a way that is mindful of the other.

If one of our children hurts his brother or sister, we first comfort the hurt child until he feels better. Then, we ask questions of each individual involved to understand the situation. If the injury could have been avoided by some basic carefulness, we assign an appropriate consequence.

Our rule turns out to be a win-win situation. The kids get to wrestle, and we have children who are thinking about each other.

If a parent does not have a there-is-almost-no-such-thing-as-an-accident policy, a child may learn that he can be cruel or careless and practice deceit by blurting out, "It was an accident," whenever an excuse is needed. On the other hand, when a parent devises consequences for accidents, and so-called accidents, he teaches his child to be forward thinking and responsible.

One day at the soccer fields, I watched an older sibling from another family picking on and hurting his younger brother. Clearly, he knew that his parent was unlikely to discipline. Every once in a while the parent would say, "Don't do that" or "Stop." The cruel child with this type of parent can say, "I didn't mean to" and nearly get away with murder. What a sad sight to see. The parent who lets this go on risks damaging the relationship between siblings for life. The pain or loss caused when a parent disciplines for an "accident" is temporary, and in my opinion, greatly preferred to the alternative, which is potentially having a bully in the house.

Taking Care of Our Things

We want our children to take care of what we own, so we make rules to help them learn how to do so. "Don't kick the soccer ball inside the house" and "put food back in the fridge," fall into this category of rules. We also say, "No drinks or food near computers or books." "Change out of nice clothing for play time." "Spray a stain or tell mom if you can't do it yourself." "Put books away properly so they won't get ripped, ruined or lost." Along with the idea that we take care of our things, we want our house to look decent and orderly, so we have rules like, "shoes must go in the shoe basket and dirty laundry in the laundry basket." When using the restroom, "flush the toilet, close the lid, wash your hands using soap, turn out the lights and close the door."

God expected people to care for items that had value to others.

> If you see your fellow Israelite's ox or sheep straying, do not ignore it but be sure to take it back to its owner. If they do not live near you or if you do not know who owns it, take it home with you and keep it until they come looking for it. Then give it back. Do the same if you find their donkey or cloak or anything else they have lost. Do not ignore it. If you see your fellow Israelite's donkey or ox fallen on the road, do not ignore it. Help the owner get it to its feet.
>
> Deuteronomy 22:1-4, NIV

This passage embodies the idea that a person should see what needs to be cared for and take care of it. Similarly, our children should not ignore something that obviously needs care or attention. However, we have to respect the fact that what is obvious to an adult may not be so to our children who are learning new things day by day.

Being responsible for the things around us is a sign of maturity. Hopefully, over time, our children will learn to consider what needs to be cared for, whether it belongs to us or not.

Asking Permission

We see value in the principle of asking permission. It shows thoughtfulness and respect, and it is a biblical concept. Submitting to God implies that followers need permission from him.

Not long after the Israelites went into the Promised Land, the people failed to ask permission before making an agreement with the Gibeonites. In Joshua 9, the Gibeonites lied to Israel. They saw how Israel was winning battle after battle. They did not want to be next to lose and they did not want to leave to find a different home, so they came to the Israelites and argued that they were not locals.

> They [the Gibeonites] answered: "Your servants have come from a very distant country because of the fame of the LORD your God. For we have heard reports of him: all that he did in Egypt...
>
> Joshua 9:9, NIV

They presented believable evidence (old bread and worn clothing), and they praised the things that God had done for Israel. The Gibeonites' lie worked and Israel made a big mistake.

> The Israelites sampled their provisions but did not inquire of the LORD.
>
> Joshua 9:14, NIV

Israel was fooled by the Gibeonites because they did not ask permission but instead did what seemed logical to them. That meant that idol worship would have a place in the Promised Land from the very beginning (Exodus 23:33). The promises Israel made to Gibeon also meant trouble later in their history (2 Samuel 21).

As with Israel, God wants to advise and direct our affairs. Parents should make sure they have God's permission before they make decisions. Children should do the same when they follow Jesus. To promote the kind of attitude that asks permission and to make sure our children are not constantly running off to do whatever they want, they are required to ask for certain privileges. For example, we ask them to get permission to take a shower. Such a requirement may not be necessary in many homes, but it is helpful in ours because we have a lot of shower-takers and not a lot of bathrooms. Asking to shower is respectful to the rest of the family, and sometimes there are other things that need to be done first. Our children also have to ask permission to use a smartphone or computer for entertainment purposes, even if the device belongs to them. (If we give permission to be on an electronic device, it needs to be out in the open where we could walk over and see what they are doing. Devices are not to be used in bed at night. We approve games, and we sometimes look over texts to check content.) In our house, a child has to ask before he eats anything between meals. We don't want a household environment in which it is a food free-for-all. We don't want our children saying, "I feel like eating, so I will," but instead to ask themselves, "Should I eat something?" Asking permission gets them a step closer to that second question. Also, it works out better for us if one parent makes all of the food decisions in our house. We have a rule that the children can't ask Dad if they can eat something, unless Mom is gone.

We would be thrilled if our children were to take initiative to do work that needed to be done at our house, but at certain times they would first need to ask. For example, if they were supposed to be cleaning the kitchen, they would have to ask to abandon the kitchen work to do a different job they thought needed to be done. Also, if the job were new to our child, we would want him to ask for advice and training in order to do the job right. When I was a child, I decided to take the tractor motor apart to try to make it work better. I got everything taken apart just fine, but my parents had to hire someone to put it back together. It would have been good for me to have asked for permission before I started that job.

Unless the situation requires an urgent response, we don't let our under-nine-year-olds pick up babies or toddlers without permission. We have observed that younger children may not be able to hold babies or toddlers safely. Also, each toddler has his own curiosities, so when siblings leave him alone to explore shows respect.

When our children are at another family's home, they are expected to ask the friend's parents for permission for the things they ask permission for at our house. For some decisions, however, they need to call and ask us rather than asking the friend's parents. For example, if they want to watch a movie or a show, they have to call home.

Learning to ask permission helps facilitate healthy relationships: it keeps kids safer and communicates respect and concern for others. Asking permission deals with fleshly desires for instant gratification and gives opportunity to seek contentment. These are valuable family lessons.

Music

Music can be a real issue in families. The vast majority of lyrics are designed to appeal to the flesh. I am not only talking about music that people generally deem rebellious. Many lyrics encourage whimsical, mindless decision-making. Further, many songs introduce romantic feelings not healthy for children or teens. Ginny and I are cautious and sober-minded about music.

Our first rule about music is that, if one of our children wants to buy a song or album, they have to ask permission. Second, we want our children to read the lyrics with us. Our children will be reminded of the ideas that a song presents over and over again, so we want the message to be a good one. We analyze the songs a radio station or web-based service plays in the same way. What groups are selected for the station? What do they sing about? Does their message glorify God? Our rule to review the words of songs forces us all to discuss, reasonably, the effect of those words. We want our children to think, not whether it is okay to listen to a particular song or artist, but whether it is best to listen.

Our policy is also that we do not want to support someone or promote his songs if his life is not outstanding in a good way. Once a child likes one song from a musician or band, he will likely want to listen to more from that individual or group. One "innocent" song can lead to others that are not so innocent. Additionally, we prefer that our children not be star-struck, even if we think the singer pleases God. We teach that no one should be regarded as more important than another. God certainly does not view the world as if there are stars. Why should we?

Critical thinking about the message is our focus when it comes to our rules about music. Our rules cause our children to discuss with us the content of a song or the message a performer presents with his creativity and life.

Communicating With Each Other

What we say and how we say it matters. Here are some of our family rules about interacting with others.

We require our children, in most cases, to use a title and last name when speaking to an adult. For example, they would say, "Hello, Mr. Jones." If a child wants to be most respectful in our society, this is the way to do it. In some instances, our children have called an unrelated adult by his first name. We don't use the title plus first name combination (e.g., Mr. Nate).

As I mentioned in the last chapter, when we ask our children to do something, we want them to respond, "yes, sir" or "yes, ma'am." When we get this response, we know that our children have heard our instructions. It is very helpful.

We want our children to say "please" and "thank you." Teaching this to a child could start before she could speak by using sign language, but we have introduced the rule to our children when they have a good language base. After quite a bit of practice, if our child does not say "please" or "thank you," he or she may not get what he or she wants. Other consequences can be substituted when we want or need them to have what they are asking for or what we are offering.

Interrupting when someone is speaking is also against our rules. When a person is writing, typing or reading, he is, in a sense, conversing. These times should not be interrupted. If our children wish to speak when we are talking or writing, they need to gently get our attention by standing next to us or by placing their hand on our arm (not by tapping, pulling, patting or rubbing). With this signal, we know to try to take a break to let a child speak.

Interruption is not always obvious. Conversation has normal pauses, and sometimes a listener thinks the speaker is done when he has not finished speaking. On the other hand, a child who is trying to fit his words in a millisecond after another person is done talking does not have the right attitude for conversation. Although technically not an interruption, it means a child is not making listening most important (James 1:19). If a child seems anxious to speak, we point it out, encourage him to listen and warn him about interrupting.

If one person asks another person a question, that person should have the opportunity to answer before others speak. The one who speaks before the answer is provided is interrupting the conversation. For example, if I ask Ginny something, the break in the conversation between the question and the response is not an opportunity for a child to talk. Ginny has the floor until she is done answering the question.

We have a rule that family members can't come into a room with words formed in their mouths. They need to first come in the room and check to see that no one else is talking. Similarly, we have a rule that a child cannot talk to someone from another room. The child must be able to see the other person's face. These rules help keep the noise level down in our house.

Every once in a while, we will have a meal or some other time during which everyone has to whisper. It has the effect of turning a houseful of busybodies into a more thoughtful bunch of conversationalists. Our children seem to like these times of whispering.

We also say, "No extra noises in the house." It is inappropriate for our children to make meaningless clamor. I am not talking about the younger children who are pretending. I am referring to those who are being noisy for the sake of being noisy. If they want to make these sounds, they can do so outside. In the house, these extra noises make conversation more difficult between people using intelligible words. These sounds interrupt people trying to concentrate. We also say, "No yelling in the house." We do not permit coarse joking or insults (Ephesians 5:4). Crude "potty talk" comments are also off limits.

Nagging is disrespectful, and it can be a real headache for parents with several children, but it also indicates a discontented heart. Our children are to ask and wait for an answer. However, if time has passed, and it seems that Ginny or I have forgotten to respond, they may ask again.

Children can become very creative when nagging. For example, a child might ask if we can get pizza when we go on an errand. After asking, he might inquire, "Are we going to leave early enough to stop to pick up the pizza?" Or, "Do we have enough money for pizza?" Or, "If you are shopping and someone gets hungry, are you going to buy pizza?" We can usually see through these planning suggestions and know that they come from a discontented, nagging heart. Since evaluating whether our children are nagging or not can be subjective, we have to consider each situation and try to decide fairly whether discipline or warning is appropriate.

Although we don't allow our children to nag or talk back, there is room in our home for negotiation and appeal. It should be done respectfully. It is worth mentioning a conversation that Moses had with God about entering into the Promised Land after God withdrew the privilege.

> At that time I [Moses] pleaded with the LORD: "O Sovereign LORD, you have begun to show to your servant your greatness and

NATE DAVIS | GOD THE PARENT

your strong hand. For what god is there in heaven or on earth who can do the deeds and mighty works you do? Let me go over and see the good land beyond the Jordan—that fine hill country and Lebanon."

Deuteronomy 3:23-25, NIV

It does not seem that Moses was nagging but respectfully asking, and the issue was very important to him. Taking the people to the Promised Land was his life's work. The request was made honorably. In this case, God was not moved: "'That is enough,' the LORD said. 'Do not speak to me anymore about this matter'" (Deuteronomy 3:26, NIV).

Finally, we expect our children to tell the truth. Deception can be very subtle, and we try to be careful to catch as much as we can. We want to consider whether a child is representing the whole truth, holding important information back or avoiding questions. Partial truths come from a heart attitude of deceit.

We are keen to watch for lying when a child is in trouble, but that is not the only time when children are tempted to bend the truth. For example, if a child tried to advance conversations with made-up information (perhaps in order to feel important), then he would not be telling the truth. In that case, we could ask if the child had made things up. We might do research together to find out if the child's claims were legitimate. If the problem continued, we could introduce rules and consequences for this kind of disregard for truth.

Our rules about communicating are part of an effort to teach our children to speak respectfully to others. We all need to have humility in our tone, gesture and words.

Mealtime Rules

Mealtime can be a bit of a challenge and coming up with the right rules can be a big help. We don't want children to play with their food. They must sit in the chair with their legs forward. (Young ones can choose to sit on their knees or on their bottoms.) All four legs of the chair should stay on the floor. Our children should not chew with their mouths open, lick their fingers, talk with food in their mouths or eat with their hands when utensils are appropriate. We don't allow children to play with toys at the table or anything that could be construed as a toy at the time.

Honestly, interrupting each other is our biggest challenge at mealtime. There are twelve of us, and we are usually having a good time.

Our children often prepare our family's meals. For safety and to keep order, those not preparing the meal must stay out of the kitchen.

What do we do with the child who refuses to eat? We don't mind if one of ours does not want to eat or does not like a meal. As a matter of rule, our children do not get any other food until they finish the food they have already been given. In other words, if one of them doesn't eat a meal, we save it until he is hungry or until the next appropriate meal. This food policy gives us the freedom to tell our children, "If you are not hungry, don't eat. You can eat it at the next meal," which is much better than, "Clean your plate." An exception would be made for inedible food. We have served meat that is very difficult to chew or have accidentally left a meal out of the refrigerator too long. These meals are thrown away. We do not serve last night's dinner at breakfast, but instead save it for lunch. We prefer not to keep cups of milk in the fridge, so children usually have to drink their first serving whether they eat any of the meal or not. Also, there are times when we ask a child to take a bite, or several bites, of food. This is not optional.

As early as sixteen months, our children began to pick and choose what they wanted to eat. It made for a difficult couple of meals, but we kept bringing the same, rejected food back to the child until he or she ate it. To protect it all from ending up on the floor, we put one bite in front of them or fed them one bite at a time. We would discipline for throwing food once that rule had been established. All of this was practiced at home, where we felt most comfortable confronting behavior problems. We have had a few struggles between the ages of one and three, but after that, our children ate almost anything.

Mealtime is a great family time. Our rules related to etiquette, interrupting and food management solve a lot of the problems that might otherwise make eating together more work than pleasure.

Crawler, Toddler and Young Child Rules

With the wee ones, we are not only asking what the rule should be, but at what age we enforce the rule. Generally, if a young child learns a new skill, he is also ready to begin learning rules related to that new ability. For example, if a child is mobile enough to open cabinets intentionally, it is a good time to start teaching him not to open them. The rule should be established, though. We teach, "Don't touch," by pulling the child's hand away from the cabinet and down to his side. After doing this several times, we direct him toward something he can play with. Before too long, the child will know that he should not open the cabinets; however, most of our children didn't stop until they realized we would introduce some additional consequences.

Several of our children have done something they knew to be wrong, like opening a kitchen cabinet, when they had a dirty diaper, were hungry or had another unmet need we did not notice. In this case, we didn't discipline them for opening the cabinet but accepted the fact that small children communicate this way at times.

A child's ability to express himself is limited during these years. Sometimes, children can't understand what parents are saying. More often, a child does not know how to communicate with mom and dad. A parent can relieve a lot of frustration for the child who is developing language by being face to face and saying, "Point your finger at what you want," "Show me" or "Take me there."

Toddlers should not stand on a chair. Our little children are not allowed to throw toys or books. They are not permitted to touch computers or stereos or things on tables or counters. We also have rules like, "Don't touch your private parts" and "Don't pick your nose."

Before the age of two, we start teaching the little ones to be still and quiet on our laps during meetings. Crawlers should be still during diaper changes. They must also learn to lie still when it is time to fall asleep. A good massage often helps wiggly legs and reading a book seems to be calming, but ours have needed a rule to stay still, too.

Of course, we expect our children to come, stop and stay next to us when asked. When we want our young children to come to us, we say, "Touch my knees." We made this rule because we saw that "Come here" was too subjective. The children were stopping before they got close enough to us.

When a potty-trained child does not take a break from playing soon enough to make it to the bathroom, we discipline. We do not do this during the period of potty training but after the child has shown that he can have self-control yet chooses to keep playing instead. Often the consequence involves missing play time, the very thing that the child was clinging to instead of going to the bathroom in the first place.

"Don't tell Mommy 'No,'" is not a viable rule. We all need to use the word no at times. Our rule is more specific: "When I ask you to do something, you can't say, 'No,' to me." We take time to establish that rule. For a while, young ones only have a few words with which to communicate, and "no" is one of them.

Between the ages of two and five years, our children have tried to have their way by using a temper tantrum. When saying, "No," escalated to yelling, we established a rule over time by explaining, "That is a temper tantrum, and it is against our family rules. Instead, use your words so we can talk about what you want." All of our children, although angry with us, were able to stop yelling when they realized that they would receive some sort of discipline for their behavior. Often, the tantrums were replaced with pouting, so we introduced a rule that they could not pout. They learned to stop pouting and throwing temper tantrums altogether, but this took time. While they were learning to control themselves, there were instances when we permitted pouting or crying by saying, "You may pout if you want to, but you have to stay here. When you are done, you can come out and play." In that case, the consequence for pouting was the loss of the privilege to play. There were times when we overlooked tantrums and pouting altogether. For example, if a child cried out for a few minutes when we left him or her with another adult, we did not discipline.

As I said in the previous chapter, the rule that a child is not to take something out of another person's hands is one of our most important for young children. Instead, they may ask for it and wait. Then, they may go to mom or dad and say, "There is a problem." This rule eliminates a lot of sibling disputes at our house.

It is difficult to make up a rule for the occasion when one child says, "She took my toy," and the other, "He wasn't using it." How does one define at what point of idleness a toy stops being someone else's toy? The situation requires a different process which, for our family, hinges on Philippians 2:3-4 (NIV, see also Romans 12:10).

> Do nothing out of selfish ambition or vain conceit. Rather, in humility value others above yourselves, not looking to your own interests but each of you to the interests of the others.

When we have to decide who would get the toy, we choose one of the two children caught in the quarrel and say, "We want you to bless your sister. What can you do to help her have a good time playing?"

The frequency of parent-child conflict is highest with toddlers and young children. We know, however, that it will not be too long until these rules will, for the most part, become second nature for our children and these struggles will wane.

Family Rules

I hope that this chapter helps you think about your family rules. Making good rules takes wisdom, the leading of the Holy Spirit, Bible study and sometimes trial and error. It is also an ongoing process. We have not stopped saying, "We need a rule for that."

We tell our children that obeying our rules is a way for them to show that they love us, just like obeying Jesus is a way to show we love him. Love should be put into action. Obedience is to be complaint-free, fast and fully finished.

We need to constantly remind ourselves that rules give us teaching opportunities. They reveal the heart, and we want to help our children see what is in theirs. Disobedience is not a personal insult to us as parents, but shows disrespect (that we knew would be there) for God and his ways. This is why it helps us to explain our rules to our children in light of the greatest commandments of God, the Two and the Ten. Having consistent and thorough rules allows us to resolve issues quickly and enjoy one another.

The world is full of rules, and humans need it that way. If we had love, we would not really need rules, and, ultimately, we want our children to love others rather than to live by rules (Romans 13:8-10). Sometimes we need to be encouraged to get our minds off rules and onto true love. For example, if a child is barking instructions at his siblings to get them to do the right thing, he is probably so focused on the rules that he has stopped loving his brothers and sisters. To God, the rules are important, but his ultimate goal is to give a new heart, a new life and love. We want to keep this in mind day to day.

For Discussion

1. Which of your rules are most helpful to your family?
2. Did you see any rules in this chapter that you would consider for your family?
3. Have you asked for advice or feedback on any of your rules? Which ones?
4. Discuss some biblical principles and consider what rules might help to teach them.

Chapter 10

WHAT DISCIPLINE IS LIKE

I find it discouraging to read of Israel's disobedience and consequent sufferings in the wilderness. When I put it in the big picture, however, I see that the nation changed for the better and the discipline gave the people opportunities they never would have had if they had been left on their own. Discipline plays a very important role in children's lives, too, allowing them to experience the benefits of self-control.

Primarily, the information in this chapter comes from passages in the Old Testament books about the Exodus, four of the Proverbs and Hebrews chapter 12 of the New Testament. These sources are sufficient for learning about the nature of good discipline, but they do not tell parents exactly how, or even at what age, to discipline a child. This is important. The Bible tells us what good discipline is like rather than telling parents exactly what it should be. Thus, with discipline parents act in faith and with discernment for their own family's particular situation.

What is the nature of good discipline? A good consequence causes temporary pain, discomfort or loss and helps to bring about a heart change that results in appropriate behavior. Heart change from discipline is not a heart replacement as is ultimately required, but discipline does cool the jets of the flesh. It helps curb a child's appetite for more and more sin. Discipline also helps a child consider wise reasoning. This is great news for the parent because it provides hope that he or she can affect a child positively from day to day.

God's Example in the Exodus

Throughout the Bible, individuals experienced consequences from God. For example, Jonah decided to obey after three days in a whale and received further correction in the hot sun and scorching wind (Jonah 1:17-2:10; 4:7-11), and Zechariah was left mute until John was born (Luke 1:18-20). In Numbers 12, the prophetess Miriam, with Aaron in tow, questioned whether Moses should be in charge because he had a Cushite wife. Miriam seemed to have a high esteem for her own clan and a low view of Cushites. God made Miriam leprous because of her behavior. Aaron realized that they had done the wrong thing: "So Aaron said to Moses, 'Oh, my lord! Please do not lay *this* sin on us, in which we have done foolishly and in which we have sinned.'" (v. 11, NKJV). At that request, God healed Miriam, but she had to spend seven days outside the camp for her purification. Aaron stayed with her.

The Bible also records many instances in which God corrected the nation he cared for as a *child* during the Exodus. It takes thoughtfulness to imitate God in his treatment of Israel because what he did was on such a grand scale. Consequences for the nation involved earlier-than-expected death for some and the untimely loss of loved ones for others. (Everyone dies, and the first death is not nearly as important as the second death, which is referred to in Revelation 21:8. God will fairly judge all who died in the events of the Exodus, whether they had a long life or short life. In the end we will forever admire how just he has been.) Although the discipline of a nation is on a very different scale than the discipline of a child, we can see principles that apply to both.

The first time the nation of Israel was disciplined in the wilderness was immediately after the rules were firmly established in Exodus 20. The Israelites made and worshipped an idol, and "they sat down to eat and drink and got up to indulge in revelry" (Exodus 32:6, NIV). After the consequence (three thousand of the guilty died by the sword and another 23,000 died from a plague), the heart of the nation seemed different for a time. For example, the people of Israel mourned that God would not go with them into the Promised Land at that time (Exodus 33:3-4) and freely gave contributions to build God's tent (Exodus 35:29).

Numbers 11 records three instances of correction—fire, plague and, surprisingly, quail from the sea. First, the people complained about their misfortune. In response to the bellyaching, the fire of the Lord consumed

Israelites at the edges of the camp (v. 1). Israel asked Moses to pray that it would stop, and it did (v. 3). That ended the complaint, but a new complaint arose. Israel wanted meat. God used the wind to blow quail from the sea into the camp from all directions (v. 31). That day, all of Israel ate meat, but God discerned that some of them had a strong craving.

> But they soon forgot what he had done and did not wait for his plan to unfold. In the desert they gave in to their craving; in the wilderness they put God to the test. So he gave them what they asked for, but sent a wasting disease among them.
>
> Psalm 106:13-15, NIV

Those with this craving died of the plague (Numbers 11:33). Over the next month, the quail from the sea became an additional means of correction. God said Israel would eat this food, "until it comes out of your nostrils and you loathe it—because you have rejected the LORD." (Numbers 11:20, NIV). The fire, the plague and the quail from the sea help change attitudes and stop complaints.

In Numbers 14, Israel decided to reject God's instruction to go into the Promised Land. God introduced a consequence:

> ...not one of those who saw my glory and the signs I performed in Egypt and in the wilderness but who disobeyed me and tested me ten times—not one of them will ever see the land I promised on oath to their ancestors. No one who has treated me with contempt will ever see it.
>
> Numbers 14:22-23, NIV

Isolation in the desert was dry, dusty and devoid of many of the simple pleasures of life. Deuteronomy 1:19, called it "that vast and dreadful wilderness," but perhaps the people's greatest angst was the knowledge that there was an alternative and that they missed it (NIV). That was a nation-turning experience.

In addition to isolation in the wilderness, "these men who were responsible for spreading the bad report about the land were struck down and died of a plague before the LORD." (Numbers 14:37, NIV). That was a loss to the people of Israel, as these were honored men from each of the clans.

Another significant lesson for parents to consider is recorded in Numbers 14:25-45 (also, Deuteronomy 1:41-46). The day after Israel refused to go into the Promised Land and God assigned a consequence, they were given this instruction: "Since the Amalekites and the Canaanites are living in the valleys, turn back tomorrow and set out toward the desert along the route to the Red Sea." (v. 25, NIV). Israel ignored that command and decided to go into the Promised Land instead. Going in after the Amalekites and Canaanites proved painful. Israel was soundly defeated.

> You came back and wept before the LORD, but he paid no attention to your weeping and turned a deaf ear to you.
> Deuteronomy 1:45, NIV

The nation experienced painful consequences because it tried to give itself a second chance to obey the first command rather than obeying the new command to "set out toward the desert."

More discipline was recorded in Numbers 16. Israel complained about Aaron's family's special job in God's meeting tent. Moses tried to reason with the complainers to no avail. So, he set up a test in which Aaron and the leaders of the complaint—253 men—would offer incense together to see if all were accepted before the Lord. At the beginning of the event, the ground opened up and swallowed the three main instigators (v. 30-32). Fire consumed the remaining 250 men who were offering incense to the Lord (v. 35). The next day, the people of Israel levied another complaint: "You [Moses] have killed the people of the LORD." (v. 41, NKJV). At that, a plague hit Israel, spreading from the front of the crowd toward the back and was ended when Aaron held a censer in the midst of the mass of people (v. 48-49). Did the people stop complaining when three families fell into the earth and 250 of them were burnt to death? No, they stopped after 14,700 of them died in a plague. It took all three of these events to bring the griping to an end. In Numbers 16, consequences were added until the nation changed.

Later, in Numbers 21, Israel held God in contempt again, so he sent venomous snakes among them.

> They traveled from Mount Hor along the route to the Red Sea, to go around Edom. But the people grew impatient on the way; they spoke against God and against Moses, and said, "Why have you brought us up out of Egypt to die in the wilderness? There is no bread! There is no water! And we detest this miserable food!"
> v. 4-5, NIV

By God's judgment, Israel's behavior warranted correction. The people found themselves in the midst of deadly snakes that caused them to quickly turn from their wrongdoing (v. 7). It was not an argument of logic that brought them to change, but the deadly bites of serpents. The snakes didn't go away immediately after Israel seemed to straighten up; however, if a snake bit, a person could look on the bronze serpent and live (v. 9).

After the snakes, Israel nearly went to war against the people of Moab and Midian. God intervened, war was averted, and there was peace between the peoples. While Israel was camped near the Moabites, some of Israel committed itself to Baal of Peor, a Moabite god, and paid for immoral relations with the women of the Moabites. That brought a plague on Israel that killed 24,000. The plague was stopped when Israel got the last rebel out of the camp (Numbers 25:1-9). In that situation, God persisted until the issue was resolved.

Throughout the Exodus, when the nation did wrong, there were unique consequences. God understood that Israel was blessed because of his discipline and that the entire world was blessed through Israel when it was not allowed to continue on the path of ruin. God did not panic, but patiently persisted with the application of rules and consequences. A parent can learn from these examples.

What can we observe from the way God treated Israel? When the nation did not follow instructions or when they broke rules, God disciplined. His consequences were right-sized for a nation and utilized several different discipline options. God used disciplinary measures that were brief, like a plague, or fire at the edges of the camp and others, like the wilderness isolation, serpents and quail, that lasted longer. When the nation did not respond to the first consequences, more followed (Numbers 11, 16 and 25).

In chapter 6, "Heart Problem," I pointed out that the Israelites often argued illogically when they wanted to resist. In these examples, we see how with correction, they responded appropriately to good reasoning. Consequences seemed necessary for logic to be considered.

Hebrews 12

Hebrews 12 shows us more of God's example and helps us understand what parental discipline is like. As students of the Bible, we should note that the purpose of Hebrews 12 is not to teach a parent how to discipline or defend a position that discipline is good no matter how it is done (it is not). The point of the passage is that God disciplines his children because he loves them, and we can learn about the nature and value of parental discipline from the passage's explanations.

The chapter starts by speaking about resisting sin (v. 1-4), and then speaks about God's deep and sincere love toward us, expressed through the pain of discipline.

> And have you completely forgotten this word of encouragement that addresses you as a father addresses his son? It says, "My son, do not make light of the Lord's discipline, and do not lose heart when he rebukes you, because the Lord disciplines the one he loves, and he chastens everyone he accepts as his son." Endure hardship as discipline; God is treating you as his children. For what children are not disciplined by their father?
>
> Hebrews 12:5-7, NIV (see also Proverbs 3:11-12)

The phrase "and everyone undergoes discipline" speaks of God's love and close involvement, and how he is a father to all who believe.

When the dads referred to in the verses used discipline, were the children forever scarred? No, on the contrary, they eventually saw that what their fathers were doing was right.

> Moreover, we have all had human fathers who disciplined us and we respected them for it. How much more should we submit to the Father of our spirits and live!
>
> Hebrews 12:9, NIV

A dad who disciplined was respected for, at the very least, that one thing. Unfortunately, not all parents are as faithful as God. Today some parents disdain discipline. Other parents aren't around. Still others yell instead of disciplining. In the Hebrews example, the fathers did the right thing. They disciplined.

Next, Hebrews tells a little about what a father's discipline was like.

> They disciplined us for a little while as they thought best; but God disciplines us for our good, in order that we may share in his holiness. No discipline seems pleasant at the time, but painful. Later on, however, it produces a harvest of righteousness and peace for those who have been trained by it.
>
> Hebrews 12:10-11, NIV

From these verses, we know that fatherly discipline was for a window of time, "a little while," but the time period is not described. We have no idea at what age it started or ended. We don't know what these fathers were doing to discipline their children, either. We do know, however, that what they did hurt. It was not "pleasant," but "painful." Notice that the pain was temporary: it hurt only "at the time." The discipline was not abusive. We should note that the fathers in this verse were not credited for using some sort of God-approved method. They were disciplining however they "thought best."

The book of Hebrews clearly legitimizes "painful" discipline, praising it for its effectiveness. In fact, discipline is used to illustrate how God shows his love for us—"the Lord disciplines the one he loves." Hebrews also promotes a response to discipline that parents would hope to foster in their children. When children are caught, confronted and disciplined, they should recommit to walk rightly, to "make every effort" and to "see to it" (12:12-15, NIV).

The message of Hebrews 12 is that in good discipline, temporary pain leads to wonderful future benefits, producing a "harvest of righteousness and peace." We might expect a person to gain righteousness through discipline, if discipline helps lead to a self-controlled life. Why would peace be a result of discipline? Perhaps it is that a disciplined person has peace with others, freedom from guilt, the ability to discover contentment, or all of these.

We observe from Hebrews 12 that if parents love their children, they must deem the concepts of biblical discipline very important. Children are better off when rules are enforced. Parents could expect that children will play better together, gain confidence from their accomplishments and be more loving. Loving parents should discipline for the sake of their children's righteousness and peace.

Proverbs and "the Rod"

To understand what the Bible says about the nature of discipline, it is necessary to do a longer study on four Proverbs that speak of the "rod" and "child" or "son." In this section of the book, I cite the KJV because the word choice for the KJV translation may lead some to wrong notions about discipline, and these ideas should be addressed.

He that spareth his rod hateth his son: but he that loveth him chasteneth him betimes.

Proverbs 13:24, KJV

Foolishness *is* bound in the heart of a child; *but* the rod of correction shall drive it far from him.

Proverbs 22:15, KJV

Withhold not correction from the child: for *if* thou beatest him with the rod, he shall not die. Thou shalt beat him with the rod, and shalt deliver his soul from hell.

Proverbs 23:13-14, KJV

The rod and reproof give wisdom: but a child left *to himself* bringeth his mother to shame.

Proverbs 29:15, KJV

The verses in Proverbs that use the word "rod", but do not speak of children, should not be included in our study (Proverbs 10:13, 22:8, 26:3).

To start off, there is no biblical context for understanding these four Proverbs about the "rod" and "child" or "son" without the morality of God in a home. When Proverbs 1:8 says, "Listen, my son, to your father's instruction and do not forsake your mother's teaching," it does not refer to any instruction, but to teaching which is committed to God's glory and his morality. The four Proverbs that use the word "rod" and "child" or "son" are meant for a home in which God's ways are honored and followed by the parent so that family members will "understand what is right and just and fair—every good path" (Proverbs 2:9, NIV).

As a starting point for our study, we must understand the style of writing and logic that makes up the book of Proverbs. Each proverb is a brilliantly concise comment that tells a person what will usually happen if he makes decisions of a certain type. They show, in their brevity, that most morality is not hard to understand and that godly wisdom is not fanciful, but down-to-earth commonsensical. We need to be careful not to ask for more information from the Proverbs than what they were intended to provide.

These four passages in Proverbs help us understand the nature of discipline and its usefulness. Central to this study will be the exploration of the meaning of four Hebrew words—*shebet* (staff), *nakah* (striking motion), *na`ar* (child) and *shachar* (to seek early).

The Staff

The four Proverbs we are considering use the Hebrew word *shebet*, and we know from its use throughout the Old Testament that *shebet* is what we think of as a herdsman's staff (e.g., Psalm 23:4). We see the *shebet* in the hands of a herdsman here: "And concerning the tithe of the herd, or of the flock, *even* of whatsoever passeth under the rod [*shebet*], the tenth shall be holy unto the LORD." (Leviticus 27:32, KJV). The *shebet* was useful on all sorts of occasions in an agrarian society, not only for herding (consider Isaiah 28:27). The staff was a common fixture, a daily-used tool. Likely, the branch of wood fit nicely in the palm of a man or woman's hand, and its owner could use it as an aid to walk on rough ground, fend off wild animals and move livestock. Sometimes the *shebet* was used to conquer, defend or rule over. For example, Isaiah 9:4 uses the term "rod of his oppressor" (KJV, see 2 Samuel 23:21, Isaiah 10:5, 15, 24, 14:5, 29, 30:3). We learn from Hebrews 11:21 that the staff was large enough to lean on (NIV, cross reference Genesis 49): "By faith Jacob, when he was dying, blessed each of Joseph's sons, and worshiped as he leaned on the top of his staff." In the Bible, there are other words that refer to a small stick. *Zĕmowrah*, *kippah*, `aleh* and *Qaneh* are all Hebrew words that suggest a woody material that is more flimsy, but in Proverbs *shebet* was the chosen one.

The student of Proverbs should understand that *shebet* was more than just a stick. In fact, more often than not in the Bible (140 to 50 in the KJV) *shebet* was translated "tribe". Here are examples of both translations of *shebet* from Genesis 49:

> The sceptre [*shebet*] shall not depart from Judah, nor a lawgiver from between his feet, until Shiloh come; and unto him *shall* the gathering of the people *be*.
>
> v. 10, KJV

> "All these *are* the twelve tribes [*shebet*] of Israel: and this *is it* that their father spake unto them, and blessed them; every one according to his blessing he blessed them."
>
> v. 28, KJV

We see here how *shebet* referred to a sceptre and how *shebet* was also translated tribe. It wasn't that the same word communicated two very different ideas (a homonym), either tribe or staff, but that the two were related. The staff was held by the one who guided the tribe (see Amos 1:5, 8), but sometimes that leadership was not good (see Ezekiel 19:11, 14, Psalms 125:3).

Since *shebet* often refers to a clan in the Bible, some people teach that these four proverbs speak of the head of a family teaching his children. They conclude that the passages are not about parental consequences at all. To them, the staff is purely a metaphor about leadership, but Proverbs 23:13-14 negates this option. It would not make sense that a metaphor or instruction was swung, and this staff was swung.

Shebet should not make one wonder whether it was meant to be literal or metaphorical, but should be thought of as a poetic choice of words that communicated both ideas at the same time. The word *shebet* tugged on heart strings associated with legacy and daily life. *Shebet* represented what parents passed on to children by their rules, instruction and discipline.

What Did the Staff Do?

Were it not for Proverbs 23:13-14, the *shebet* would have been inanimate. It is the only passage of the four that says anything about what the *shebet* did. The Hebrew word translated in the KJV "beatest" and "beat" (*nakah*) means to strike, or smite. The KJV choice of words for the translation is unfortunate because it implies something violent and abusive. The NIV translation, "punish", also misses as it ignores the motion involved with *nakah*.

The best way to try to understand *nakah* and *shebet*—striking with the staff—in Proverbs 23:13-14, is in light of the life of a herdsman. Should we imagine that herdsmen beat their animals? No, nor should we imagine that it was always swung at the same speed. We could suspect that an experienced farmer knew how to prod a particular animal in a particular situation. In a farming context, *nakah* would have been thought of as whatever was appropriate, not what English speakers generally mean when they use the word *beat*.

We should also consider the meaning of the phrase, "he shall not die" in 23:13. Is "he shall not die" a prescription for extreme, near death punishment? It is not. The point of the verse is to compare things that don't cause death to things that do, and there is a reason to bring up dying in this context. Because a sinful lifestyle may well lead to an early death, discipline might help to save a child's soul (Proverbs 19:18, Deuteronomy

21:18-21). Discipline falls into the immense category of things that don't cause death, but failing to discipline can lead to it. We should conclude that the *shebet* was swung (in whatever way was right), not to deliver an extreme beating, but to discipline when necessary.

The lack of detail leads one to believe that Proverbs 23:13-14 referred to accepted practices of the day, using words common to agrarians. I am not saying that Proverbs told parents to treat their children like animals, but that the people for whom these proverbs were written would have understood *nakah* and *shebet* in the context of their lives, and that if we want to understand them we have to consider how these verses of encouragement fit with their vernacular and experience.

Let me elaborate on the difference between working with farm animals and raising children. If a parent tries to train a child the same way he trains an animal, he will be ignoring what God's Word tells us, that humans are made in the image of God (Genesis 1:27). Humans are spiritual beings, designed to love and be loved. They are capable of reason, and they are not bound to live in the moment but can imagine the future. People were made to be persuaded. If someone were to say that carrots and sticks work for horses and should also work for children, or if someone were to say that children need to be "broken," then they are wrong. Instead of training children like pets, parents should care for them as if they were unique creations, made in God's image. Without a doubt, the book of Proverbs focuses on logical persuasion, treating humans as willful, rational individuals whose decisions have future physical and spiritual implications.

How Old is a Child?

The three verses that talk about the staff and a "child" use the Hebrew word *na'ar*, which was used in the Bible to refer to a large age range. For example, in Exodus 33:11, Joshua was described as a *na'ar* before he was chosen to spy out the land. He was approximately twenty years old (Numbers 1:3, 13:8, 14:23-24 and 32:11-12). On the other hand, Moses was described as a *na'ar* when he was found by Pharaoh's daughter in the Nile river (Exodus 2:6). Samuel was a *na'ar* when his mom gave him over to the service of God (1 Samuel 1:22-25). Samson was a *na'ar* from the womb (Judges 13:5).

One might argue that the *na'ar* in Proverbs refers to a much older child because Proverbs addresses sons who would be tempted by wayward women (2:16), who were big enough to join bands of thieves (1:11-14), may have been married (5:18) and may have been working (6:9-11). However, the argument fails because the person who was old enough to be dealing with these issues would have also been old enough to be thinking about the children he would be raising. In that case, giving him advice about dealing with young children would be appropriate.

Using the term *na`ar* did not necessarily mean that the *shebet* was to be used on a *na`ar* from infancy to age twenty but that those who were disciplined fell somewhere within that time period. The word does not tell us anything more. Why is that important? The vagueness leads one to believe that these were primarily verses to encourage parents in something that they already understood rather than trying to tell them how to do it. Rather than being consumed with the makeup of the rod, the swinging or the child's age, we should think more about the benefit and reason behind discipline.

I think that many Christian parents wonder at what age they should start and stop disciplining. The Bible does not offer a precise formula, and nor will I. However, I do believe that there should be many years in which a child's misbehavior is met with parental consequences. Even when a parent has stopped assigning consequences, he should continue to ask judicial questions that help his children evaluate their behavior.

When Was the Staff Useful?

Perhaps the greatest truth to reap from these four proverbs is the understanding about when to discipline. Parents would do well to focus on this. The staff was useful "betimes", *shachar*, in Proverbs 13:24. The word means "to seek early," or to "long for." For example, in Psalm 63:1 David said, "early will I seek [*shachar*] thee: my soul thirsteth for thee." In the same way that David sought God early, a parent is to seek to discipline his child when necessary. The best we could say is that this referred to an ongoing, loving pursuit of a parent. Similarly, Proverbs 29:15 indicates that a child should not be "left [to himself]," implying a high level of attention to "the [staff] and reproof". Finally, Proverbs 22:15 implies that the "[staff] of discipline" is to be used when a child has foolishness in his heart. To sum it up, parents are to be earnestly paying attention in order to discipline on the occasion that a child's outward behavior is showing foolishness in his heart.

It is no small thing when a verse gives us an understanding of the workings of the heart as we see in Proverbs 22:15: "Foolishness [is] bound in the heart of a child". In English, the word "foolishness" takes on varying degrees of badness. It can mean lacking sense, ridiculous and trifling, but in the Proverbs "foolishness" (*ivveleth*) describes one who lacks sense about the rules of God. The concept is not excitement, silliness or giddiness. The foolishness referred to in Proverbs 22:15 is sin, rebellion against one's maker's ways and nothing less. According to Proverbs 22:15, sin is bound up in the heart of a child, and the cords cannot or will not be severed by the child. The child is stuck: sin is secured there. It takes a parent to set him free. When a parent is not consistent in his discipline, he will permit the tied-down sin to remain. Sometimes, I think this mischievousness shows up on the countenance of a child's face. He might keep thinking, "What can I get away with next?" He does not live to play, pretend, learn and wonder, but feels obligated to establish whatever power he can by constantly testing his parents. The internal battle that rages will consume his attention. Children's tendency, when they discover a restricted activity is appealing to their flesh, is to focus on that restriction. Parents might talk to them, warn them, redirect them, negotiate with them or offer them rewards, but their attention will likely be drawn back to doing what they should not do. Consequences force children to deal with these desires and gain some control.

The language of Proverbs 22:15 implies setting a child free, not breaking his will. It is not the behavior modification proposed by B.F. Skinner, nor does it seek to be the classical conditioning of Ivan Pavlov. Further, those who imagine that sin is like a baseball and that spanking is the parent's bat to knock it out of the park ("...the rod of correction shall drive it far from him") have misunderstood the process to their children's detriment. A better metaphor would be that discipline is the push needed to get over a tall wall, the hand needed to get out of a hole, or as the verse suggests, the set of hands needed to untie a binding rope. Children will need help to overcome the temptations of the flesh. Discipline engages the will, giving them the boost that is needed to get them over the hump.

Knowing the purpose for discipline is vital to the proper development of its application. When children disobey rules, parents must discipline so that sinful intentions will be more likely to be addressed by them. Consequences sober children up from the inebriation of the flesh, giving them the opportunity to experience life in a good way; and they provide the ability to learn, focus, listen, build friendships, think, lead and follow. Should moms and dads be trying to catch their children doing something wrong? Absolutely. The alternative is to ignore or miss bad behavior, leaving children stuck with the sin bound in their hearts. Children do well when a parent responds to behavior problems.

If parents prescribe consequences only when there is danger or for the most blatant rebellion, they show they do not understand the purpose and benefit of discipline. Parents should long for their children to break free from sin in the short and long term. Thus, it makes sense for a parent to seek early (*shachar*) the opportunity to discipline. Good rules and reasonable consequences along the way are far better for children and their relationships with their family than waiting until things get really bad.

In spite of the nature of fallen mankind, a family can be peaceful and joy filled. It is truly the grace of God. Having and raising children is a glorious experience; and in the event children rebel against their parents' good rules, their parents can help them turn right around.

The Four Proverbs

Considering the issues of what (*shabat*), who (*na'ar*), how (*nakah*) and when (*shachar*), it is clear that Proverbs speaks of corporal discipline (discipline that is felt in the body), but the details are left quite vague. *Shebet* was a familiar, well-used tool that also represented what one generation passed on to the next. *Na'ar* was a child of unspecified age. *Nakah* meant to strike with a swinging motion. *Shachar* meant to seek early.

A person is overreaching if he claims the four proverbs we are studying refer to modern-day spanking. It would be presumptuous to say that the staff of discipline was a switch or a branch to be used on a child's bottom. The verses don't provide what many want—a detailed description of a God-ordained corrective technique. By God's design they give us what they give us, and nothing more.

Proverbs 13:24, 22:15, 23:13-14 and 29:15 can be presented in general terms. Proverbs considered irritation of the nerve cells in the skin to be a small price to pay for good character. Pain signals from the flesh, joined with words of importance and sound instruction help parents free their children from entangling sin. Consequences are to be used from time to time, and at the right time, and the benefits soundly outweigh the costs. Parents should earnestly seek to discipline in order to free their children from tied-down sin, saving them from death and hell and the family from turmoil. These four passages in Proverbs were written, not to provide specifics, but to encourage readers to be good parents.

Although the passages bring up corporal discipline, we should not assume that all correction must be felt on the skin. Instead, parents should follow God's example of using various kinds of consequences. Foremost, all who consider these four passages should keep in mind that the goals of the discipline were love (13:24), freedom (22:15), life (23:13-14) and wisdom (29:15).

Discomfort

Biologically, pain is an electrochemical transmission that the body produces on its own. If our nerves did not manufacture the signals, or if our brain were to ignore these signals, as in the disease of congenital insensitivity, then pain would be truly unreal. When one of my children got hurt, a medical doctor told him, "That is your leg telling your brain something that it already knows," which is the truth about pain. Further, most pain in life is a relatively mild distraction. Although not much consolation in the moment, nerves usually stop sending pain signals after a couple of minutes. Painful correction instituted by a loving parent would be similarly mild.

It is important for parents to put corporal discipline into the right context. Our children come back from mountain bike rides and show us the blood and bruises from their falls. If they were not nearly exhausted, they would go out again without hesitation. At fourteen, my son Micah wrote a short, humorous poem about mountain biking.

The birds chirp in the air,
The wind blows through my hair,
And the rock that is stuck in my arm is still there,
But I don't care.

To him, the pain of the pebble imbedded in his scratched skin was, relative to the perceived value of the experience, inconsequential. Also, our boys and girls join other children for a rough and tumble game of soccer, willingly placing themselves in front of a fast-flying ball or throwing their own body between the ball and another player under full steam. The pain that they experience is real, but it is outweighed by the desire to be fully engaged in the game. Your children may not be as tough as mine, or they may be tougher. This is not a competition. It is, however, important to put relatively mild pain in the proper perspective.

There are a lot of things that do create enduring pain. A parent who is indignant, self-centered, angry, anxious or arrogant will do lasting harm. The parent who brings the darkness of the world into a home—immorality, lying, drunkenness, drugs, crude speech, and licentiousness—will scar the hearts of his children. The parent who believes life's goal is to prove one's genetic superiority in a game of survival of the fittest in which humans are encouraged to satisfy "animal instincts" causes his child to objectify other humans and to chase after the wrong ambitions. The unchecked sibling who bullies his brothers and sisters for years on end for his own entertainment will cause misery. These are where real damage is done, and these have nothing to do with the momentary unpleasantness a child might feel from reasonable parental discipline.

Me Against You?

One verse sums up well the way God presented himself to the people of Israel in their disobedience. God said, "…you will suffer for your sins and know what it is like to have me against you." (Numbers 14:34, NIV). When God said these words, he was preparing to send the people of Israel into the desert for forty years. The loving discipline of the Father was going to create a change in the situation. Of course, the whole time God was very much for them. The phrase "me against you" is only part of the story: "For the LORD your God is a merciful God; he will not abandon or destroy you or forget the covenant with your forefathers, which he confirmed to them by oath." (Deuteronomy 4:31, NIV). Mercy would be God's response. However, the nature of discipline is that the one receiving the consequence may feel that the disciplinarian is taking a stand against his will.

Parents don't need to put on a show in order for children to see that their behavior has caused a change in the situation. They only need to act judicially and implement appropriate consequences. With the hardship, children's minds will likely register that their parents will not tolerate the conduct.

Unfortunately, some parents seem to be always against their children. Being mean is not necessary or helpful. Other parents never want to confront, always acting as if nothing is wrong. This will not do, either. Loving parents have to take a stand against their children's misbehavior. When children disobey, they must confront them with discipline.

Discipline Defined

God has shown us how he disciplined individual adults and the nation of Israel. We have learned a little about how he disciplines believers from the book of Hebrews and that it is similar to a father's discipline. Further, God provides information about the nature of discipline in four Proverbs about the "rod" and "child" or "son." It is not possible to hold to the Bible and believe that discipline is only teaching. It involves teaching and consequence (loss, hardship or pain).

The purpose of discipline is to be helpful. Understanding this helps parents avoid misconceptions. Good consequences are never aimed at paying for sin, making things right or justifying a child back to his parents or to God. Jesus' work on the cross does these things, not discipline. A parent should not "make an example" of a child. Also, a parent should never think of discipline as something that will toughen up his child or prepare him for a harsh world.

Some parents will do just about anything but use the principles of discipline spoken of in the Bible to help a child work toward compliance. In lieu of good consequences, parents may be tempted to use bribes, manipulation, yelling, begging or negotiation with a child. These cause harm. Furthermore, insulting is not good discipline. Passive aggression, like the silent treatment, is not good discipline. Threatening, like, "If you don't get in the car, I am going to leave you here," is not good discipline. It is a lie (one would hope) and shows disregard for the responsibility God places in parents.

Although many have focused on what type of consequence should be used, as if that were the secret to child training, the Bible leads one to believe that it is more important to understand the nature of discipline. Good disciplinarians acknowledge the sin problem in children's hearts and do what is necessary to help escort that problem out of their lives. Parents who discipline well are firm enough to give children a sense of what it is like to go against rules. With the help of discipline, they lead their children away from the enticements of the flesh and toward righteousness and peace.

For Discussion

1. Has your understanding of discipline changed through studying these verses? If so, how has it changed? What passages referred to in this chapter add most to your understanding?
2. How would you describe what discipline is like?
3. Discuss what it would mean to seek early to untie entangling sin in a child's heart.
4. What forms of discipline would you use in your home? Are they consistent with biblical parameters?
5. Was your parent or guardian's discipline helpful to you in the long run? Would your life have been different without their discipline?
6. Is there a time in your adult life when you experienced the natural consequences of your decisions? Is there a time when you experienced the discipline of God? How did it turn out?

Chapter 11

Practical Discipline

God's Word broadly supports the type of consequences meant to help a person put off sin and run toward righteousness. Because the Bible tells us the nature of discipline rather than specifics about what consequences to use, I feel comfortable only listing potential options and letting parents wrestle with these decisions for their own families. This chapter makes mention of several disciplinary methods that have been tried by others in the past, but parents should carefully consider whether each of these ideas matches up with the biblical principles we explored in the previous chapter, and if so, how it would look to implement them. The consequences are divided into six basic categories which include constraint, loss of privilege, natural consequences, logical consequences, exercise and corporal discipline.

Aids to Discipline

Before starting on a list of discipline methods, I want to consider some ideas that do not constitute discipline as defined by the principles of the Bible. The ideas listed in this section are good ideas. Parents could use them in conjunction with discipline or when they are introducing a new rule, but they should not be used in lieu of discipline when rules have been broken. For example, when there is disobedience, parents and children can problem-solve, discussing what might help a child to obey next time. The best route to take is not only to ask how to prevent the behavior in the future but also to enquire about the source of the behavior. What types of hopes, concerns or desires did the child harbor in his heart that caused him to break a rule? Identifying the problem, brainstorming solutions and then trying the best solution can be helpful. Consider these other useful ideas.

Explaining the purpose for a rule again does not hurt. An explanation might even merit an impromptu family meeting to discuss the importance of a particular rule. Of course, teaching can also be in the form of questioning. For example, a parent can ask, "Can you come up with three good reasons we have the rule you broke?"

Repeating or practicing the right way to do something after disobedience can help a child. A parent could simply say, "Go back and do that the way you think you are supposed to do it." Or, if a parent told a child to do something and the child did not respond, then he might be asked to say whatever response the parent expects (e.g., "Yes, sir") ten times for practice sake. Or, a child who slams doors could close one as quietly as possible several times while the parent watches.

Keeping track of disobedience can also help a child. He could write down each wrong done during the day and review the results with a parent in the evening or the next morning. Reasoning about past behavior is discussed more in Chapter 13, "Reason."

Redirecting a child from unacceptable activities to acceptable activities is not a consequence either, although it can be a beneficial step for a child who is breaking a rule (similar to 1 Corinthians 10:13). For example, if a four-year-old is found with something he is not supposed to touch, a parent might realize that the child needs some help focusing on acceptable play. After a discussion and consequence, a parent could suggest a toy to play with or could play with the child for a bit to get him started. Of course, redirecting helps when a child has not disobeyed. If a parent sees that a child is struggling or frustrated, the parent could redirect the child before he does wrong.

Parents should not consider an apology to be a sufficient consequence; however, if a child hurt or wronged another, asking for forgiveness is necessary. If a child does not know how to apologize or is unlikely to do so thoughtfully, his parents should help him think it through. A parent might say, "Imagine I am your sister. What would you say to apologize?" "I am sorry" is a statement of how the offender feels, but it is not enough. The offended deserves more. The one who wronged another should admit what he did wrong and ask, "Will you please forgive me?" Apologies could also include empathy and a sincere confession: "I see that I hurt you, and it was my fault." A person who is apologizing might also offer to make things right: "What can I do to fix this?"

Last, but not by any means least, parents could pray with children who have disobeyed, asking God to help them make good decisions. Also, parents could ask God to help them do their job well.

None of the valuable practices above are disciplinary in nature because they do not result in a significant loss of time, privilege or comfort. These should be done but should not be substituted for discipline.

Constraint

Some reasonable disciplinary techniques involve constraint. Sitting still and quiet or staying put to write or work are included here. We may also think of grounding, which means a child is stuck at home. For younger children, being held still or being required to hold a hand for a certain period of time would fall into this category, too. One could say that this type of discipline has some similarities to what God did for Israel when he sent them into the desert for forty years.

One common restricting consequence is to make a child sit still (perhaps with his hands clasped) without activity for several minutes. Some have suggested that the number of minutes a child would have to sit would match the age of the child. A four-year-old would sit for four minutes. A parent might call it a time out or a thinking chair. It should not be called anything like a naughty chair or dunce chair as that would be an attempt to use derogatory manipulation to change behavior. Of course, parents don't need to call it anything particular at all. A parent can simply say, "I want you to sit still here until the timer goes off." Sitting alone is not only a time to reflect, but a loss. It means losing the privilege to play. If a child refuses to sit still and be quiet, time could be added or restarted as a consequence. Or, other disciplinary measures could be used to enforce the rule.

Constraint may be helpful correction for a very young child, too. For example, if a parent wants a crawler to stop touching something on a coffee table, he might hold that child's hands by his side for ten or more seconds after the child touches something on the table. It is easily repeatable and can be associated with the rule not to touch a particular item. After the consequence, redirecting a child to a different activity is helpful.

Sometimes, being confined has had a writing activity along with it. When I was young, a child who disobeyed would not get to go to recess, but instead would find himself writing, over and over again, something like, "I will not speak without permission in Miss Wilson's class." Similarly, a child could be assigned a research paper like, "What does the Bible say about lying?" Or, instead of saying an apology face to face, a child might have to write out a thoughtful letter.

At times, being restrained to a location has had work added to the mix. Obviously, the work would have to be unexpected or a task that belonged to another child.

Many parents have used grounding as a constraining discipline, but there are some drawbacks. For example, grounding might end up penalizing another who did not do anything wrong. If a child was to go to a birthday party and now can't because she is grounded, then the birthday girl would miss out to some degree. Also, if a child has a lot of fun at home anyway, grounding may not have the desired effect. Finally, grounding for an extended period of time may take quite a bit of effort on the parents' part. Parents might prefer a consequence that doesn't last as long, if a substitute will accomplish the same aim.

Constraint and the next category, loss of privilege, are the most widely accepted forms of discipline today. Moms and dads should seriously think about what options to include in their discipline from these categories.

Loss of Privilege

If, as a response to disobedience, a parent prohibits an activity that his son or daughter would normally have the right to do, it is a loss of privilege. For example, if a child disobeyed right before his family was headed to a fun evening at the bowling alley, then that child might have to sit on the sidelines for part or all of the activity as a disciplinary consequence.

Loss of privilege could be for a time or until the child restrains a certain behavior for a set period. For instance, if a child has a problem waiting to speak in conversations, a parent might tell him that he can resume a certain fun activity only after he has gone 24 hours without interrupting.

A parent should be careful that substitutes don't render the loss of privilege ineffective. For example, telling a child he can't join in a fun family game, but letting him go to his room to play on an electronic device may hardly be considered a loss. Similarly, if a child is not permitted to drive but can ride with a friend or sibling wherever he wants to go, he is not likely to be burdened much by the consequence.

When privileges are withheld, it is important to make sure that siblings don't miss out. To say that no one in the family is going to a game or party because of the disobedience of one is unjust, and it may cause siblings to want to get back at or hold in contempt the one who did the wrong.

Skipping a meal or snack is a type of loss of privilege, and it is uncomfortable. Certainly children have been sent to bed without dinner. (Dehydration is many times more dangerous than hunger.) If parents have a wiry bunch of energetic children, they might prefer to keep them eating. As an alternative to skipping a meal, a child could get broccoli, dry toast and yesterday's chicken while others eat pizza.

When using withholding privilege as a disciplinary measure, it is preferable to withhold things that add little or no benefit to a child's wellbeing. One boy on a recreational soccer team I was coaching could not come to several games because of disobedience at home. Soccer was a positive experience for this child. It helped him develop self-control and he needed the exercise. Unfortunately, his parents did not utilize another consequence but made him sit at home during soccer games as discipline.

Loss of privilege can be a reasonable method of discipline. Parents can talk about what options fit in their own family. They can also ask children to propose privileges that would be lost in the case that they disobeyed.

Natural and Logical Consequences

Parents should consider how natural and logical consequences might help a child. A natural consequence occurs when something undesirable happens to a child all as a result of his own actions. When a child wrecks his bike and scrapes his knee after he was told not to ride the bike, he has experienced a natural consequence. With a logical consequence, however, the parent matches the discipline to the disobedience.

Very often with natural consequences, the pain of the incident is sufficient to turn the heart of the child so that he can listen to wisdom. After the child is cared for and calms down, a parent could simply point to the pain as the discipline: "If you had obeyed, you would not have gone on your bike and your knee would not be bleeding. You need to obey."

A parent should generally not rely on or hope for natural consequences because he can't control the amount of discomfort or pain a child feels. A mom or dad should not say or think anything like, "I hope he falls and hurts himself. That will teach him." Or, "He will learn not to touch that stove when he sees how hot it is." However, not all natural consequences are unmanageable. For instance, hunger as a result of refusing to eat a certain food would typically be safe.

Some natural consequences might be ineffectual. For example, if a child is careless with a toy, and it is ruined, then a parent could let the loss be the consequence; however, the child might think, "I didn't care about that toy anyway." Suddenly, the consequence is ineffective. Similarly, if a child fails to keep up with necessary assignments in school, a parent might think that the child's low grades will serve as a natural consequence, but this is a poor parenting choice. If he is defiant and says, "I don't really care," what has he learned? He has deduced that life is fine without education. It would be far better for a parent to teach him to study by coming up with a few rules that help him focus daily.

If a child carelessly or intentionally damages a neighbor's property, that property should be restored as a natural consequence. Restitution does not always involve money. If a child is careless and hurts another, that child might be required to wait on the hurt person and do his work if possible. Sometimes recompense may be a more severe consequence than what would be needed. Other times it may not be enough. Parents may have to add more discipline in some situations, and at other times they may need to help with the work or cost of making things right again.

A parent should be aware of natural consequences because they do happen from time to time and, sometimes, the loss or discomfort is sufficient. Adding another consequence to the natural one would be too much.

Logical consequences are superior to natural ones because they involve thoughtfulness rather than chance. Our Heavenly Father matched the discipline to the disobedience when he said that refusing to go into the promised land after forty days of spying would result in forty years of wandering (Numbers 14:34). The correlation between the forty days and forty years helped Israel remember how they disobeyed. This was also a logical consequence:

> The judges must make a thorough investigation, and if the witness proves to be a liar, giving false testimony against a fellow Israelite,

then do to the false witness as that witness intended to do to the other party.

Deuteronomy 19:18-19, NIV

The one who lied received the consequence that he wished the accused to receive, which was logical.

Here are some logical consequences that might pan out in a home: Toys not put away will be stored in a box and not used for a certain period of time. Or, a parent could say, "For every toy left out when the timer goes off, each of you will do five push-ups." If a child is too loud or interrupts during a meal, a parent might make him sit quietly until everyone has finished. A child who has neglected a work assignment could be required to do additional work. If a child nags, a parent may not let him have what he is nagging about.

To sum up, parents need to understand that the pain or loss from a natural consequence may be sufficient correction. Parents should also consider ways to logically connect a child's disobedient action to the discipline. Logical consequences are to be preferred to natural ones.

Exercise

Exercise has been used for correction, especially on athletic teams and in the military. A parent might use physical conditioning for consequences in the home as well. Exercise may be considered corporal because it involves the body, although most people don't think of it that way.

While I was away from home at basketball camp, my disobedience compelled a leader to make me sit against the wall with my legs at a ninety-degree angle as if I were sitting in an invisible chair. That was hard and it helped me make better decisions that evening. Similarly, holding the top position of a push-up, halfway up in a sit-up or holding a heavy book above one's head is difficult. Burpees (push-up, stand up, jump) are an exercise that could be used as discipline. Runs that require a person to get from one point to another in an allotted period (perhaps five minutes to run around the house a certain number of times) might help wake a child up and shake off a bad attitude. Health issues, such as asthma, should be taken into consideration when thinking about exercise as a consequence.

Repetitive exercise might be combined with verbal commitments to change. For example, if a child were to do pushups, he might also stop at the top of each to say, "I will do what my mom asks me to do right away."

Exercise is generally accepted as reasonable discipline, and it helps release pent up energy that might otherwise make future obedience more difficult. Parents should consider the options for discipline in this category.

Corporal Discipline

Aggravation of the skin has been used for correction. Most common to Americans is "spanking." The British use the term "smacking." Both are delivered on a child's bottom, but a swat on the bottom is not the only form of discipline that aggravates the skin. Smacking or flicking a hand might be considered acceptable to some. Others might consider a careful pinch on the shoulder to be okay.

For spanking, different implements have been used—a ruler, stick, switch, belt, paddle, the hand, etc. Some things that people have used for chastisement seem harder to control. For example, a long belt or a hard paddle would be more difficult to actuate carefully than a rubbery ruler or the palm of one's hand. Some have hypothesized that if there is no implement when spanking, the children will connect the discomfort more directly to the parent in a negative way. Others feel that using a hand can more tightly regulate the pain delivered. In any case, a parent would be wise to test the method he is going to use on his own person before administering it to a child.

Many parents have been quite thoughtful about how to use corporal discipline. Some supporters of this type of consequence suggest it be used as a back-up only, meaning that it is used only to enforce another form of discipline like time out. Some say it should be reserved for certain types of disobedience like lying or fighting. Some parents make it an ordeal with several semi-formal steps. Many suggest finding a private place in the home for such discipline and that it is best for a particular stage in a child's life (e.g., ages two to eight).

Not all corporal discipline should be acceptable to parents. No chastisement should invoke physical trauma (e.g., bruising), mental anguish or general fear of one's parents. A parent should not smack his child on the face, which would be disrespectful and may cause skittishness. Pulling on the arm should be avoided because it can cause dislocation of the elbow or shoulder. Wrenching the ear can damage cartilage, creating an unattractive condition known as cauliflower ear.

There are good reasons to use something other than corporal discipline in some situations. For example, when a child is already hurt or exhausted, it would not be appropriate. A very young child might become confused if spanked. Some children might not respond to something like spanking, or at least won't respond well. Other consequences, like loss of privileges or exercise may be more "painful." Asking a child whether he would rather be spanked or sit alone for ten minutes would give some indication of how painful he considers spanking to be compared to the loss of ten minutes of play time.

Many have found and still do find corporal discipline to be a beneficial tool for helping a child become free from entangling sinful desires. At the same time, if a parent is consistent with rules, judging, other discipline, testing and reasoning, it might be that corporal discipline is seldom or never necessary.

Extreme Philosophies about Spanking

People have believed wrong and strange ideas about corporal discipline. For example, the phrase "beat the devil out of him" came from a belief that disobedient children had demons that could be removed by beating (see Mark 9:14-29 for setting children free of demons). Also, some parents have concluded that one has to keep spanking until his child is clearly crying because the KJV version of Proverbs 19:18 says, "Chasten thy son while there is hope, and let not thy soul spare for his crying." This is an unfortunate conclusion and a misrepresentation of what the verse actually says. The last word in the sentence translated by KJV "crying" is *muwth* and it means "to die." The verse is more like Proverbs 23:14, in which the child is saved from death because of the parent's discipline (to "deliver his soul from hell" (KJV)). The NIV more accurately translates Proverbs 19:18, "...do not be a willing party to their death." Thus, if corporal discipline is going to be used, the pain should be only enough to have a decent chance of getting a child temporarily unstuck from a rebellious attitude, and nothing more.

Those who believe that spanking is the only true, God-ordained form of discipline have an extreme view. Many who hold the spank-only philosophy focus on the four Proverbs that we studied at length in the previous chapter. Their inaccurate interpretation of these verses says that spanking is God's way and the only acceptable form of discipline for the Christian family. Parents who only have spanking as an option will be stuck wondering if they should spank their children for everything, even the smallest infraction. This type of zeal could wear on parents, children and family relationships. Instead, parents who adhere to a spank-only philosophy might decide to let most bad behavior pass without a consequence. In that case, children may regularly and intentionally break rules that don't lead to spanking. Another option for parents is to eliminate all rules except those that seem most grievous. In such a case, many good principles may go untaught. It bears repeating, parents should have several disciplinary options at their disposal. Any time parents decide to use only one type of discipline, they are ignoring God's example.

The polar opposite of those who believe the spank-only philosophy are those who want to outlaw all corporal discipline. In 2001, the United Nations Global Initiative to End All Corporal Punishment of Children was launched. At the end of 2016, 51 countries had outlawed corporal discipline in all situations, including in the home.[9] In the U.S., Delaware has taken the position that all of this sort of discipline is child abuse.[10] There, a parent causing "pain" to a child under the age of three could end up in jail for two years, and the government has the power to take children away from their parents as well. Unfortunately, removing corporal discipline as an occasional option for parents is becoming more and more a matter of public policy.

Spanking can be done in such a way that it reasonably irritates the skin, which is within the biblical guidelines for discipline. It should not be illegal. At the same time, corporal discipline should not be thought of as God's only way. His example is much richer than that. Parents would do well to avoid these extremes in their own philosophy.

Studies on Corporal Discipline

From time to time, an article will be published exclaiming that corporal discipline causes children to grow up violent, depressed and maladjusted. Here is the truth: statistics can be and are misused to deceive. To understand

---

9. Global Initiative to End All Corporal Punishment of Children, "Ending Legalised Violence against Children: Global Report 2012," *Global Initiative to End All Corporal Punishment of Children*, (2012): 3, http://www.endcorporalpunishment.org/assets/pdfs/reports-global/Global-report-2012.pdf

10. Senate Bill 234, 146th General Assembly (Delaware, 2011 - 2012), https://legis.delaware.gov/BillDetail/21145

the deception, it is important to first understand the difference between correlation and causation. When events tend to happen together, they are correlated, but it is sophomoric to conclude that one certainly caused the other (causation). Many things happen at the same time, and for good reason, when one does not cause the other. Without the idea of causation, one might say that ambulances are extremely dangerous because a lot of people die in them. Or, one might note that in the springtime lightning is highly correlated with the greening of grass and the blooming of flowers. Should he then say that April lightning brings May flowers? No, it is the showers that bring the flowers. Lightning is highly correlated, but it is not in any way the cause of the plant growth.

Proving causation requires a tightly controlled study with a significant data set. Those who claim that corporal discipline causes harm often rely on large data sets that offer little control. The study known as the Fragile Families and Child Wellbeing is one such data set.[11] These types of studies cannot establish causation, but researchers seem willing to jump to that conclusion. Consider this example from the analysis of the "National Epidemiologic Survey on Alcohol and Related Conditions" collected between 2004 and 2005: "Harsh physical punishment in the absence of child maltreatment is associated with mood disorders, anxiety disorders, substance abuse/dependence, and personality disorders in a general population sample. These findings inform the ongoing debate around the use of physical punishment and provide evidence that harsh physical punishment independent of child maltreatment is related to mental disorders."[12] The first part of the statement, "associated with", is true because researchers can certainly observe a modest correlation between the presence of physical discipline and grown children's maladjustment. The second part of the statement is not true because the studies referenced don't prove any causation. The findings don't "inform", and they certainly don't "provide evidence".

---

11. Karen Tourangeau, Mike Brick, Lauren Byrne, Thanh Lê, Christine Nord, Jerry West, and Elvira Germino Hausken, "Early Childhood Longitudinal Study, Kindergarten Class of 1998–99 (ECLS-K)," *Third Grade Methodology Report (NCES 2005–018)*, (2004), U.S. Department of Education. Washington, DC: National Center for Education Statistics.

12. Tracie O. Afifi, Natalie P. Mota, Patricia Dasiewicz, Harriet L. MacMillan, and Jitender Sareen, "Physical Punishment and Mental Disorders: Results From a Nationally Representative US Sample," *Pediatrics* 130 No. 2 (2012) 184–192, http://pediatrics.aappublications.org/content/130/2/184

Here are a few explanations for what might be happening with the results in studies that correlate unwanted outcomes with something like spanking. Parents with belligerent dispositions may be more likely to adopt some form of corporal discipline. Even if they are non-abusive, their example and influence leans toward violence and other antisocial behavior. In those homes, children would be growing up with one or more parents who tend to be aggressive, or even violent, toward others. In a study that batched all users of physical discipline into a general category, physically aggressive parents could easily sway the outcome. Or, it is possible that the group of parents who are firmly against corporal discipline have a higher percentage of very involved parents while the group that would consider corporal discipline includes more disengaged, cold or bossy parents. Or, it is possible that children with a disposition to do the wrong things (those more likely to experience something like spanking) are also more likely to develop problems later in life, while children with compliant dispositions (those less likely to be spanked) do better.[13] Whatever the case, studies on spanking that do not employ sufficient scientific control should not be used to draw conclusions about the efficacy and long-term outcome of corporal discipline.

Researchers should know that correlation does not prove causation. They should know that many factors account for a child's experience and that their conclusions must absolutely be tempered by their control of these factors in their studies. However, some seem comfortable with the idea of arguing something like, "April lightning causes May flowers." It appears that, for some, commitment to a social goal has clouded good scientific judgment.

Are these correlative studies on corporal discipline virtually worthless? As far as determining the merits of something like spanking, yes. Correlative studies are helpful for determining how controlled studies should be designed in order to pinpoint cause and effect. Unfortunately, with corporal discipline, they are often used as propaganda pieces to advance the cause of those involved in the anti-spanking political movement.

Dr. Robert E. Larzelere (University of Oklahoma), Dr. Diana Baumrind (University of California, Berkeley) and others speak out against studies in which conclusions are drawn from correlations. They also point out that

13. Robert E, Larzelere, Ronald B Cox, and Gail L Smith. "Do Nonphysical Punishments Reduce Antisocial Behavior More than Spanking? A Comparison Using the Strongest Previous Causal Evidence Against Spanking." *BMC Pediatrics* 10 (2010), https://bmcpediatr.biomedcentral.com/articles/10.1186/1471-2431-10-10

studies with tighter controls reveal different conclusions. [14,15,16] A 2013 study done by Dr. Marjorie Lindner Gunnoe (Calvin College) found that children who were spanked fared far better than those who were not.[17,18]

One should not be fooled by the claims that corporal discipline is always bad or is worthy of being outlawed. At the same time, one should not assume that corporal discipline on its own leads to better results. For something like spanking to be effective, parents should devote themselves to the parenting principles found in the Bible.

Right Sized Discipline

When God dealt with Israel, consequences were effective but not a permanent deterrent. He could have inflicted enough pain on the nation to keep each of them living in constant terror for the course of the forty years they were in the desert. Instead, his discipline was such that Israel felt enough at peace to later defy his word. According to God's example, discipline should be significant enough to constitute a reasonable attempt to help a child comply at the time, but not more. If children repeat offenses, it doesn't mean that their parents are failing. It actually means these parents are encountering something similar to what God experienced when his consequences were sized right for the nation of Israel.

Some parents believe that discipline should be significant enough to make a "lasting memory" in a child's mind. The parent might think, "I'll teach him never to do that again," or read a child the "riot act" or "give him a piece of my mind." For example, he might sell the dog because

14 Robert Larzelere, "I Have Researched the Topic of Spanking: Critique of Anti-spanking Study (Straus et.al.), (1997), http://www.experienceproject.com/stories/Have-Researched-The-Topic-Of-Spanking/1782068

15 Diana Baumrind, "A Blanket Injunction Against Disciplinary Use of Spanking Is Not Warranted by the Data", *Pediatrics* 98 No. 4 (1996), http://pediatrics.aappublications.org/content/98/4/828

16 Robert Larzlere and Diana Baumrind, "Are Spanking Injunctions Scientifically Supported? *Law and Contemporary Problems* 73:57 (2010), http://scholarship.law.duke.edu/cgi/viewcontent.cgi?article= 1566&context=lcp

17 Marjorie Lindner Gunnoe, "Associations between Parenting Style, Physical Discipline, and Adjustment in Adolescents' Reports". *Psychological Reports* 112 No.3, (2013): 933-975, http://journals.sagepub.com/doi/abs/10.2466/ 15.10.49.PR0.112.3.933-975

18 *Fox News*, "Study: Spanked Children May Grow Up to Be Happier, More Successful." January 04, 2010. http://www.foxnews.com/story/2010/01/04/study-spanked-children-may-grow-up-to-be-happier-more-successful.html

the kids consistently fail to care for it. If a parent believes that he would discipline a child in such a way that he would never think of doing it again, then he is not following God's example.

With right-sized discipline, parents have to be persistent. Lessons that children learn may need to be relearned in a short period of time. A parent can say, "Oh, you are so frustrating," but this is the wrong response. The better response to common disobedience is, without expressing surprise, "This is disappointing. Let's keep working on it." Parents have to take their job one step at a time, judicially.

Like God, parents may also have to apply additional discipline if the first attempt does not help a child fully break free from a rebellious attitude. At the age of three, defiance often comes in the form of yelling and screaming. If parents apply discipline, a child might scream even louder. Parents need to be steady, calm, and persistent; and they need to have a deep chest of disciplinary options. One day when I was away from home, Ginny sent me a sweet video of our then three-year-old exclaiming with bright eyes and evident joy, "I got my happiness back!" It was a result of repeated discipline. He was no longer in a grumpy funk. However, repeated correction requires thoughtfulness and is not always appropriate. For example, as I have already written, when a child is exhausted, a parent should make great effort to usher him to bed as quickly as possible and show him tenderness along the way.

God shows us what it is like to avoid over-the-top discipline and how to persist with patience when disobedience is repeated. Parents should be comfortable with the idea that their discipline might be such that their children will disobey again later.

Following Through

God didn't flounder but was consistent when he disciplined the nation of Israel in the Exodus. For example, he followed through on his promise that the generation of Israelites who disobeyed the command to go into the Promised Land would not do it later. Deuteronomy 2:14-15 says, "Thirty-eight years passed... By then, that entire generation of fighting men had perished from the camp, as the LORD had sworn to them." (NIV). Also, God would be resolute if Israel chose to disobey in the future.

Many disasters and calamities will come on them, and in that day
they will ask, "Have not these disasters come on us because our God
is not with us?" And I will certainly hide my face in that day because
of all their wickedness in turning to other gods.

Deuteronomy 31:17-18, NIV

If God had let Israel off or lightened the consequences after assigning
them, his ability to forewarn the group he treated as a *child* would have
greatly diminished. Instead, God was consistent. Parents, likewise, should
be looking for disobedience, thoughtfully asking judicial questions,
offering time for appeals and establishing consequences carefully.

Practical Discipline

This chapter is not about punishment, which is payback for a crime.
It's about discipline meant to help the one who has done wrong. If a child
is captive to the flesh, he will be unlikely to think outside of his view of
life without discipline. Parents should use correction to free their children.
When a parent thinks about how to respond to an issue of disobedience,
he should be certain that he has no desire or duty to punish his child.

The biblical view of discipline flies in the face of the parent who takes
pleasure in the brilliance of his correction or brags to others about how
well his consequences worked. The parent who looks at discipline as the
way to win child-parent power struggles has a hierarchical view and sees
his children as lower echelon. It becomes an us-versus-them atmosphere,
which is not what God had in mind. The biblical goal of discipline is to
help a child, who is considered a friend, break free from the sin bound in
his heart (John 15:15, Hebrews 12:5-6, Proverbs 22:15).

Rather than giving specific "how-to" instructions, the Bible leaves
correction to the parent's judgment. This chapter offers six general
categories of discipline that a mom or dad might consider. These include
constraint, loss of privileges, natural consequences, logical consequences,
exercise and corporal discipline. Some good responses to disobedience
may not meet the criteria of discipline, but are good add-ons. Practicing
the right way, keeping track of daily wrongs, solving problems together,
redirecting a child to new activities, additional explanation, giving
apologies and praying could all be helpful for a child.

When parents choose what consequences will be used in their house,
they should remember that true discipline always involves some sort of

hardship. If parents' response does not involve loss or discomfort, children will likely be casual about engaging their will. Instead, discipline should be such that they will learn to struggle against temptation.

For Discussion

1. Can you think of a time when practicing the right way, keeping track of daily wrongs, solving problems together, redirecting a child to new activities, additional explanation, giving apologies or praying together after disobedience helped or would have helped your child?

2. Discuss the elements of apology listed in this chapter (see "Aids to Discipline" section).

3. Which categories of discipline do you draw from most? Why do you choose consequences from these categories?

4. Do you have and utilize several methods of discipline?

5. What steps should be included in the process of assigning a consequence for a child's disobedience?

6. Do you have any questions or suggestions about discipline?

Chapter 12

TESTING

In the Exodus, God treated Israel as a father should treat his child. He tested the nation. Often, the Bible uses the process of removing the dross from precious metals to describe testing.

> This third I will put into the fire; I will refine them like silver and test them like gold. They will call on my name and I will answer them; I will say, "They are my people," and they will say, "The LORD is our God."
>
> Zechariah 13:9, NIV

> The crucible for silver and the furnace for gold, but the Lord tests the heart.
>
> Proverbs 17:3, NIV

The best way to remove impurities from metals is to heat them until they become liquids. While hot, the impurities surface and can be removed. Similarly, testing provides a way to see and remove bad attitudes. Often, tests create what a parent might consider to be a "teachable moment," a time when a child can learn a life lesson by experience. It should be noted that tests are not meant to lead to failure for the one tested. Children, when tested, can succeed, but whether in failure or success, testing is valuable to a child.

God knows the heart. Parents do not have such omniscience. When a child undergoes a test, the parent and child learn a little something about what the child has harbored in his heart. This is the first benefit of testing. The second benefit is testing's ability to turn a situation in which a child's interaction with another is subjective (e.g., tone of voice or a certain facial expression) to a situation in which obedience is objective (specific commands). Third, testing is a good preparation tool, readying one to obey in more challenging situations. Finally, testing gives a person the opportunity to make humble realizations about life. Testing may produce more than one of these benefits at a time.

Deuteronomy 8 mentions four benefits. God's tests of Israel in the desert were "to humble you *and* test you, to know what *was* in your heart, whether you would keep His commandments or not." (v. 2, NKJV). First, the wilderness offered a chance to see what was in the hearts of the people. Second, the test would result in objective obedience or disobedience—"whether you would keep his commandments." Third, God would use the test to prepare Israel "that He might humble you and that He might test you, to do you good in the end." (v. 16, NKJV). Fourth, God allowed Israel to go hungry so that manna could bring the people to the awesome revelation "that man shall not live by bread alone; but man lives by every *word* that proceeds from the mouth of the LORD", and the testing in the wilderness was to keep Israel from saying, "My power and the might of my hand have gained me this wealth." (v. 3, 17, NKJV). These tests brought humble realizations.

To Know What Is in Your Heart

In Numbers 20 and 21, Israel was again without water. After God provided it (and Moses and Aaron were corrected for becoming angry and disrespectful toward God), the nations around Israel became contentious. That was a testing circumstance. Edom would not let them pass through their land, which obliged them to find a way around (Numbers 20:21, 21:4). As they did, the Canaanite king Arad attacked them. After defeating Arad, the people continued on their out-of-the-way route. Eventually, the test brought out what the people had harbored in their hearts. The Israelites even sniveled about manna, saying, "We detest this miserable food" (Numbers 21:5, NIV). At that point, the disobedient attitude of the nation became clear, which led to discipline: "So the LORD sent fiery serpents among the people, and they bit the people; and many of the people of Israel died." (Numbers 21:6, NKJV).

In the same way that God used the Israelites' trials to expose their attitude, a parent who notices some questionable behavior can test a child to discover the truth about his heart of hearts. Through testing, a parent will get a glimpse of what a child has harbored in this secret place.

Objective Obedience

Even though God knows everything, he did not generally judge Israel on their heart attitude alone. Instead, he created a circumstance that would put the Israelites' hearts into action. Manna provided this kind of test. Manna couldn't be stored, except for the rest day. On the rest day, they were not to gather it.

> Then the LORD said to Moses, "Behold, I will rain bread from heaven for you. And the people shall go out and gather a certain quota every day, that I may test them, whether they will walk in My law or not.
>
> Exodus 16:4, NKJV

God came up with a circumstance that would test Israel's willingness to obey. Did Israel pass the test? It sounds as though some Israelites did and some didn't; but as a whole, they didn't. Therefore, God asked: "How long will you [Israel] refuse to keep my commands and my instructions?" (Exodus 16:28, NIV). The tests made it objectively clear to the people of Israel that they had disobeyed.

If a parent is to discipline, a rule must have been broken. A parent should not say something like, "I need to discipline you because you seem crabby to me." Instead, if a parent notices that a child has a bad attitude, he should give a very specific instruction that will test the child's willingness to obey objective commands. Then, if he disobeys the commands, discipline would be appropriate.

Preparation

God says that he will test those he loves to prepare them for future obedience.

> My brethren, count it all joy when you fall into various trials, knowing that the testing of your faith produces patience. But let patience have *its* perfect work, that you may be perfect and complete, lacking nothing.
>
> James 1:2-4, NKJV

Testing was used to prepare a person to do what was right.

Jacob had twelve sons, one of whom, Joseph, was tested many times (Genesis 37-41), preparing him to be chief assistant to Pharaoh at age thirty (Genesis 41:46). One might also imagine that testing helped Joseph welcome his brothers, who had, years earlier, hated him enough to sell him as a slave (Genesis 45).

Like God, parents can test their children to prepare them for an upcoming event. Before going someplace where children need to sit still, a family can sit and practice. If a family is headed to grandma and grandpa's house, practicing saying "please" and "thank you" may be helpful. Parents should know that children do not necessarily need to practice the exact activity they will face as a temptation. The benefit from the preparation can develop an attitude of obedience that will translate effectively to other activities. For example, if a child's heart is set free from entangled sin when he is doing work around the house, he is very likely to enjoy that freedom when the family leaves the home for a fun activity.

Humbling Realizations

Job's painful test was uncommonly tough, but God knew that, unlike most others, Job could handle it (Job 1:8-12, NIV). The experience led Job to a new realization about God. At the end of the time of testing, God said to Job, "Brace yourself like a man; I will question you, and you shall answer me." (Job 38:3, NIV). As it turned out, Job was overwhelmed by God's questions, and he had a humble realization.

> Then Job replied to the LORD: "I know that you can do all things; no purpose of yours can be thwarted. You asked, 'Who is this that obscures my plans without knowledge?' Surely I spoke of things I did not understand, things too wonderful for me to know."
>
> Job 42:1-3, NIV

Job experienced tremendous loss and discomfort, yet in the end, he spoke of wonderful things. Job's eyes were open to new understanding that he deeply appreciated.

Parental testing should never be painful or harsh. Under no circumstances should a parent imitate anything like what God did with Job. Parents must realize that they will rarely be able to design a test that leads a child to humble realizations. One consideration would be a vacation that challenges a person, like a long backpacking adventure or mission trip. Occasionally, a situation may arise at home that provides a child with clarity on issues of life as well. For example, when it came time to dig up the septic system to fix it, I made sure that the child who likes to avoid such things was in the thick of it with me. He did fine with the test, and I think it helped him realize that he could serve others when things literally stink. The discovery was not as profound as the kind of test God could design, but it was a little hurdle we were able to jump over together.

Testing a Child

When should a parent test? If, on the same day, a child disobeys family rules several times, a parent should consider testing. If a child seems to be unkind, defensive, or selfish, testing may be in order. Sometimes, a certain look from a child may indicate the need to test. The child constantly asking for entertainment or the teen pressing for an answer, "Can I go? I need to know right now," might need testing. A parent should consider it when an upcoming situation is dangerous. For example, a teen might benefit from testing before driving a car. If a child does not seem to be thinking through a situation logically, testing may help. If a child is working really slowly, is spacing out, is slow to answer questions or expresses a sense of entitlement, a parent should think about testing. If a child is "bouncing off the walls," is talkative, has emotional outbursts or shows signs of discontentment, a test should be considered. When children have had a nice, long playtime on their own, it may be wise to follow it up with a test. Children who seem to be arguing with each other may need to be tested, too.

What are some tests? Playing within a defined boundary, like on a rug, bed, chair or swing is a reasonable test for a young child. A parent might say, "I want you to go color by yourself for ten minutes because I think that you could use some time to calm down. Then you can come out and play again. I will start the timer." Or, "Sit still with me for a little bit." Or, "Put away all of your toys." Bickering siblings can be made to play while holding hands as a test. For some children, playing a game that requires exercise may be useful for assessing the heart. Any job that needs to be done can be a test. If a child is begging for a fast answer to some school work, a parent could test by saying, "I would like to see if you can solve this problem by yourself. Look in your book to see if you can learn how to do it."

If a four-year-old starts banging two toys together, it may not be clear if it is part of playing or if he wants to be destructive. In this case, a parent could show the child how this might damage the toys and then test with simple, objective instructions like, "Come touch my knees" and "Go touch the door." A parent might ask the young child to go back and forth between the door and his knees several times to make sure he is willing to do what he is asked.

To practice is also to test. For example, a parent could ask a potty-training child to stop playing and run to touch the bathroom door. The instructions would test the child, and he is practicing what it takes to stop playing in order to use the toilet. Anything children learn, like a musical instrument, handwriting or folding laundry well might also serve as a test.

Parents should let children know that from time to time, they will test them to see if they will obey. It is also healthy for parents to follow up tests with a conversation. A mom or dad might say, "I asked you to do that to test you, to see how you would respond. How do you think you did?" After the discussion, parents can point out the benefit of the test and suggest that the children be thankful for it (James 1:2).

Parents should not offer inappropriate materials or put children in situations that stir up perverse desires as a test. This is not testing but tempting.

Parents must watch carefully to see how their children do in a test because the whole point is to find out if they are in a funk and, if so, to set them free from it. If parents do not intend to discipline when children fail tests, then the parents should not bother to test.

Life is full of tests, not only the kind that come from parents. Each experience tells us whether our heart is inclined toward God or against him. It would be good for our children to understand this reality.

Ongoing Tests

Manna was introduced to see if Israel would obey simple instructions (Exodus 16:4). Every day the people of Israel were tested in the same way. Decades later, the exact same test showed whether Israel would be content and thankful for what God was providing (Numbers 11). In this way, manna was an ongoing test. There are other examples of ongoing tests in the Bible as well. For example, "They [the nations remaining in the Promised Land] were left to test the Israelites to see whether they would obey the LORD's commands, which he had given their ancestors through Moses." (Judges 3:4, NIV. See also, Judges 2:22, Judges 3:1). Israel would have to trust and obey God to defend itself. The climate of the Promised Land would provide a similar challenge to the people. They would have to trust God for rain (Leviticus 26:19, Deuteronomy 11:10-19; 28:12, 24).

Parents can facilitate ongoing testing. A child could do daily exercise, like a run around the neighborhood with mom or dad to get the morning started. The greatest advantage of daily duties and chores is not getting the work done, but providing a regular test. For small children, the test of playing in a designated area could be practiced every day at a certain time. Putting several siblings in one bedroom can provide an ongoing test as well.

Sports teams, although not often thought of as a test, can serve this purpose. Exercise, teamwork and skill training require determination. Parents may have opportunity to help their children through issues like bragging, work ethic, getting along with others and earthly focuses. The activities could be a test for the parents. Are they able to remain cool headed, keep all things in perspective and make wise decisions about how much time and money this activity should consume?

Like God, a parent should consider instituting ongoing tests; however, when testing becomes part of the daily routine, a parent may be more likely to neglect his duty to look for successes and failures. Moms and dads must remember to evaluate how children are doing during the tests, or the activities will not serve their purpose well.

Help

One of the most important aspects of good parental testing is that it is intentional. Sometimes a parent's mistakes or bad behavior put a child through unintended tests. For example, a negative, antagonistic attitude toward children may well leave them feeling like most interactions with their parents are a test. All such tests should be avoided:

> Fathers, do not provoke your children, lest they become discouraged.
> Colossians 3:21, NKJV

Children's lives should be governed by parents' helpfulness, with occasional times of testing. At all ages, children should hear, "I will help you." Like those who sent the second letter to the Corinthians, parents should "open wide" their hearts to their children.

We have spoken freely to you, Corinthians, and opened wide our
hearts to you. We are not withholding our affection from you, but
you are withholding yours from us. As a fair exchange—I speak as
to my children—open wide your hearts also.

2 Corinthians 6:11-13, NIV

Moms and dads should have a heartfelt attitude of helpfulness.

The topic of how to help and love is hardly a small one; in fact, it
covers everything that is good. I want to address three areas where it seems
possible for parents to miss the mark—understanding childhood, keeping
busy and providing encouragement.

In generations past, when people had larger families, when extended
families still gathered on Sunday afternoon and when homes had front
porches where families interacted with their neighbors, children had
far more opportunity to observe child development. Unfortunately,
many of us did not grow up caring for a younger sibling, neighbor or
cousin. Today, a lot of us have almost no hands-on experience with
young children until we have our own. We need to find out what
typical capabilities and concerns are to be expected from age to age. For
example, parents should not interpret what children say and do as if they
were thinking, reacting or behaving like adults (1 Corinthians 13:11).
Parents must teach children almost everything, and teach them more
than once. Children don't even do well at intuitively identifying things
that are dangerous. Sometimes parents jump to the conclusion that
children have already thought life through. This might be expressed in
the confrontational question, "What were you thinking?" The answer is
that they were thinking whatever they learned in the few years they have
been alive. Additionally, parents would do well to remember what it
was like to be lost, unsaved, without Jesus and without hope (Ephesians
2:12). Even a child in a Christian home may experience some of the
same feelings.

Development goes in cycles of struggle and relative peace. When
children get to a major turning point in development such as crawling,
walking, talking, potty training, starting school, etc., they often become
easily frustrated. For example, when a child is developing verbal
communication, he will likely become more emotional about whether
others understand his wants or needs. Communication can become quite
impassioned. If a parent shows he is trying to understand, the child will

usually calm down. A parent should get down to eye level or pick the child up high enough to look right into his eyes. He should repeat what he thinks the child is trying to say. If he can't understand, he could ask the child to point to it: "Show me."

While children struggle through these stages, they need to be touched and to be moving. Tickle, wrestle, spin, swing, hug and massage. In fact, pediatric occupational therapists use some of these as successful treatments for children with developmental problems. A parent should not neglect to provide this kind of touch and activity. When he was three, one of our children insisted that he was stronger than me. After many fun times of wrestling to see if he could escape my grasp, he finally conceded that I was stronger (but that he was "getting stronger and stronger"). I am convinced that the resistance tests were therapeutic for him.

Talking is important, too. At every stage of childhood, parents should listen well to their children because they want and sometimes need to be heard and understood. Parents should stop what they are doing long enough to listen. When children and parents have a chance to talk, parents should ask honest questions rather than taking over the conversation. Parents should communicate as one friend to another, no matter a child's age. If parents enjoy children in this way, communication will be natural rather than contrived. Talking does not have to be one on one. For example, family meetings and meals are valuable times to communicate with one another.

Above all, parents should love their children at every stage. They should read to them, fall asleep with them sometimes and play with them because play is part of the "work" of growing up. Homes should be made child-friendly and fun. Children should be allowed to wade in the creek and get their clothes all wet. Parents should help them be fascinated with the world and thankful for all its moving parts and critters, helping them appreciate the Creator.

If parents can remember their own childhood well, they will be able to empathize, which is a great starting point for loving children as they grow up. Loving with time and attention is a necessity. To be helpful parents, moms and dads should consider how to understand life from a child's perspective.

Another way to help children is to have a schedule to avoid idleness. Consider that the sin of Sodom was pride, comfort and spare time.

> Look, this was the iniquity of your sister Sodom: She and her
> daughter had pride, fullness of food, and abundance of idleness;
> neither did she strengthen the hand of the poor and needy.
>
> Ezekiel 16:49, NKJV

Sodom is a pretty extreme example, but the principle of being aware of idleness should be noted. (Also, in 1 Timothy 5:13, young widows were instructed to avoid idleness.)

Many children have stretches of time when they are busy running from one place to another. This has some benefit, but it can be too much. It is easy to be too busy. Other times, children wake up wondering what they will do with themselves all day. Parents should help children find productive activities during the slow times. It helps to have a schedule.

Parents should not be afraid to fill some of a child's day with work. Hard-working children are assets to the family and can derive purpose from their ability to contribute. I believe much teen depression is a result of self-centered living and the idea that children are a liability to the family. Instead, children should hear, "We need your help" and "The work you just did really helps our family."

Children could do most of the laundry, cleaning and cooking (certainly they contribute significantly to the need for cleaning and cooking). Older children could spend some time taking care of younger children. They could "strengthen the hand of the poor and needy." They could start a business, work for the family business or remodel the house. When children are busy in these ways, they will likely spend more time working alongside their parents, which is important, too (see Proverbs 10:4-5).

Especially for younger children, a lack of schedules can be trying. Having an evening schedule like book, bed, a hug, a kiss, a prayer and a backrub can help a child. When a parent says, "We can't do the book tonight. It has gotten too late," it may test a child a little.

Parents should consider age-appropriate schedules that help a child fill her days with worthwhile activities. These should include fun times, creativity and work that helps others.

In addition to being empathetic to a child's developmental needs and making sure a child has a moderately busy schedule, parents should encourage their children. When the Bible says that we should encourage one another, should we imagine that it is advocating that believers tell one another how great they are and what a phenomenal job they have done?

No, encouragement is, first and foremost, telling someone that God will get him through and make him able and therefore give him courage. Here are encouraging words from Scripture:

> But since we belong to the day, let us be sober, putting on faith and love as a breastplate, and the hope of salvation as a helmet. For God did not appoint us to suffer wrath but to receive salvation through our Lord Jesus Christ. He died for us so that, whether we are awake or asleep, we may live together with him. Therefore encourage one another and build each other up, just as in fact you are doing.
>
> 1 Thessalonians 5:8-11, NIV

Encouragement is built on the concepts that Paul mentioned here. It compels a person to do things the right way. We all need to be encouraged to do what pleases the Lord (e.g., Ephesians 4:1, Philippians 1:27, Colossians 1:10). The biblical idea of encouragement is to compel another to serve God, to persist, to love deeply and to seek righteousness.

Parents sometimes focus their encouragement on the child or his performance rather than on God or his ways. "You are so big! Look at you! You did the best job I have ever seen!" This sort of cheerleading might make a child feel good in the short run, but some children who receive it may begin to live in order to gain the praise of other people. A parent who is trying to make a child believe, "You are really something special," is not helpful to the cause of Jesus. Further, some children will find such praise disingenuous and manipulative and will avoid the type of good behavior that causes a parent to heap it on. If a parent's praise consistently points out how well a child does something, then he will learn to value performance rather than the inherent worth of others. He will begin to compare himself rather than to enjoy others. Unfortunately, many of us have been conditioned to think this way. It makes us look around and ask, "Who is doing a good job?" instead of, "Who needs to be encouraged or helped?"

Rather than making a child feel special, a parent should point out how a child did the right thing and was helpful. A parent might say, "You cleaned up the back yard. That helps the whole family." "You put your clothes away. That helps keep the house organized and looking peaceful." "You are learning math. That may help you work to support your own family someday." These are valid ways to encourage children to pursue good goals and cause them to think about helping others rather than about themselves. Also, a parent should remind his children, "And whatever you do, do it heartily, as to the Lord and not to men" (Colossians 3:23, NKJV). Children should be encouraged to live for an audience of one, not for the praise of people.

This section of the book pursued three ideas that help parents make life a little easier for their children—understanding how children think and feel at different ages, providing meaningful activities rather than idle time and giving the right kind of encouragement. As parents think about how to test their children, they should also think about how to test only when necessary. By thinking about how to be helpful, they will avoid a lot of unintentional testing.

Testing and Help

Testing has four benefits. It allows parents to discover children's heart attitude. It turns subjective behavior into something objective that parents can judge. It prepares with practice when time and effort can be devoted to discipline and teaching. It provides humble realizations.

Moms and dads should take the results and findings of tests and adjust accordingly. For example, if tests reveal that a child is engrossed in himself first thing in the morning, then reason, review, teaching, special rules and ongoing, daily tests could be applied. Parents should not wear children out with testing. Between tests, parents should provide help, love, friendship and encouragement. When they are neglectful, irresponsible or disengaged, it provides a test for sure, but these are not good tests for children.

Testing and help should go together. For example, one day our three-year-old boy was jumping off the couches. He was wired, so I asked him to sit on my lap to test him. He did quite well, and while he was there, I asked what he liked to do most that day. Then, we talked about what he might like to play with next. He chose to play with a ball, and he did so quietly for about fifteen minutes. After that time, I had an opportunity to play with him. He threw the ball, and I caught it in a bucket. In this case, testing and help were working together for my child's benefit.

For Discussion

1. How would you describe the difference between testing and discipline?
2. Describe a time when you have experienced one or more of the four purposes for testing mentioned in this chapter.
3. What would you consider using to test your children? How might tests change as a child grows older?
4. How do you limit unnecessary testing for your children? In what ways do you help your children when testing is not needed?
5. Have your actions put your children to a test they should not have had to endure?

Chapter 13

REASONING

Deuteronomy is a book of getting ready to go someplace in order to do something. When Moses tried to get Israel ready to live in the Promised Land, he did far more than say, "Here is rule number one" or "Because God said so." He "undertook to explain this law" (Deuteronomy 1:5). Deuteronomy is a book of logical persuasion about future obedience. The book is unique because it is mostly a transcript of Moses' speeches. If Exodus, Leviticus and Numbers are the game (recorded history), Deuteronomy is the rallying halftime talk. As a coach can rouse a team to victory, a parent can prepare a child with inspiration and reasoning. When we think of Israel as the child, God as the Father and consider ourselves as his imitators, we can see that Deuteronomy is awash with insights for parents.

Preparation is a very effective tool for accomplishing God's goals for children. Often, it leads to obedience and blessing. When a child chooses not to listen to warnings, his rebellion becomes even more obvious.

What can parents say in order to prepare their children to make good decisions? Parents should be thinking it through before a birthday party, worship, hangout time with peers, or a vacation with family or friends. Parents should be prepared to speak to their children about life decisions. Deuteronomy provides guidance. From the book, we learn how to be proactive parents.

Anything true is worth reasoning about. I have, for the most part, limited this presentation to ideas found in Deuteronomy. I don't mean to communicate that these are the only issues that a child could reason through. Families should take time to discuss, learn about and even debate all sorts of important points in light of the Scriptures.

Warnings

The instruction "be careful" shows up repeatedly in Deuteronomy. The phrase expresses the quintessence of reasoning in the speeches of Moses to the nation that God was treating as a *child*. Of course, the words "be careful" do not have to be present in order to give fair warning. "They are not just idle words for you—they are your life" certainly exudes caution (Deuteronomy 32:47, NIV). The principle of caution and carefulness abounds in this great record of speeches, and it should abound from the mouths of parents, too.

Parents need to think seriously about how to warn their children, not primarily in the sense of being safe, but in terms of making the very best God-pleasing decisions. Consider how a parent might use one of these phrases from Deuteronomy during the day with his children.

> Observe them [God's rules] carefully. (4:6, NIV)
> Only be careful, and watch yourselves closely so that you do not forget the things your eyes have seen or let them fade from your heart (4:9, NIV)
> Acknowledge and take to heart this day that the LORD is God in heaven above and on the earth below (4:39, NIV)
> Learn them [the rules] and be sure to follow them (5:1, NIV)
> …be careful to obey (6:3, NIV)
> …take care to follow the commands, decrees and laws (7:11, NIV)
> Be careful to follow every command (8:1, NIV)
> These are the decrees and laws you must be careful to follow (12:1, NIV)

For various reasons, some parents don't really worry about warning their children. Maybe they presume that they will learn on their own, are concerned that thoroughly-warned children will not fit in with peers, or have decided that they are going to act badly whether they are warned or not. Maybe these parents are too busy with other tasks. Or, some parents might be hesitant to tell a child to be cautious because it might bring to light the parent's own hypocrisy. All of these reasons are parenting mistakes. God wants parents to warn their children to be careful about everything they say and do.

The world sends the message that parents should try to be cool rather than cautious. Perhaps this type of casual attitude might even be erroneously credited to Jesus, who said, "...do not worry about your life" (Matthew 6:25, NIV). When he said that, he gave examples of what we were not to be concerned about, but what some miss is that he also told us what must be a concern to us: "But seek first his kingdom and his righteousness" (Matthew 6:33, NIV). Jesus said that God's righteousness should be first, which is consistent with the cautions in Deuteronomy: "So be careful... do not turn aside to the right or to the left." (Deuteronomy 5:32, NIV). Statements like, "Be careful, or you will be enticed" are to be the mindset (Deuteronomy 11:16, NIV). So, we should not worry about what people normally concern themselves with, and we should be careful, not careless or carefree, with right and wrong.

In Deuteronomy, the reason to be careful was not a focus on the rules alone, but so that people could love God with everything they had (Deuteronomy 6:5). When a person focuses on the rules, he asks, "What does the Bible say I can and can't do?" In this case, he is focused on himself. Liberty in Jesus happens when a person asks, "What should I do to love and please God?" The answer to the question ends up in carefulness and concern about doing what is best.

Reasoning about Past Behavior

In Deuteronomy 1, Moses reminded the people of Israel of their rebellion in the past. Clearly, he didn't want the nation to repeat any of the same mistakes. The example in Deuteronomy suggests that a parent can and should bring up missteps a child has made before to prepare him for a situation that lies ahead.

Also in Deuteronomy 1, Moses reminded Israel that they had accused God of evil intent: "The LORD hates us; so he brought us out of Egypt to deliver us into the hands of the Amorites to destroy us." (Deuteronomy 1:27, NIV). That was wrong! This was the God "who went before you [Israel] in the way to seek you out a place to pitch your tents, in fire by night and in the cloud by day, to show you by what way you should go." (Deuteronomy 1:33, NIV).

Consider these other reminders of Israel's past behavior. In Deuteronomy 4:10, Moses said, "Remember the day you stood before the LORD your God at Horeb." (NIV). That was the time that they made a golden calf and worshipped it. Later, in Deuteronomy 9:7, Moses said, "Remember this and never forget how you aroused the anger of the

LORD your God in the wilderness. From the day you left Egypt until you arrived here, you have been rebellious against the LORD." (NIV). Over the next twenty verses, their rebellion was recounted for them in detail.

Remembering mistakes was and is only a tool for preparing a child. One should not make it a means of belittling. Love "keeps no records of wrongs" (1 Corinthians 13:5, NIV), so whatever a parent must share about past behavior ought to be forgotten, in so much as it is possible, when a child no longer struggles with this type of disobedience.

> He who covers a transgression seeks love, but he who repeats a matter separates friends.
>
> Proverbs 17:9, NKJV

If a child's behavior changes, he does not need the warning, so it should not be mentioned, or relationships may be damaged.

When my teenage child was going to spend time with peers, I warned her about "I know, I..." statements. I had observed that when my child started a sentence with, "I know, I...," she was likely to brag or complain. She was showing that she was more interested in herself than in the person to whom she spoke. The reminder of past behavior helped her prepare for spending time with friends. When my child stopped saying, "I know, I...," I used a more general warning for the whole family. "We are going into a dangerous situation," I said. "Can anyone tell me what is so dangerous?" The answer was, "Our own mouths!"

Reasoning about past behavior helps children obey in the future. Parents should follow God's example and help them think through old mistakes when there is an approaching opportunity to be careful.

Reasoning about the Future

If a child is going to learn to govern himself, he must understand the principles of blessings and painful consequences. A parent can present this type of reasoning at all communicative ages. The key is for parents to be in the habit of pointing out blessings and negative consequences and for children to learn to think about everything and how it will play out in the long run. We can learn from God's example.

In Deuteronomy, God, through Moses, extensively reasoned about the consequences of future decisions. The book covers this reasoning in chapters 4, 6, 11, 28 and 32 (see also Leviticus 26). Here is a condensed list of what was promised, both positive and negative. If the people of Israel did as God said, he would "keep his covenant of love" (Deuteronomy 7:12, NIV). Moses said to the Israelites that otherwise, God "will destroy you from the face of the land", that is, banish them from the Promised Land, which was where the people lived and, as they were an agrarian society, was the source of their livelihood (Deuteronomy 6:15, NIV, see also 32:19). This land was their key to independence. Conquerors and kings would not take this land from an obedient Israel: "No man will be able to stand against you", and "terror and fear" would come to those around them (Deuteronomy 11:25, NIV, see also 6:18 and 11:24). In fact, they would acquire new land. However, if they disobeyed, they would lose their property, as God would "scatter you among all peoples" under "cruel oppression" (Deuteronomy 4:27, 28:33, NIV, see also 4:2, 6:18, 28:36, 64, 68).

If Israel did not "serve the Lord your God joyfully and gladly in the time of prosperity", a powerful and relentless nation from far away would defeat them by besieging all the cities (Deuteronomy 28:47, 49-50, 52). The siege would be horrific (Deuteronomy 28:30, 51, 53-57; 32:25). The experiences would be so bad that they would leave Israel with great mental anguish. "The sights you see will drive you mad", Moses warned (Deuteronomy 28:34, NIV). Captivity would be bad, too: "In hunger and thirst, in nakedness and dire poverty" the Bible says, the Israelites would serve those who "put an iron yoke" on their necks (Deuteronomy 28:48, NIV). This time of correction would leave Israel with "an anxious mind, eyes weary with longing, and a despairing heart" (Deuteronomy 28:65, NIV, also v. 66-67). All who could work would be taken away as captive slaves. The older generation would not see them again: "you will wear out your eyes watching for them day after day, powerless to lift a hand" (Deuteronomy 28:32, NIV, see also 28:30, 41, 63). They would bring these circumstances on themselves. On the other hand, obedience insured that "it may go well with you and your children after you" (Deuteronomy 4:39, NIV, see also 11:21).

Moses said that God "will love you and bless you and increase your numbers. He will bless the fruit of your womb", which would cause them to "increase greatly" (Deuteronomy 7:13, 6:3, NIV, see also 28:4). The fruitfulness of the womb was described as "abundant prosperity", but if they followed other gods, they would not have a lot of children (Deuteronomy 28:11, 18, 62).

God promised prosperity in other parts of life. The Israelites would have longevity (Deuteronomy 5:33, 6:2, 24), success in work (Deuteronomy 28:3, 6, 8), abundance of produce, many work animals and large herds (Deuteronomy 7:13, 11:14, 28:4-5, 11). Moses said that God's generosity would be on "everything you put your hand to" (Deuteronomy 28:8, NIV).

If they disobeyed, God said through Moses that the sky "will be bronze, the ground beneath you iron" (Deuteronomy 28:23, NIV, see also 28:17-18, 22). Locust and worms would eat their crops (Deuteronomy 28:38, 39, 42). Robbers would take whatever was left. If they did not follow God, they would be "unsuccessful in everything" (Deuteronomy 28:29, NIV, see also 28:20).

God would also be willing to bring diseases upon a disobedient Israel, such as plague, wasting disease, painful boils, festering sores and the itch (Deuteronomy 28:21-22, 27, 35). These would be "severe and lingering illnesses" (Deuteronomy 28:59, NIV, see also 32:24). These diseases would affect the mind and the body. God would strike them with confusion, madness and blindness (Deuteronomy 28:20, 28). If they obeyed, they would be "free from every disease" (Deuteronomy 7:15, NIV).

Recall that God's goal for the people of Israel was that they be "blessed more than any other people" (Deuteronomy 7:14, NIV). For his glory and the spreading of his good reputation, he wanted to establish Israel as "his holy people" and bless them so that they could be a blessing to other nations (Deuteronomy 28:9, NIV, Genesis 12:2-3).

> Then all the peoples on earth will see that you are called by the name of the Lord, and they will fear you.
>
> Deuteronomy 28:10, NIV

Making Israel a great nation was completely a win-win proposition. God would set Israel "high above all the nations on earth", make them impenetrable to enemies, and make them "the head, not the tail" (Deuteronomy 28:1, 7, 13, NIV). At the same time, God would have a living testimony to his goodness, righteousness and love, so that every nation in the world could get in on it. The truth is that even if Israel was a pathetic nation, God could use the situation to show his greatness. Even if Israel became "a thing of horror and an object of scorn and ridicule to all the nations", God could get credit for being just (Deuteronomy 28:37,

NIV, see also 28:25). [19] These consequences did not occur all at once, but were persistent and progressive. The people of Israel would have had plenty of time to turn to God and therefore avoid the biggest losses.

Parents should ponder the privilege that God gave the nation by warning the people how he would respond to their moral decisions. God reasoned with specificity about what would come in the case of obedience or disobedience. Of course, these awful pains were meant to bend the will of a nation, not an individual. Turning a child's heart requires much, much less than changing the collective heart of millions of stubborn adults joined together in a culture of rebellion. Parents should, however, acknowledge that obedience in their family is a great experience and that disobeying is uncomfortable.

Proclaiming Blessings and Consequences

In Deuteronomy, God set a clear choice before the nation he treated as an adopted *child*.

> See, I am setting before you today a blessing and a [painful consequence][20]—the blessing if you obey the commands of the LORD your God that I am giving you today; the [painful consequence] if you disobey the commands of the LORD your God and turn from the way that I command you today by following other gods, which you have not known.
> Deuteronomy 11:26-28, NIV

> This day I call heaven and earth as witnesses against you that I have set before you life and death, blessings and [painful consequences]. Now choose life, so that you and your children may live and that you may love the Lord your God, listen to his voice, and hold fast

---

19. There was justice at play in God's consequences for Israel. God drove out the people in the land he had promised to Israel because the people were perverse (See Leviticus 18 and 20). How could he let Israel remain if they were doing the same things? God said, *"Like the nations the LORD destroyed before you, so you will be destroyed for not obeying the LORD your God"* (Deuteronomy 8:20, NIV).

20. English translations use the word "curse" in these verses in Deuteronomy, but the passages are really speaking of negative consequences ultimately meant to bring about good. What was happening when Israel experienced a "painful consequence" in Deuteronomy? The goal of these painful consequences was to turn the heart of the nation back to the love of the Father. This certainly speaks of something very different than a witch's curse or a cuss word (modern English meanings).

> to him. For the Lord is your life, and he will give you many years in
> the land he swore to give to your fathers, Abraham, Isaac and Jacob.
> Deuteronomy 30:19-20, NIV

To solidify this concept of blessings and painful consequences, God
provided Israel with an experiential learning event. The nation covered
two mountains and shouted out the blessings from one and the painful
consequences from the other.

> When the LORD your God has brought you into the land you
> are entering to possess, you are to proclaim on Mount Gerizim the
> blessings, and on Mount Ebal the [painful consequences].
> Deuteronomy 11:29, NIV

The instruction was repeated in Deuteronomy 27. On Gerizim six tribes
were to "bless the people", and on Ebal six tribes were to "pronounce
[painful consequences]" (27:12-13, NIV). Each mountain had a million
people or more on it, chanting out the good things that would come by
walking with God and the bad things that would come with rebellion.
God's reasoning was participatory, and the grandiose event must have
been a memorable experience for those involved.

Parents' job is to present two choices clearly to their children, fostering
a child's ability to reason. A dad might say, "If you obey me today, your
day will go better," but it would be more important to say, "If you obey
God, you will have a good life. Obey and be satisfied, or disobey and be
discouraged." Or, "If you are willing to do what God says, God will bless
you over time."

Parents' most important warning to their children should be about
eternal life, the coming judgment and Hell (Hebrews 9:27-28). The Bible
makes several parallels between Israel's entrance to the Promised Land and
a person's entrance into eternal life (e.g., Hebrews chapters 3 and 4, 12:22-
24, Revelation 21:2). Parents should be warning about Hell and telling
their children about the New Jerusalem (Heaven), where those who escape
judgment will live forever. Having made it clear, parents can compare the
abundant life in Christ (John 10:10) to the darkness and dead-living of sin
(John 3:19). They can explain that disregard for the Ten Commandments
leads to ruinous problems in life. For example, they can talk about how
small lies are the foundation of lifestyles of sin, explaining that those who
abuse drugs, cheat or act lazy, are often experts at lies, small and large.

Lying becomes a way of life. This is a good reason for a child to learn to identify and resist every temptation to misrepresent the truth.

Breaking God's rules has obvious practical consequences, but it also causes problems in the spiritual realm. A parent could say, "If you don't obey God, you open yourself up to the torment of Satan and the demons. They will degrade you and hurt you." (see John 10:10 and 1 Corinthians 5:5).

Comparisons of blessings and negative consequences can be brought into everyday living. To a young child who still takes naps, a parent might say, "God made us so that we need to rest. Resting helps you grow up. If you go to sleep quickly, you will have more time to play. After you rest, you will be happier, and it feels good to wake up from rest. But if you aren't still so that you can fall asleep, I will have to discipline you." These preparations help children.

Just as the warnings in Deuteronomy were given before disobedience, parents' warnings must also be given before a child breaks a rule. Parents who regularly warn instead of disciplining after children disobey will teach their children that they can get away with wrongdoing at least once. It would not be helpful for children to think this way. However, a warning any time before disobedience is appropriate.

Parents should give warnings when they observe that children's attitudes or intentions are questionable. For example, at an athletic practice I had a feeling that my then-six-year-old was considering complaining, so I called him over, knelt down where our eyes could meet and quietly warned him not to have any complaining in his heart. The practice tested him and he passed, perhaps, in part because he knew judiciousness and discipline were consistent in the rest of his life.

Parents should warn of the consequences of all types of decisions, but the blessings of God should also be held in great esteem in a Jesus-following home: "Thank you, God, that you showed us your principles. We followed them and life is so much better now." A parent might say, "When you learn to obey, all sorts of other things will work better." If a child is into competing or performing, a parent could say, "Because you have learned some self-control, you are able to practice with determination. Self-control is a blessing from God, and you should consider how it can help you love others throughout your life." Or, "If you get married someday, following these rules will strengthen your marriage." Or, "Obeying God makes for better relationships and brings peace to one's soul." Or, "The opportunity to show love to another person is a privilege in and of itself. 'It is more blessed to give than to receive.' We would not have known this without Jesus' help." (Acts 20:35, NIV).

Today, some speak of positive reinforcement, but it isn't comparable to blessings. These come over time and, therefore, are a matter of reasoning rather than positive reinforcement provided by an immediate reward. Motivating with instant rewards is not the biblical example, but there are practical problems, too. For example, if obedience is rewarded (e.g., "If you're good during the meeting, I will give you candy on the way home"), a child might develop the mindset that he will be tyrannical if the parent does not pay him well enough for obedience. Rewards teach children to focus on stuff rather than on people. Children might relish the prize rather than doing what is right to honor and respect others. Instead of offering rewards, parents should talk to their families about following God in the long run, so that they can be blessed long term.

God did not promise utopia for Israel. He promised that they would be productive, they would enjoy their large families, they would have a reasonable reward for their work, and they would be healthy and safe. When speaking of blessings, a parent should not over promise. We can be content with what God provides and contentment is a real blessing. Blessings are not like experiments that faithfully repeat themselves in a lab. Sometimes things get turned around as Solomon pointed out: "...there are wicked *men* to whom it happens according to the work of the righteous." (Ecclesiastes 8:14, NKJV). Jesus told us that the Father "causes his sun to rise on the evil and the good, and sends rain on the righteous and the unrighteous" (Matthew 5:45, NIV). In life, instant results from a given action are not guaranteed, but there are activities that raise the probability of success or failure. With this understanding in mind, we should reason with children about blessings to come, and this is the best of them all: "I will walk among you and be your God, and you will be my people." (Leviticus 26:12, NIV). God's presence is the ultimate prize.

Parents will get a great deal of help from Deuteronomy when considering how to warn their children, but this kind of reasoning about the future is abundant in Proverbs as well.

> My son, do not forget my teaching, but keep my commands in your heart, for they will prolong your life many years and bring you peace and prosperity. Let love and faithfulness never leave you; bind

them around your neck, write them on the tablet of your heart. Then you will win favor and a good name in the sight of God and man. Trust in the LORD with all your heart and lean not on your own understanding; in all your ways submit to him, and he will make your paths straight. Do not be wise in your own eyes; fear the LORD and shun evil. This will bring health to your body and nourishment to your bones. Honor the LORD with your wealth, with the firstfruits of all your crops; then your barns will be filled to overflowing, and your vats will brim over with new wine.

Proverbs 3:1-10, NIV

Obedience results in blessings. Similarly, Proverbs warns of the negative consequences that will come to the disobedient.

Proverbs also suggests at what age parents should start teaching children these blessings and consequences.

When I [Solomon] was my father's [David's] son, Tender and the only one in the sight of my mother, He also taught me, and said to me: "Let your heart retain my words; Keep my commands, and live. Get wisdom! Get understanding! Do not forget, nor turn away from the words of my mouth. Do not forsake her, and she will preserve you; Love her, and she will keep you. Wisdom *is* the principal thing; *Therefore* get wisdom. And in all your getting, get understanding.

Proverbs 4:3-7, NKJV

Notice how the core of the message to the younger one ("tender") was similar to the advice given to the older ones: "Keep my commands, and live. Get wisdom!" Wisdom is the ability to apply knowledge gained in order to self-warn. Before Solomon had a younger sibling ("the only one in the sight of my mother"), David was teaching him to understand how decisions will turn out and to pursue what is best. One should not underestimate the reasoning ability (or at least the innate desire to reason) of two- or three-year-olds. At the very least, parents should try to explain life in terms of wisdom.

Proverbs and Deuteronomy deal very specifically with cause-and-effect thinking. They both encourage one to obey in the future. In Deuteronomy the nation of Israel was offered the choice, by its own actions, to be either blessed or ruined; and in Proverbs the individual was offered the choice to be either blessed or ruined. A parent should present these kinds of warnings to his children regularly, referring to both small, daily and major, whole-life decisions. A parent's strategy of warning should start early and carry on year after year.

Reasoning about Maturity

Generally, people want to be mature, or at least they don't want to be immature. By growing older, a child can get the mental capabilities to do grown-up things, but only by persistent pursuit of righteousness is one able to truly mature.

> Anyone who lives on milk, being still an infant, is not acquainted with the teaching about righteousness. But solid food is for the mature, who by constant use have trained themselves to distinguish good from evil.
>
> Hebrews 5:14, NIV

Maturity is what God wants from everyone who follows him, and parents should help boys become godly men and girls godly women. A disobedient seventeen-year-old can't decide to be instantly developed in Jesus because maturity is not a matter of age but of behavior, blessing, knowledge, wisdom and experience with the Spirit of God and the Word of God. Growing mature is a cumulative process.

Parents could refer to the growth of the nation God treated as a *child* in order to show how obedience and maturity are related. When we think of a nation maturing, we think of it growing in population and order, which is recorded for us in the Bible. Israel's growth, or lack thereof, is worth analysis.

As part of the prospering, God hoped Israel would grow larger and larger.

> The LORD your God has multiplied you [from Abraham and Sarah to a great nation], and behold, you *are* today as numerous as the stars of heaven. May the LORD, the God of your fathers, make you a thousand times as many as you are and bless you, as he has promised you!
>
> Deuteronomy 1:10-11, NKJV

A thousand times Israel's population would have been two billion or more. For this reason, the land that God promised Israel went from Egypt to Iraq.

"To your descendants [Abraham's] I give this land, from the river of Egypt to the great river, the Euphrates."

Genesis 15:18, NIV

God had hoped Israel would multiply in order to cover the areas we now call Syria, Lebanon, Jordan, and large parts of Iraq, Egypt, Turkey and, likely, the Arabian Peninsula. Israel had the blessing to multiply if it obeyed, and as it grew God would have provided land as needed (Deuteronomy 7:22). The parts of the Bible that talk about large families, multiplying, children and the blessing of the womb are plentiful (more than forty) [21] and worth our consideration. Humans were born to love, and love welcomes children and counts them as a blessing (see Psalm 127:3). This is what God had in mind for Israel.

Did Israel grow and mature as a nation? Numbers 1 and 26 record two different censuses of the Hebrews. The first was taken about two years into the Exodus (Numbers 1:1). The second was taken on the plains of Moab (Numbers 26:3), Israel's 43rd and final stop on the way to the Promised Land (Numbers 33:48-49). Numbers 1:46 gives us the precise number of men who were twenty years and older and were able to fight at the beginning of the Exodus. There were 603,550 such men. [22] How did the first census compare to the census taken about forty years later? Did Israel grow significantly in the desert? Numbers 26 states that the results of the latter census of fighting men came to 601,730 (v. 51). They did not grow: they shrank. Certainly they could have grown. Seven of the tribes did, adding 16.5% over the forty years on average. The other five tribes lost an average of almost 25%.

---

21. Some of these verses are direct commands to have many children. Others speak of the blessing of having a large family and the disappointment of not multiplying much. In all cases, the context communicates that motherhood and an abundance of children should be greatly desired. Genesis 1:28, 9:1,7, 13:16, 15:5, 17:20, 20:17, 22:18, 28:3, 29:31- 30:13, 35:11, 41:52, 46:18, 47:27, 48:4, 49:22-26, Exodus 1:7,12:37, Leviticus 26:9, Numbers 5:28, Deuteronomy 6:3, 7:13, 28:4, 11, 15-18, 62, 30:9, 1 Samuel 1, 2:5, 2 Samuel 6:20-23, 2 Kings 2:21, Job 1:1-3, 10, 42:10-17, Psalm 72:16, 105:24, 113:9, 127:3-5, 128:3-6, Isaiah 54:1, Jeremiah 23:3, 29:4-13, Ezekiel 16:44-45, 19:10, 36:11, Hosea 14:8, Malachi 2:15, Mark 10:29-31, Luke 7:35, 1 Timothy 2:15, 5:14

22. This number was roughly equal to the number of families in the camp of Israel since men who were able to fight were also likely heads of households. This is a lot of families, a lot of people. To give an idea of the total population, we could consider that in the United States in 1950, males age twenty to fifty years old made up about 20% of the total population (about 22% in 2015, http://esa.un.org/unpd/wpp/Download/Standard/Population/). If there was any similarity, Israel would have been about three million people.

David took another census about four hundred years after the last wilderness census. Israel had 1.3 million fighting men, excluding Levi and Benjamin (2 Samuel 24:9, 1 Chronicles 21:6). It might seem like a lot, but it is not nearly what it could have been. If we apply an annual growth rate of 1.18%, which happens to be the 2010-2015 global growth rate, over four hundred years Israel's 600,000 men would have reached more than sixty-five million.[23] Israel's growth was dismal after it entered the Promised Land. Had the nation obeyed, it would have spread out toward the Euphrates River, but that is not what happened.

Why didn't Israel grow as it could have? The nation's behavior made it necessary for God to institute painful discipline over and over again. Disobedience wasted time for growth (Deuteronomy 28:15, 18). If the nation had decided it wished it had grown, Israel would not have the option to instantly add people to its ranks. Maturing as a nation required consistent obedience and blessing. This lesson can be shared with children, who should fix their sight on the long-term goal of maturity. The lesson is all around us in creation. Things grow as they are nourished over time and without proper nutrients, they don't grow well. Parents can teach children that the nutrient that causes one to mature in Jesus is submitting to him in everything.

You Teach Them to Your Children

Today, families are not together as often as in the past. The industrial revolution and the information age have affected the way we think. When families had farms or trades, life was different. Families worked, lived and learned together. This is the lifestyle context for the instruction:

> Hear, O Israel: The LORD our God, the LORD is one. Love the LORD your God with all your heart and with all your soul and with all your strength. These commandments that I give you today are to be upon your hearts. Impress them on your children. Talk about them when you sit at home and when you walk along the road, when you lie down and when you get up. Tie them as symbols on your hands and bind them on your foreheads. Write them on the doorframes of your houses and on your gates.
> Deuteronomy 6:4-9, NIV (see also Deuteronomy 11:18-20.)

---

23. While in Egypt, Israel grew at an annual growth rate closer to 2%, from 70 to 603,550 in 430 years (Genesis 46:27). The equation for calculating potential population is $Population400 = Population0(1+rate)years$.

In our modern society, people specialize. Mom and dad make the money and keep the house, school teachers educate, youth pastors spiritualize and children focus on academics, entertainment and talents. We need to consider how we can live in the modern world and still heed Deuteronomy's instruction for parents to be fully responsible to "Teach them to your children". We must be intentional, and lifestyle changes may be needed to help facilitate Deuteronomy's instructions.

In the passage above, Moses was saying that parents should communicate God's ways to their children whenever possible, wherever possible. Parents were to wear the message, inscribe it on their house and gate and talk about it when sitting, lying down or walking. When God said that parents and grandparents were to teach children while doing things they did every day, he was suggesting that teaching took time. Parents were to stop and explain why God wanted them to be loving or truthful in a specific situation or to explain again why something was wrong when a child couldn't see it that way.

This command was not for a priest or judge, but for parents and grandparents, and the teaching was to continue for generations to come.

> Only be careful, and watch yourselves closely so that you do not forget the things your eyes have seen or let them slip from your heart as long as you live. Teach them to your children and to their children after them.
> ...hear my [God's] words so that they [Israel] may learn to revere me as long as they live in the land and may teach them to their children."
>
> Deuteronomy 4:9-10, NIV

> These are the commands, decrees and laws the LORD your God directed me [Moses] to teach you to observe in the land that you are crossing the Jordan to possess, so that you, your children and their children after them may fear the LORD your God as long as you live by keeping all his decrees and commands that I give you, and so that you may enjoy long life.
>
> Deuteronomy 6:1-2, NIV

Again, this job belonged to parents and grandparents.

The Ten Commandments are central in the verses we are now considering. When the truth finally occurred to me that our children needed to know the Commandments by memory, I gave them a challenge: no family member gets breakfast until he can list them. It was a fun morning, a race to memorize, with everyone helping each other; but it was not a once-and-done lesson. We also sing the Ten Commandments song together, and we use the commandments when our children get in trouble: "Which one of God's rules did you break?" Further, we talk about what the Commandments mean and why they are so important. Coveting, for example, affects how we relate to other people and is a sure sign of ungratefulness and discontentment.

The instructions in Deuteronomy explained that parents and grandparents were not merely enlisted to teach the Ten Commandments, but everything that went along with them—the history, personal life experience, blessings and desire for righteousness.

> In the future, when your son asks you, "What is the meaning of the stipulations, decrees and laws the LORD our God has commanded you?" tell him: "We were slaves of Pharaoh in Egypt, but the LORD brought us out of Egypt with a mighty hand. Before our eyes the LORD sent miraculous signs and wonders—great and terrible—upon Egypt and Pharaoh and his whole household. But he brought us out from there to bring us in and give us the land that he promised on oath to our forefathers. The LORD commanded us to obey all these decrees and to fear the LORD our God, so that we might always prosper and be kept alive, as is the case today. And if we are careful to obey all this law before the LORD our God, as he has commanded us, that will be our righteousness."
>
> Deuteronomy 6:20-25, NIV

The conversation about the Ten Commandments was to lead a parent to talk about the miracles and faithfulness of God. It was not about passing information only. It was about giving logical and persuasive presentations throughout life. It was about answering questions fully and about reasoning.

Furthermore, the events and teachings of the festivals in Israel would confirm all that a child was hearing from his parents at home.

> "...when all Israel comes to appear before the Lord your God at the place he will choose, you shall read this law before them in their hearing. Assemble the people—men, women and children, and the

aliens living in your towns—so they can listen and learn to fear the Lord your God and follow carefully all the words of this law. Their children, who do not know this law, must hear it and learn to fear the Lord your God as long as you live in the land you are crossing the Jordan to possess."

Deuteronomy 31:11-13, NIV

The nation gathered together to hear the Bible read. The children were not to be left out because reading the Bible would lead to the reverence of God. They "must hear it and learn to fear the Lord your God".

I want to mention a few ideas for honoring God's commandments in these Deuteronomy passages. Perhaps these are good starting points for thinking about what a family would do. Family meetings, both spontaneous and regularly scheduled, are great times for talking, teaching and encouraging. What should take place in these meetings? Parents could reason with their children concerning blessings and painful consequences. Or, the family could discuss how wise Jesus is and what he has done in their lives and in history. They could watch and speak about an important video on biblical truths or study the Bible together. Parents could talk about the activity coming up next and how one could walk in the Spirit rather than the flesh in that situation. Or, a family could sit and have a discussion about whatever comes up. Parents should consider utilizing the family meeting time to teach their children.

Home schooling is a lifestyle choice that can greatly increase opportunities for a parent to reason with children along the way. It puts parents and children together and provides ample opportunities to integrate Deuteronomy-style teaching into the curriculum. Home schooling isn't as hard as people often think, and the commitment is largely offset by resources that would otherwise be spent when a child attends a traditional school (meetings, meals, travel, dealing with temptations and behavior problems, volunteering, etc.).

Some today are promoting a style of worship they call "family integrated," which is a way of saying that worship meetings, in so much as is possible, involve the entire family. This may be a good way for parents and children to learn to revere the Lord and mature together.

Following the instructions of Deuteronomy requires that parents and children be together and that life coaching take place regularly. Parents should arrange their children's activities, work and education in such a way that they, personally, can teach the ways of God. Parents and grandparents should be proactive, anywhere teachers. They have to be careful to reason about God's rules and his record as Deuteronomy says. They must capitalize on the time they have with their children and grandchildren. Thinking about how best to accomplish these goals is a worthy exercise and children will be blessed to have parents and grandparents who do so.

The Blessing of Good Parents

Israel was under the watchful eye of God the parent, as physical and spiritual needs were met.

> The LORD your God has blessed you in all the work of your hands. He has watched over your journey through this vast wilderness. These forty years the LORD your God has been with you, and you have not lacked anything.
>
> Deuteronomy 2:7, NIV

God provided for Israel's needs and then some. For example, in Deuteronomy 3:19 Moses said to the Gadites and Reubenites, "I know you have much livestock." (NIV). God did not only provide for physical needs, but so much more. We should reflect on what Moses said of Israel's unique circumstance.

> Ask now about the former days, long before your time, from the day God created human beings on the earth; ask from one end of the heavens to the other. Has anything so great as this ever happened, or has anything like it ever been heard of? Has any other people heard the voice of God speaking out of fire, as you have, and lived? Has any god ever tried to take for himself one nation out of another nation, by testings, by signs and wonders, by war, by a mighty hand and an outstretched arm, or by great and awesome deeds, like all the things the LORD your God did for you in Egypt before your very eyes?
>
> Deuteronomy 4:32-34, NIV

God did something spectacular, and they were the centerpiece of the events.

In the passage above, the question, "Has any other people heard the voice of God speaking out of fire, as you have, and lived?" is a reference to the presentation of the Ten Commandments (Exodus 19:9,16-19 and 20:18-21). God was revealing righteousness and helping Israel foster an interest in it. The Israelites could proudly say that God gave them what "will be our righteousness" (Deuteronomy 6:25, NIV). God did not merely provide for the nation's physical needs. He also set forth rules to instruct them in what was just, kind and loving. Who wouldn't want to be a child of this father?

If Moses could say that the nation God treated as a *child* in the desert was remarkably fortunate, why can't we tell our children something similar? If parents live by and teach God's principles, their children are unique beneficiaries. Other families do not provide this.

> The secret things belong to the Lord our God, but the things revealed belong to us and to our children forever, that we may follow all the words of this law.
>
> Deuteronomy 29:29, NIV

Those who do know God have something amazing, and their children are privileged. Parents need to be able to effectively promote this truth and should brag on the Lord's faithfulness and ability. Time must be taken to tell children how good it is to have caring parents willing to teach them, judge their behavior and reason with them. "Megan, why are you so happy?" I asked. "I don't know," she answered. "Well, I know why," I said. "You are in a family that Jesus got a hold of, and that makes all the difference." If parents are willing to obey God, they can tell their children that they are fortunate to have them because they are.

Reasoning

Parents would do well to read the entire book of Deuteronomy with their role in mind because God, through the mouth of Moses, reasoned with the nation he treated like his *child* to prepare it for what would come next. Foremost, the message was that Israel should be careful to obey, not only some things, but everything. They were reminded about those times in the past when they had not obeyed. At some length, positive and negative consequences were spelled out. If the people of Israel were to follow God in the future, they would have plenty of food, security, babies and freedom. If they rebelled against God, they would starve, be attacked, end up a small nation and be enslaved. Clearly a choice was put before them. The book of Proverbs gives similar warnings, but for individuals rather than for the nation of Israel.

Parents should follow this example and prepare their children to obey. It is not optional, but God commands parents to do the warning and reasoning. They are responsible for teaching their own children and leading them to maturity. Grandparents should also play a role in communicating these truths.

Final Word

I am so thankful for God's example and his Word. I can say without hesitation that God is the one to imitate. This is why successful parenting requires a life governed by love, a thorough and thoughtful search of the Bible and the help of the Helping Spirit.

Of the seven observations I made about God the parent in this book, I am concerned that some parents will be stuck in fair judging, rules, consequences and testing and will neglect reason, trust in God and the heart solution. The former are facilitators, really, and the latter get to what matters eternally. Parents should not neglect the latter. Perhaps others will do the opposite, tending to focus on reason, trust in God and the heart solution and will neglect judging, rules, consequences and testing. These parents may fail because they will lose influence and neglect the practical parenting that effectively shows children they need a new life in Jesus. Instead of either extreme, parents should consider God's full example and imitate him.

Although God's ways are not complicated, I have found myself messing them up from day to day. This is not how I want it to go. I care that my children always see the Spirit of God in me. I want it to be my constant pursuit. I do know one thing that helps: every time I read this book, my mind is set straight, I see parenting mistakes I have made, and I look forward to something better, which is why I hope you will read *God the Parent* again, too. If you found it helpful, why not put a reminder on the calendar to read it again soon?

God bless you and your family. I am confident that as you earnestly pursue him, he will prove himself faithful to you and your children.

For Discussion

1. Is the mindset in your home "be careful" with God's rules?

2. Do your children know the Ten Commandments? The Two Greatest Commandments? Do you have any suggestions for parents who want to teach them to their children?

3. How might you carefully reason about past behavior with a child?

4. How would you help your children think about life in regards to blessings and negative consequences?

5. What words would you use to encourage your child to pursue maturity, to "grow in wisdom and stature, and in favor with God and man" (Luke 2:52, NIV)? What practical steps would be helpful?

6. How would you promote the idea that, thanks to God, your children are fortunate to have you as a parent?